———————

INSCRIPTIONS AND
REFLECTIONS
Essays in
Philosophical Theology

ROBERT P. SCHARLEMANN

INSCRIPTIONS
AND
REFLECTIONS
Essays in
Philosophical Theology

University Press of Virginia
Charlottesville

THE UNIVERSITY PRESS OF VIRGINIA
Copyright © 1989 by the Rector and Visitors
of the University of Virginia

First published 1989

Library of Congress Cataloging-in-Publication Data

Scharlemann, Robert P.
Inscriptions and reflections.

(Studies in religion and culture)
Includes index.
1. Philosophical theology. I. Title. II. Series:
Studies in religion and culture (Charlottesville, Va.)
BT40.S28   1989   230'.01   88-33912
ISBN 0-8139-1225-3

Printed in the United States of America

CONTENTS

PART THREE
THE QUESTION OF PLURALISM

FOREWORD

Robert Scharlemann in a wide range of publications has assessed and interrogated the basic framework of the Western tradition in philosophy and theology and has provided fresh and important insights into the possibilities for theological reconstruction in our period. The essays composing this book, with cumulative force, supplement this work and clarify its import for contemporary discussion of the relevance for theology of recent theories of discourse formation.

The essays in Part One, "Ontology and Theology," complemented by chapter 16, are clearly an original rethinking of the problematic of philosophical theology. Scharlemann's understanding of theology as an "afterthinking" (*metanoesis*) and an inversion of traditional ontology is a unique English-language contribution to the current discussion that stems from German hermeneutical theology and French deconstructionist philosophy. But his work involves much more than merely a description of the present scene in Continental philosophy and theology. With extraordinary clarity he has developed through a very complex argument a theological concept of *alterity* that is as radical as that which is a part of the theology of Karl Barth, though it is developed not out of a theory of revelation but out of his account of how the name "God" functions in formal discourse.

Though many of Scharlemann's insights resemble those that are central to deconstructionist thought, he demonstrates that it is the radical function of the word *God* in theological discourse that gives access to meanings that transcend any merely semantic order of reference. And he insists with great cogency that, insofar as the Western theological tradition bears witness to realities that are beyond the range of discourse itself, it requires a revisioning of both language and theology that will inevitably entail new ways of exploring the possibilities of current and future theological enterprise.

The essays in Parts Two and Three augment the more purely theoretical insights of Part One. Here, as Scharlemann discusses and analyzes the work of such thinkers as Barth, Tillich, Hegel, and Jüngel, he helps us to place his own reflections in relation to the larger conversations making up modern theological tradition. The chapters on music, *Faust,* and the biblical tradition can be read as independent essays; but in many interesting ways these pieces disclose the richness of import belonging to his basic theoretical work.

Indeed, we confront in this book a body of thought that is virtually without analogue in contemporary American theology, for there are few people in the theological community who are working with fundamental issues in the theory of discourse formation, at either a philosophical or theological level; and the recent publications of theologians representing a deconstructionist sensibility are much less directly concerned with the funded Christian theological tradition than is Scharlemann. Moreover, most of the important figures in Christian theology have not at all seriously addressed the new questions being posed by post-Heideggerian and poststructuralist thought. But this is precisely what Scharlemann is undertaking to do in these essays, as in his recent book *The Being of God.*

His style is clear and readable, even while his arguments are complex and philosophically demanding. Because of its clarity and readability, this collection of essays provides theological readers with a unique opportunity to engage some of the most important philosophical problems facing contemporary theology, even if they are without previous initiation into recent philosophical debate. And those readers who approach these essays from a philosophical or literary perspective will be fascinated by the ways in which a radical kind of theological investigation intersects with the sort of inquiry being carried forward by the avant-garde in contemporary philosophy and literary theory.

The carefulness and soundness of Scharlemann's scholarship are in every way exemplary. His thorough knowledge of the history of

Western philosophy and theology is equaled by his alertness to
the current intellectual scene, so that he is forgetful neither of the
tradition nor of his own situation. And thus he presents a body of
work that is at once thoroughly theological and thoroughly secular. So we may say that he offers indeed an apologia for theology in
a predominantly secular culture.

Charles E. Winquist
Thomas J. Watson Professor of Religion
Syracuse University

PREFACE

One way of describing the task of theology is to say that it is to inscribe the name "God" upon any name, the tale "God is" upon any event, and the judgment "God is God" upon any identity. But how can such inscription be done without eradicating those names, events, and identities that come into play on their own? In the essays collected for this volume, I have set forth some principles and applications which indicate a way in which it has seemed to me to be possible to do so. The way is at best a path and not a strict method. The collection is called "inscriptions and reflections" to indicate that the essays represent attempts at such inscription as well as reflections on whether and how it can be done.

The chapters that appear in part 1 under the heading "Ontology and Theology" are those which are most directly concerned with the principles involved, understood both historically and constructively or systematically. Part 2 brings essays that represent specific applications or treat specific questions concerned with aspects of science and art. The themes treated by no means exhaust even basic issues, but they are illustrative of one way of understanding the connections of science and art to theology. In part 3, the question of pluralism, in many ways the most urgent of theoretical questions, becomes a focus of attention. How is it possible, within a framework of thought and from a definite standpoint, to reckon with the alterity of the other standpoints? Can that about which one thinks be a unity without also being a manifold? How is the many-ness of the one related to its oneness?

Since the essays, which were originally prepared as articles or as lectures, were not written with a view to being published together, there is a certain amount of repetition in them and there are more than a few gaps. I have tried to reduce the number of gaps by including articles that supplement one another; but, in the hope that the amount of repetitiousness is not intolerable (and that readers will be patient enough to put up with the recurrence of the same examples in several essays), I have eliminated only a few of the repetitions. Almost all of the essays, however, have been revised in minor ways for this publication.

ACKNOWLEDGMENTS

Chapter 1, "Onto- and Theo-logical Thinking," was presented as a paper to the Duodecim Theological Society in 1986. It is based upon an earlier essay, entitled "Being Open and Thinking Theologically" and published in *Unfinished . . . : Essays in Honor of Ray Hart*, ed. Mark Taylor (Chico: Scholars Press, 1981), pp. 111–24.

Chapter 2, "The Identity of God and the *Crucifixus*," appeared in *God: The Contemporary Discussion*, ed. Frederick Sontag and M. Darrol Bryant (New York: Rose of Sharon Press, 1982), pp. 261–77; it is reprinted by permission of the publisher.

Chapter 3, "The Being of God When God Is Not Being God: Deconstructing the History of Theism," from *Deconstruction and Theology* by Thomas J. J. Altizer, Jr., et al., © 1982 by The Crossroad Publishing Company, is reprinted by permission of The Crossroad Publishing Company.

Chapter 4, "Being 'As Not': Overturning the Ontological," was presented as a paper for a discussion group of the hermeneutics of Paul Ricoeur at the annual meeting of the American Academy of Religion in 1981; a slightly abbreviated version appeared under the same title in *Dialog* 21, no. 1 (1982): 114–20; it is reprinted by permission of the editor.

Chapter 5, "Does Saying Make It So? The Language of Instantiation in Buber's *I and Thou*," appeared in *God in Language*, ed. Robert P. Scharlemann and Gilbert E. M. Ogutu (New York: Paragon House Publishers, 1987), pp. 114–27; it is reprinted by permission of the publisher.

Chapter 6, "Hegel and Theology Today," appeared in *Dialog* 23, no. 4 (1984): 257–62; it is reprinted by permission of the editor.

Chapter 7, "Schelling's Impact on Protestant Theology," was presented to the Nineteenth Century Theology Group at the annual meeting of the American Academy of Religion in 1984 and was published in the papers of that group.

Chapter 8, "The No to Nothing and the Nothing to Know: Barth and Tillich and the Possibility of Theological Science," presented as an address at the annual meeting of the American Academy of Religion in 1986, appeared in *Journal of the American Academy of Religion* 55, no. 1 (1987): 57–72; it is reprinted by permission of the editor.

Chapter 9, "Constructing Theological Models," appeared under the title "Theological Models and Their Construction," in *The Journal of Religion* 53, no. 1 (1973): 65–82, © The University of Chicago Press; it is reprinted by permission of the University of Chicago Press.

Chapter 10, "Biblical Tradition and Liberal Learning," appeared in *Dialog* 19, no. 1 (1980): 99–105; it is reprinted by permission of the editor.

Chapter 11, "Theology and Music," is a slightly revised version of a paper presented to a Conference on Sacred Music at the University of Iowa in 1967; it appeared in *Response* 9, no. 2 (1967): 66–72.

Chapter 12, "Goethe's and Berlioz's Faust," is a slightly revised version of a symposium paper presented at the University of Iowa in 1979.

Chapter 13, "Demons, Idols, and the Symbol of Symbols in Tillich's Theology of Politics," appeared in *Religion et culture: Actes du colloque international du centenaire Paul Tillich (Québec 18–22 août 1986)*, ed. Michel Despland, Jean-Claude Petit, Jean Richard (Laval: Les Presses de l'Université Laval, Les Editions du Cerf, 1987), pp. 114–27; it is reprinted by permission of the editors.

Chapter 14, "The Argument from Faith to History," appeared in *Religion in Life* 48, no. 2 (1974): 137–49, © 1974 by Abingdon Press; it is reprinted by permission of the publisher.

Chapter 15, "Pluralism in Theology," appeared in *Journal of Ecumenical Studies* 5, no. 4 (1968): 676–96; it is reprinted by permission of the editor.

Chapter 16, "One of the Many and the Many of the One," was delivered as a plenary address at the fifth conference in a series sponsored by the New Ecumenical Research Association under the title "God: The Contemporary Discussion" (1986).

PART ONE
Ontology and Theology

1

ONTO- AND THEO-LOGICAL

THINKING

HEIDEGGER'S ESSAY on the ontotheological constitution of metaphysics, which raised the question of how God got into philosophy and made the suggestion that the godless philosophy of today
might be closer to the godly God than is any metaphysical theism,
introduced a theme that more recently has been taken up by the
deconstructionists. In one sense, Heidegger was only reiterating
what Barth and Tillich and other dialectical theologians in the
early 1920s had already said, Barth in his speaking of theology as
both impossible and necessary and Tillich in speaking of overcoming the concept of religion in the philosophy of religion. But
Heidegger put the matter as a question for philosophy, not just a
question for theology, and as a question about the very foundations of Western thought. Unlike some of the deconstructionists,
Heidegger did not conclude that theology was no longer possible,
as though it had at one time been possible but was no longer so.
But he did raise anew the question of what kind of thinking it
might be. Is theology, as he stated in *Phenomenology and Theology* (1928), an ontic science, namely, the science of that mode
of existence made possible by Christian faith? Or is theology, as
Tillich's method of correlation implies, a mode of thinking not
subordinate to but on a par with ontology, not an ontic science
but a theological knowledge?

In pursuing an answer to these and related questions, I should
like to propose that a distinctively theological thinking has the
nature of an "afterthinking" (*metanoein*) in which ontological
thinking is rethought and inverted. This is not meant to be a de-

scription of everything that one might find in books of theology, but it is meant to say that there is a kind of thinking that distinguishes theology as such from other modes of thought. It is a theontology not on the basis of an identity of God and being, as in ontotheological metaphysics, but on the basis of a difference between them. All of this will take us into some rather abstract considerations, but I hope the example at the end of the chapter will help to make things clearer and more concrete.

Ontological Thinking

The initial task is to indicate what is meant by "thinking" and "being" and by "ontology" as a thinking in which thinking is identical with being.

Thinking. To think is to present something to mind as it is on its own; it is to make oneself conscious *of* something *as* what that thing *is* in itself. Within thinking so defined, there are three distinguishable modes or phases: objective thinking (as formulated in a judgment like "That is a tree"), reflective thinking ("That is the truth"), and reflexive thinking ("This is thinking"). They are distinguished from one another by the kind of object to which they are directed.

Thus, one is not "thinking" when one is dreamily gazing out the window and one's eye tracks a rabbit running across the lawn or a leaf drifting down from a tree onto the ground. In such a dreamy state, the eye follows the movement of the rabbit and leaf without getting them into focus *as* the rabbit and the leaf that they are. If the daydream is interrupted by the ringing of a telephone, the aroused dreamer can still recall the dreamy state and, through recalling it, think of the rabbit and the leaf as what they were; but this synthesis of a dream appearance into a thought of reality does not belong to the dreamy state itself. Such a state is, strictly speaking, a prethinking—a consciousness not entirely disconnected from thinking, since it can be recalled, and yet only capable of objectifying its content when the reverie has already passed; the synthesis or interpretation, in which the reality is presented to mind as what it is on its own, is performed on the dreamy observation only retrospectively.

The retrospective thinking that can objectify the content of the dreamy state by recalling it is also the mode of thinking at work in our understanding of the everyday world as a world of things that are there. To think of a tree, a stone, a person, and the like, is to present them to mind as they appear in reality to be; objective thoughts are thoughts *of* things which, as things, are different from the thoughts of them. The relation indicated here—when one says that a thought *is of* a thing but *is not* the thing—is the "intentionality" of thinking, which is the basis of its objectivity, and the "otherness" of being. If we could not distinguish, in our thinking, between the thought of a tree and a tree, we could not think objectively at all.

Intentionality and otherness are characteristic of the *objective* thinking of things in the world. *Reflective* thinking has to do not with things that are other than the thought of them but with relations between the intentionality and the otherness. A tree (a stone, a person, and so on) is an object of objective thinking; "truth," by contrast, is the name of an object of reflective thinking. For truth does not appear as another thing in the world alongside the trees and stones; it appears, rather, "upon" or "at" the otherness of the thing and the intentionality of the thought. The Aristotelian definition of truth as the correspondence between understanding and reality can be disengaged from the particular notion of resemblance (as though the mental intention had to be a picture resembling the appearance of the object) and can be understood to say that truth is a reflective object: we perceive truth as the sameness in the difference between the thought and the thing. When we think of something so that the way in which we think of it is the same as the way in which it shows itself to be on its own, even though it is as such different from our thought of it, then what appears with that objective thing is the reflective object truth.

Objective, or mundane, thinking has to do with trees and such; reflective thinking has to do with truth, goodness, and such; *reflexive* thinking (or "speculation [mirroring]," as it was called by the speculative idealists) has to do with objects that are identical with the thoughts of them. To think of thinking differs from thinking of truth and thinking of a tree because, when we think of thinking, the activity and the object are exactly the same. We think of a tree but understand that the thought of the tree is not the tree itself; we think of truth but understand that truth is different from the thought of truth; we think of thinking and understand that thinking is the same as the thought of thinking.

When thought is reflexive, thinking and being are identical in the sense that that of which one is thinking is nothing other than the thinking by which one thinks of it. To think about thinking is to present to mind thinking as thinking, or the being of thinking. But what thinking is on its own and what we are doing when we think are exactly the same. Hence, in reflexive thinking there is an identity between thinking and being that does not appear in reflective or objective thinking. The thought of a tree is not an example of a tree; the thought of truth is not a case of truth; but the thought of thinking is a matter of thinking. In reflexive thinking there is an identity of thinking and being because what we are doing when we think is a case of that about which we are thinking. That makes reflexive thinking ontological—both a thinking and a being, a thinking that is a being and a being that is a thinking.

There is, to be sure, an identity of thinking and being even in reflective thought, but only an identity between our being and our thinking, not an identity between our thinking and the being of that of which we are thinking. This identity in reflective thought is shown, for example, in the fact that "being open" and "telling the truth" can be nearly synonymous expressions. If a person has made an assertion, the question "Are you being open when you say that?" amounts to the same as the question "Are you telling the truth when you say that?" What we *say*, when we make an assertion about something, is an expression of objective thinking; what we *tell* along with what we say makes a reference to reflective objects. We can say that there is a tree in the middle of the parking lot; what we tell, when we say that, is either the true or the false. Our telling and our being are, however, identical in a way that our saying and our being are not identical. When we tell the truth, we are being open; when we tell the false, we are not being open. To be open is not the same as to say that there is a tree; but it is the same as to tell the truth. Hence, *when* we tell, we are ourselves, in one way or another. Making an assertion is to enact thinking, by putting it into words; it is to say something about something. To say something is, at the same time, to tell something else (the true or the false); and to tell the true or the false is to be open or closed. The assertion discloses the being of the object, by saying what it is, and simultaneously it makes known a reflective object, by telling the truth, and the being of the teller, by showing the teller as open.

In that sense, we cannot say something about something without constituting an identity between what we are thinking and how we are being. This is not an identity between *our* thinking and *its* being but between our thinking and our being. Just for that reason, as it seems to me, Heidegger's effort in *Being and Time* to arrive at the meaning of being by an interpretation of the being of Dasein could not reach its goal. The most one can attain by an existentialist analysis of the identity of thinking and being in reflection is the meaning of the being of our thinking but not the meaning of being. Heidegger could get at the meaning of the being of Dasein, but he could not divest Dasein of its *da* in order to arrive at the meaning of being. The meaning of our thinking, if our thinking is *Sorge*, may well be shown to be temporality. But temporality as the meaning of the being of being-there is not yet the meaning of being as such.

Reflective thinking is, in other words, ontological to the degree that the mode of being of the teller and the act of telling are the same; but it is not ontological to a degree that the being of the teller, the telling, and the told are all identical.

Being. To think is to present to mind something as it is on its own. It is directed toward the "being" of things. "Being" is to be understood here as different from percepts (of particulars or singulars) and from abstract thoughts (of generals or universals). We do not perceive being nor think it abstractly but "understand" it as the unity, or connection, of the singular with the universal. The singular is what we perceive ("this thing here-now"); the universal is what we abstractly conceive ("a woody perennial plant with one main trunk . . ."); and being is what we think or understand ("this 'as' a woody perennial plant"; "this 'as' a tree"). Being is the synthesis in the object that makes it possible for us to understand a singular (perceived) *as* a universal (abstractly conceived), just as thinking is the presenting to mind of a singular as a universal. In a judgment ("This is a tree, i.e., a woody perennial plant . . ."), being (which we understand) is expressed by the copula connecting the subject (the singular which we perceive) with the predicate (the universal which we abstractly conceive), and the connection is always at the same time a temporalizing ("is," "was," "will be").

Now, the identity of thinking and being in reflexive thinking is an identity in which the act of the thinker (which is an act of thinking, that is, of joining a singular with a universal through the synthetic "as") and the object of the thought (which is the being of thinking, that is, a unity of a singular act with an abstract concept ["what I am now engaged in is a joining of a singular with a universal"]) are just the same. The percept involved here is the awareness one has of one's own act while performing it; the con-

cept is the abstract notion of "joining singular and universal"; and
the thought or understanding is the actual joining of the singular
and universal. In thinking, what I am doing is joining singular and
universal; what the object of that thought is, is the joining of singular and universal; and what I am while doing this is a juncture
of singular and universal: I am, in act, a case of what thinking as
such is. (One needs to make a reservation here by noting that the
identity is not complete: I am *a case of* the thinking of being and
the being of thinking, but I am not simply the thinking of being
and the being of thinking. However, one need not go into that reservation further, despite its importance for marking historically
the point at which speculative idealism faltered, because it will
not be necessary for the main purpose, which is to delineate the
features of theology as an afterthinking.)

Theological Thinking

What is theological thinking in reference to this ontological thinking? Four different types of answer have been proposed to this question by theologians influenced by Heidegger. One type makes a
proposal to the effect that theology thinks holy being as ontology
thinks being. John Macquarrie's *Principles of Christian Theology*
is an example of this type, for Macquarrie uses a Heideggerian
conception of ontology in order to recover a version of natural
theology as the foundation for symbolical theology.[1] The relation
of God to being is specified here as the relation of holy being to
being. What remains somewhat unclear is whether this relation is
that of species to genus, so that the scope of "being" is logically
larger than the scope of "God," or whether the difference lies only
in the relation to being. "Holy being," or "God," differs from
"being" in this latter case not in the way that a maple tree differs
from a tree as such but in the way that a tree which is the object
of observation differs from a tree which is an object of response (as
when, say, its falling leaves are not just falling leaves but a re-
minder of one's mortality). Heinrich Ott, similarly, in saying that
theology is to think God as ontology thinks being, the former a
thinking by faith and the latter a thinking by philosophy, leaves
unanswered questions having to do with the relation between
being God and being at all.

A second type, represented in Ray Hart's *Unfinished Man and
the Imagination*, inserts theology in an ontological "crack": the
openness of self to world and the openness manifested in the dif-

ference between being and entities are the place where the being of God appears to imagination.[2] God is not identical with the ontological structure but appears in the open region between the elements that constitute that structure. Were one to follow the path here delineated, theological thinking would have the character of a reflection on the images in which God is perceived. As a form of thinking, theology would not be distinct from any other thinking; its distinction would lie only in the way its object is presented to it—through the imagination that fills in the open region in being.

A third type can be found in Ricoeur's hermeneutic of religious symbols, and in the speculative idealism that is its precursor. Here theology is an ontological thinking in which the unformed content of prethought, expressed in religious myths (or, for Schleiermacher, in feeling), is brought together with reflexively formed thought. Theological thinking synthesizes the mythic reality with the reflexive form, so that reflexive thinking is a mirror of the reality content that is given in myth but is lost when thinking becomes critical; it is then a self-conscious apprehension of things as objects over against a self. To a pure, prenoetic beholding (the "mythical consciousness," if one will), the image of deity counts as the reality of deity; and it is this naïveté that theological thinking is to recover in a second naïveté or mediated immediacy. Fritz Buri's conception of theology as a self-understanding of faith probably fits into this same type.

Similar to the third type is a fourth type, represented preeminently by Tillich's method of correlation. It differs from the third type by the way in which it coordinates ontology and theology and connects them as coordinate. It is similar to the speculative type in seeing the task of theology in the mediation between critical thought and religious symbols. As a form of thinking, however, theology is a second-order thinking (a thinking about thinking), in which ontological thinking and religious symbols are related to each other through an interpretation that lets ontological thinking have the character of a sign-thing (a "question," which points to but does not point out) and lets religious symbols have the character of realities that point out only by pointing to. Theology itself, as a second-order thinking, is a reflective thought that does not appear to differ from other reflective thought. Yet that is surely too Kantian for Tillich's own intentions; so it is not entirely clear (despite Tillich's own agreement with that description of his conception of theology) that that is what Tillich origi-

nally envisaged when he began work on the correlating of ontology and theology.

These four types seem to exhaust the possibilities. How else
could theology be related to ontology if ontology means the thinking of being as such? Does not being as such have to include the
being of God? Is not ontology, then, the fundamental discipline
since it has to do with the unity of the singular and the universal
aspect of anything at all—is not the being of God (that by virtue
of which or by reference to which God "is" God) included in being
as such?

The only remaining possibility, so far as I can see, is to understand theology as an afterthinking, or *metanoein,* of the thinking
of being. Thinking is always a thinking *of* something *as* something; it is never a pure beholding or a nonsynthetic intuition but
always a synthesis performed with either the hermeneutical "as"
of anecdotal understanding (when we see a tree we do not explicitly see something as a tree, though that is implicit in the understanding) or the apophantic "as" in explicit judgments (which distinguish the subject from the predicate and connect them with
a copula). But the elements of a synthesis can be inverted. This
leads me to propose that theological thinking is an inversion of
ontological thinking, so that *to think theologically is to think of
the thinking of being (ontology) not as our thinking of being but
as the being of God when God is not being God.* What does such
a formulation intend to say?

Let me start with a quotation from Moltmann's *The Crucified
God.* The title of that book was suggested, if I am not mistaken,
by a statement in Heidegger's *Phenomenology and Theology* of
1928: "The entity that is manifest . . . only for faith and that, as a
revelation, is what even 'times' faith at all is . . . Christ the crucified God."[3] But whether or not there is that connection with
Heidegger, Moltmann gives an illustration of the inversion of
thinking when he remarks: "Faith must think of the suffering of
Christ as the power of God, and the death of Christ as God's potentiality."[4] The suffering of Christ is, surely, not the power of
God, and the death of Christ not God's potentiality. To think of
the suffering of Christ (which is not the power of God) in that way
(i.e., as the power of God) is, accordingly, to think of the suffering
of Christ as other than what it really is. Moltmann's coupling of
such thinking with the word "must" is, admittedly, out of place
(for we "must" think of things as they are, but we "can" think of
them as they are not); moreover, what is inverted here is not on-

tological but ontic thought. Even so, the statement does give a guideline for understanding the inversion that occurs in theological thinking. To understand something theologically presupposes this kind of turn, as a turn from thinking to afterthinking. A second example might be provided by John the Baptist's injunction if one were to translate "Repent! For the kingdom of God is at hand!" with the words "Think again! This is the kingdom of God"—what the hearers think of as other than the kingdom of God, when they think of a reality as it is, is to be rethought as the kingdom of God.

Transferred from ontic to ontological planes, afterthinking is the rethinking of our thinking of being as the being of God. Nothing is required to make such an inversion other than the freedom of thinking itself. We just can think of thinking as other than itself—nothing prevents us from doing so. But this possibility remains empty, merely a formal inversion, if there is no extra-noetic reality to which it is related. Standing in the presence of a tree, I *can* form the thought "This is a bear," but then I am not thinking of the thing as what it is on its own. Hence, a major question for theological thinking, if it is to be an inversion of ontological thinking, is how the otherness of reflexive thought (named "the being of God") is presented *to* thinking to be thought about. Without its being so presented, the thought of the thinking of being as the being of God when God is not being God is not a thinking *of* anything but only a play with its own synthetic elements—it has no more bearing on reality than does the thought "This is a bear" when I am in the presence of a tree.

So the question is this: To what reality is this metanoetic thought related? To what is the thought of the thinking of being as the being of God when God is not being God a response? It seems to me the answer to this question can be found if we look at the double function of language. On the one hand, language formulates thinking; on the other hand, it donates being. It is both form and datum, the medium for grasping the forms of reality as well as the medium for giving the real to thought. This is reflected in there being two languages for the ontological structure (the structure contained in the thinking of being). That is to say, the self-other structure of the thinking of being can be put into words in two different ways. Put into words in one way, it is expressed by them; put into words in another way, it is given by them. For every relation of the self to reality there is both an account and a second account. In the one account, we assert something about reality (what we can say of it on our own); in the second account, reality is made the datum for us. What we can say on our own and what we can be told by another represent the two accounts. Through saying we can express our thought of something as what it is—our thought of its being. Through being told, we can be given the reality as a present power. Language is both the medium in which I think and the medium in which I am given to think. So there is a language that says what is thought, and there is also a language that gives what is to be thought.

It is this second kind of language that enables afterthinking to be more than a formal possibility. For this language proposes to thinking something that can be thought through the inversion of the thinking of being. Let me use as an example two ways of talking about the *Sein zum Tode* that is the existential mode of thinking—the thought "We-are-to-come-to-an-end" that is the implicit direction of the thought of anything at all. There is a language in which we can assert this finitude as the finitude it is. Such a language is existential language. When I speak of finitude by speaking of the "I-am-to-come-to-an-end" as the possibility most my own, I assert the finitude of the thinking of being. I alone, and only I, can veritably end only by not being able to do so as I. In a Heideggerian phrasing, death is the possibility of the impossibility of having any possibility of being in the world. Authentic existential language is the language in which one can say what finitude as a free possibility, the possibility most my own, is. Its counterpart, the language that gives the reality of which it speaks, is christological language. Christological language is the language in which the free possibility is *told to me*, just as existential language is the language in which it is *said by me*. Objectively, the phrase "the cross of the Christ" and the phrase "the death of everyone and anyone" refer to the same event, the universality of the human destiny of coming to an end. But the latter puts it into words that one can say *of* anyone, including oneself; the former puts it into words that can be said *to* one (which one can hear) of oneself and anyone. "Christ died" speaks of the same event as does the anecdotal "everyone dies" and the authentic "I alone, and only 'I,' always can die." But the christological language *gives* the reality that the everyday and authentic language *asserts*. Through the christological language one receives the reality that one asserts, or intends, when using the ordinary or authentic language.

The christological in this sense does not, however, involve any inversion of the existential. Here it is intended to illustrate the difference between donative and assertive language, but not the difference between thinking and afterthinking. Its point is to show that the existence of a language which can give the power of reality to be thought is what makes it possible for afterthinking to be more than a formal change in thinking itself.

An Illustration: The Thinking of Finitude

Suppose that we designate the theme of our thinking as "mortality" or "finitude" and, by using some material from Heidegger's discussion of the theme, follow the way in which mortality is interpreted in ontic language, existential language, ontological language, and, finally, theological language. The statement "Everyone dies" formulates the thought of finitude as an objective reality; the existential assertion "I alone, and only I, can always die" formulates the thought of finitude as an extreme ontological possibility; the christological declaration "Christ died" makes into a real datum the reality to which the everyday and the existential thinking is related. Finitude is expressed in this that I am always to-come-to-an-end. To-come-to-an-end is the extreme possibility of the thinking of being. On the one hand, it is an impossibility— for what I can never do, as I, is really end, though I can do such things as end this chapter. On the other hand, it is a possibility— for I can say "I end" and try to think it. "End" is the not that I can always do. So, strictly speaking, I am the one who can always come to an end but who can never end. End is what I always can do but only negatively; it is always that which I, as I, can not-do, the negative possibility.

"Being toward death," that is, thinking of the end, which hangs over existence, is a phenomenon that Heidegger used to show the difference between everyday and authentic forms of understanding. It can also serve here to show the difference between ontological and theological thought. All understanding is pervaded with the thought of an end; it is always understanding finitely. In Heidegger's characterization death, mortality as an existential phenomenon, is the possibility of having no possibility of being in the world. It is interpreted by everyday talk in the third person as meaning "Everyone dies," implying that everyone dies, but for the time being not I. In the time being, the end occurs but is not something that I as I can or do do. Such an everyday understanding is ambiguous. What in the end, though not for the time being,

is always the possibility most my own, is set forth as a public occurrence—something that is always happening to anyone else but
is never what I can do; what is essentially always a possibility,
never an actuality, is treated as something that has always already
occurred to So-and-So by now; and what is always a possibility is
treated as a novelty. These are the features of the phenomenon as
interpreted in the *Gerede,* the *Zweideutigkeit,* and the *Neugier* of
the everyday, or ontic, understanding.

This public interpretation is interpreted in turn as a disguising
of the phenomenon, a flight from it, an avoidance of its reality;
the ontic way of speaking of finitude is interpreted as a flight from
it, and the flight from it is interpreted as a symptom of the loss of
one's own self in the world. So the public interpretation, which
treats finitude as an ontic phenomenon in the world (something
that is always occurring in the world), is properly, or *eigentlich,*
reinterpreted: death is not a phenomenon occurring in the world
but rather everyone's very own "I can," a blueprint of what is
most one's own, not referable to another and not surpassable. It is
the extreme possibility for everyone, not in the general sense of
"everyone, though for the time being not I" but in the sense of
"everyone as 'I' on 'my' own." The movement from understanding the meaning of finitude through the ontic thought "Everyone
dies" (or "All men are mortal") to understanding its meaning
through the thought "I alone, and only 'I,' always am-to-end" is
a process of interpretation involving a difference in the "as" of
thinking of the phenomenon. Ontically, finitude is thought of as
a universal occurrence—"everyone dies, *man stirbt einmal.*" At
the end, properly, it is thought of as the possibility that only I
and I alone have always as possibility and never as actuality. This
completes the movement from unreflected thought to ontological
thought of the same phenomenon. To think of mortality as the
fact that everyone perishes from the world is to think of it ontically; to think of it as the possibility most one's own is to think
of it existentially; to think of it in such a way that one's thinking of it is also one's being it (I think of my thinking of what
finitude is as itself a mode of being finitely: the mode of possibility) is to think of it ontologically.

The last step of the interpretation already has the character of a
certain turnabout in thinking, an *Umdeuten,* as Heidegger called
it, because the subject of the phenomenon which, at the beginning, was "everyone but not I" is, at the end, "I and I alone" and
because what was read, at the beginning, as an occurrence taking

place again and again is read, at the end, as an ability, the extreme limit of what I can do. "I can come to an end" is then understood to mean not that something may, by chance, happen to me, as it happens to everyone else, but rather that come-to-an-end is what, as I, I can always do but never actually do do. It is the utmost of what I can do as an "I can," the last horizon of possible being. (That I can think of my being able to think of my being able to not-be as my being able to not-be is the reflexive thought that is simultaneously an unsurpassable power to be finitely.)

Before taking the next step, by inverting the ontological, it may be helpful to recall here the modes of thinking outlined in the first part of this chapter. (1) Objectively, we think of the being of things by understanding them as they are. When I understand this-thing-here-now (the thing I have in mind or in view) as a tree and understand a tree as a woody perennial plant, I am thinking ontically, or objectively. Mundane objects are "entities," syntheses of singulars, of which we are directly aware, with universals, which we grasp as abstract forms, by means of the copula of being. Existentially, we think of the being of the self by understanding what "I" as such can do. The synthesis of "I" with this-one-here in "I am this-one-here," which constitutes the being of a person, joins the subjectivity of which we are immediately aware in the thought "I" with a temporal location (embodiment). Persons in that sense are potentialities rather than entities, the *can be*'s of the self as "I." (2) When I think of the assertion "This is a tree" as true, I am thinking reflectively. Reflective objects like truth are not syntheses of concrete singulars with abstract universals but, rather, syntheses of realities with meanings (e.g., truth as the connection of the "is" of a proposition with the "is" of the entity). Reflective objects are, thus, not "entities" but transcendences (they are bridges between reality and meaning). (3) Reflexively, we think not of entities or transcendences but of our thinking-of. Thus, to think of the thinking of anything as a synthesizing of a synthesis is to think reflexively. The reflexive object is always ontological, a unity of thinking and being; and reflexive thinking is likewise ontologically a unity of thinking and being. To think of the thinking of being is at the same time to be the being of thinking.

Mortality, or finitude, is a *mundane* object when it is thought of as the death that occurs in the world, and it is an *existential* object when it is thought of as the not-be that I can always do, my power to be-not. It is an *ontological* object when I think of my

finitely thinking of being as what it is, namely, my being finitely;
I think of my thinking finitely as my own "I am-to-end." The
mundane, existential, and ontological thoughts of death are traversed in Heidegger's analysis of being-to-die. What is the *theological* thought of the same phenomenon? The formulation, I have
suggested, is this: To think anything theologically is to think of
our thinking of its being as other than our thinking of its being,
namely, as the being of God when God is other than deity. How is
this applied to the theme of finitude or mortality?

Mundane thinking, because it disguises mortality, is itself a
way of thinking of death not as what it really is (namely, the possibility most one's own); but this is a disguise, not an inversion of
the thinking of being. Authentically, one thinks of it as death,
that is, as the possibility most one's own. The authentic thought
is also ontological: to think "I am not thinking" is to be at one's
end, it is to enact the possibility that is pure possibility. To think
this possibility theologically is to think of the pure possibility of
my thinking of anything (namely, the thinking of "I am not thinking") *as* other than itself, namely, as the pure actuality of God's
being in the world (my "can always" as God's "is already"). The
phenomenon of which we are thinking when we think of our not
thinking is the phenomenon of the extreme possibility most our
own. It is the phenomenon given such names as "finitude," "mortality," "*Sein zum Tode*," and "sickness unto death." To think this
phenomenon over, to afterthink or rethink it, means to think of it
as other than what it ontologically is. This is what we do when
we think of it not as the extreme possibility of the thinking that
is most our own but as the extreme actuality that is most other—
the actuality of God (who is not-I, not-this, and not-nothing either) when God is not being God (or is most other than God).

If this *metanoesis* is to be more than a formal inversion, however, the thought of our pure possibility (the possibility of "not")
as the actual reality of God must arise as a response to some enabling language, some language that donates the reality which the
thought projects. In Christian theology, it seems to me, this is the
function of the narrative of the resurrection of Jesus when that
narrative is donative language. Thus, if the narrative of the death
of the Christ is a christological language, which presents the reality of which existential language projects the possibility, then the
narrative of the resurrection of the Christ is a theological language that grants the reality projected by the inversion of ontological language that is the expression of *metanoesis*.

2

THE IDENTITY OF GOD
AND THE *CRUCIFIXUS*

Das primär für den Glauben und nur für ihn Offenbare
und als Offenbarung den Glauben allererst zeitigende
Seiende ist für den "christlichen" Glauben Christus, der
gekreuzigte Gott.
— Martin Heidegger

WHAT KIND of thinking is it that makes an identity between the
meaning of the name "God" and the historical reality of the crucified Jesus? And what kind of being is the being involved in this
identity? It is not enough here to answer that these are the "thinking" done by faith (instead of, say, by *scientia*) and the "being"
that belongs to the object of faith (rather than to an empirical or
a metaphysical object). On the contrary, these questions demand
a reflection on how theology thinks at all. Picht's work toward a
thinking that is a thanking, Jüngel's effort to rehabilitate the doctrine of analogy, and Ricoeur's theory of metaphor, which relocates metaphor in the copula of discourse rather than in a word,
all recognize this demand.[1] The present chapter sets forth a conception of theological thinking that, while differing from the
three mentioned, undertakes to follow the same general direction. The direction is indicated both by how the being with which
they are concerned is a certain unity of being and not being and
also by how the being of God appears in the midst of the being of
the world.

Here I shall propose, first, that the being of God is not a "being
like" (as in Ricoeur's explication of metaphor) but a "being . . .
as," in which what follows the "as" serves as an ostensive definition of God by showing where (or, better, when) in the world God

is and also as what deity is what it is. The differences set off against each other—between an analogical or metaphorical "being like" and an ostensive "being . . . as"—within theology are not finally exclusive of each other but are related to each other in a dialectical whole. Second, I shall propose that the identity between God and the crucified Jesus is not only a matter of "being . . . as" but also that it is a "being . . . as" that overturns the thinking of being so that the thought of this identity is a μετανοεῖν, an afterthinking, and its object is being in the sense of "being other," or the free appearance of being that Picht describes as a hovering over the abyss of nothing. Hence, the thought of God as the crucified is a "being . . . as" that is simultaneously a "being other": "God is God as the crucified Jesus," or, expressed analogically, "God 'comes to' being-there as Jesus is-not-there" (this latter a paraphrase intended to express Jüngel's rehabilitated *analogia entis*), and this "being . . . as" is the being of God when God is not being God. In order to explicate this, it will be helpful to recall what is meant by the terms "thinking" and "being" in the first place.

First Thesis: The Being of Thinking

The being of thinking, which appears in language as logos, is the unity of showing and defining (naming and predicating).

The word *thinking* designates a mental activity that is to be contrasted with prethinking, or dreaming, and also with a mechanical performance. It is not thinking, but a prethinking state, when we dreamily gaze out the window and our eye tracks the movement of a falling leaf; it is not thinking, but mechanical performance, when we are reading words from a book while our mind is elsewhere or when we repeat conventional opinions without appropriating them through an effort of our own. It *is* a matter of thinking, however, when, with our attention upon an object, we form the thought "This is X." ("That is a tree." "This is a dog.") Thinking involves holding something before our mind and directing attention to it so that the mind shapes itself in accord with how the thing shows itself. It is the conscious activity in which "I" (that is, any self in the power of what is expressed through the first-person singular pronoun) relate myself as a subject to another as an object by reference to the being of the object. "Being," here, refers just to the connection, indicated by the "is" of judg-

ments, between singular ("this") and universal ("dog"), that is, between the percept and the notion of the object. Being appears
upon a physical object as the union of what is perceived and what
is cognized. To think of something is, thus, to present to mind its
being—not its physical appearance, as when we see or recall how
it looks, or its abstract notion, as when we define what we see,
but the connection between the two. One way of doing so may be
through a transcendental image (as Kant called it) or through an
intuition of essence (in Husserl's phenomenology), as when we
mentally picture some generalized tree that contains a schema of
all trees without being a replica of any particular one. But there
are other ways of doing so too; for the being of things is given not
only to the intellect in an image but also to will and feeling. Hence,
"thinking," as used here, includes activities of planning, willing,
hoping, feeling, and the like, as well as of understanding. Each of
them, as an activation of thought, may intend a connection between singular and universal. But the focus of attention here will
be upon being and thinking in relation to intellectual faculties.

This definition of thinking is reflexive; it results from an activity of thinking about thinking, in which the process of thinking itself is made the object of the activity of thinking. In reflexive thought we direct ourselves to the being of thinking, that is,
to being as it appears in the process of thinking itself. But since
thinking is not a physical object, we cannot present its being to
mind by forming a transcendental image, as may be done with
physical objects. Instead, the being of thinking is manifest in language, and manifest as the unity of showing and interpreting, or of
naming and defining. The unity of sensation and cognition, which
is the being of physical objects, does not appear in the process of
thinking; for there is nothing to perceive, but only something of
which to be inwardly aware as we engage in the activity, and there
is therefore nothing to cognize through perception. How then can
the invisible process of thinking be thought at all? How can the
being of thinking be presented to mind? How can we say what
thinking "is"? We can do so to the extent that the being which
appears upon objects in the synthesis of sensation and cognition
("This is a tree; a tree is a woody perennial plant . . .") appears to
thinking itself in the synthesis of the words that show their referent with the words that interpret or define what is shown, a synthesis that appears in words that are less deictic than names and
more deictic than abstract rules. I would take Tillich's use of
what he called the metaphor "ground of being" to be an example

of such a synthesis in words; for the term is less ostensive, or deictic, than the name "God" but more so than the abstract notion
of being-itself, and it contains a schema for the name "God" as
well as for the rule of thinking that the concept of being-itself
implies.

Thus, whereas we can think of the being of a tree because we
can form a general image that is both an abstraction from particular details of perception and also a concretion of the abstract notion, we can think of the being of thinking because we can form
a metalanguage that is both less ostensive than the language of
nouns and more ostensive than the language of abstract rules;
and in this metalanguage the being of thinking becomes manifest.
That is to say, the being of thinking appears in a synthesis of language with itself rather than, as with objects, in a synthesis of
sensation and cognition.

All thinking is synthetic. To think of something is always to
think of it *as* what it is, to present it to mind *as* what it presents
itself in reality to be. But just this synthetic character is what provides a distinction in the kinds of thinking that are possible. For
we can think of thinking (that is, present the being of thinking to
mind) in different ways by rearranging the elements that constitute it. These possibilities are the following:

1. We can think of thinking *as such;* we can think of it as thinking.
2. We can think of thinking *as other* than itself; we can think of it
as being, that is, as the being of the world or as Dasein (the self-
reflective being manifest in human being).
3. We can think of thinking *as other* than itself and than its own
other (being); we can think of it as the being of God.

It is clear that in (1) we have the idea of a critical logic; in (2) is
the idea of ontology, from which both physical science and the
analytics of Dasein are derived; and in (3), the idea of theology,
when the word *God* signifies something or someone other than
the unity of thinking and the structure of the thinking of being.
Physical science is based upon the identity of the forms of thought
with the appearances of the physical world, just as the interpretation of Dasein is based upon the identity of what one is with how
one thinks; both of them presuppose the identity between thinking and being which is expressed in the reflexive thought that
thinking is being and being is thinking. Science, therefore, represents a certain inversion of thinking, for it thinks of thinking not

as thinking (that is, as our activity of making the synthesis) but as being (that is, as the synthesis taking place or existing independently of our thought). This is the thought of the being of the world. Furthermore, when thinking and being are one and the same, as they are in reflexivity (thinking of thinking), we have the idea of our being, the being of Dasein; for when we think, we are, and what we are is the same as how we think. In Dasein, unlike in physical objects, being appears not as the connection of a perceptible singular ("this") with an abstract universal ("tree") but as the thinking which enables the universal "I" to be united with a particular embodiment ("this person here")—that is the sense of *cogito ergo sum*. Existential self-understanding, therefore, also represents an inversion of thinking, for it too is based upon a thinking of thinking as being. Science and self-understanding both presuppose the ontological idea of thinking as being; and, accordingly, this first inversion of thought constitutes the structure of the thinking of being.

The second inversion—which is, in effect, the conversion of thinking to afterthinking, of νοεῖν to μετανοεῖν—comes with the idea of the being of God, when "God" means what is wholly other than our thinking and than the being of the world or of Dasein. This idea is formed by thinking of thinking as other than both itself (in the thinking of being) and its own other (being). To form the idea is to think of thinking as other than the constitution of the ontological structure. For this inversion, the word *God* names what is not-I and not-this. Yet thinking is always done by an "I" and is always about a "this." Hence, the idea of God, as the idea of one who is wholly other, cannot be formed as a conception at all. Instead, to grasp the conception, we must break with thinking by thinking of our thinking as wholly other than itself; that is to say, we must think of it not as our thinking of being but as the being of God. This is not a thinking, but a conversion of thinking, the real *metanoia* of thought; for when we think of our own thinking not as thinking (which ontically it is) nor as our being (which, ontologically, it uniquely is in human being) or the being of the world (which it is in the objects that we think and know as such) but as the being of God, that is, as the thinking which is other than our thinking (because it is of God) and the being which is other than our being and the being of the world (because it is not the object of our thinking), then thought is turned inside out. To "think" thus is to afterthink.

The conversion to afterthinking is made with the thought of

thinking as other than itself, as the being of God. But this transition is only an abstract possibility, without real import, if it is not brought about by something real. Thinking can make the transition on its own, to be sure. Indeed, if the question is asked how afterthinking is possible at all, one answer is to say that the possibility lies in the freedom of thinking itself—the power to form a thought is also the power to invert the elements of thought so as to form an afterthought of the same. With the aid of language, the mind just *can* think of thinking as other than itself; it has the freedom and the power to do so—through thinking it can transcend the whole thinking of being. In a limited way, this freedom is there even in the thought of physically present objects. A person viewing a tree must normally think of it as it presents itself in reality, namely, as a tree; one cannot think of it as a stone if one is to think of *it* as it shows *itself*. Yet the same person can think that the tree, if cut into lumber, provides material for a house, and in that way the mind thinks of the present tree as other than it presents itself, as potentially other than how it actually shows itself, although, in this case, the potential other is still a physical reality. But such inversions remain mere possibilities as long as their origin lies only in the act of the mind itself and not in a response to reality. Hence, something else, something besides the freedom of thinking, is needed in order to make afterthinking a mode of apprehending—an after*thinking* instead of a complete break with reality. This other requirement is the existence of a language which enables thought to make the turn to afterthought as a response to reality, a language that gives the reality to thinking in a "donation" that is, for the thinking of thinking, the same as what a sense "datum" is for the thinking of physical objects. What language is it, then, that "donates" the reality corresponding to the afterthought "Our thinking is (not thinking but) the being of God"? Let us say it is the declaration "God is not God," the declaration that the essence of God's freedom is to be there as other than deity.

The two sides of the matter can now be put together. From the side of the freedom of thought, the transition to afterthinking occurs when we think of the activity of thinking as other than itself. From the side of the donation of reality, the transition occurs when it can be said to us, by our own or by another person, that God is not God, that is to say, when the being of God is presented to mind as other than deity. "Thinking is not thinking" and "God is not God" correspond to each other, the one formulating the freedom that is a power of thinking on its own, and the other formulating the freedom of God (the freedom to be or not to be deity) that is the real donation to which the thought responds.

To *think* that thinking is other than thinking, and to do so in correspondence with the giving of deity in freedom, is to join thinking and afterthinking as well as being and being-other. This juncture serves as the basis of the correspondence between afterthinking and being-other so that afterthinking does not replace thinking, as an alternative to and substitute for the whole of thinking, but is actually joined to it, enabling thinking to be completed in afterthinking or to be "in the world" without being "of the world"; μετανοεῖν does not do away with νοεῖν but adds a dimension to it. The combination of the two—of the whole of thinking and being with the other of that whole—is contained in the two propositions:

(A) "Thinking is thinking as other than itself" and
(B) "God is God as other than God"

These two propositions express the thought and the afterthought of the relation of thinking to afterthinking and of God to non-God, or, in more traditional terminology, of the transcendence to the immanence of God. The first proposition (A) formulates the nature of thinking in its own freedom; the second (B), understood as donating speech, formulates the divine freedom existing as grace. For to think of thinking is to think that thinking is something; and to combine thinking and afterthinking is to form the thought "Thinking is thinking as other than itself." Moreover, if this thought corresponds to reality, then what it corresponds to is something or someone; and to combine being with being-there is to say "God is God as other than God." Here, I would suggest, we have the analogy upon which theology rests:

$$\frac{\text{God's transcendence (God's being)}}{\text{immanence (being-there)}} :: \frac{\text{thinking}}{\text{afterthinking}}$$

in which the point of comparison is the openness of each member of each side to the other member, and of each side to the other side. The analogy can be read as saying, "God is God as other than God when thinking is thinking as other than thinking." This amounts to saying that what corresponds to the conversion of thinking to afterthinking is the nondeification of deity. It is not an analogy of being in which we say that God is to divine being as we are to human being (where the concept of being is common to both sides of the relation), but it is the analogy of otherness, according to which the openness of thinking that is executed in afterthinking is "the same as" (not "like") the openness of God that happens when deity appears as nondeity.

Second Thesis: The Being of God

The being of God in the world is a "being . . . as."

Tillich formulated the basic theological proposition, which combines the realm of symbols with the realm of concepts, as the statement "God is being-itself," which asserts that what the symbol "God" presents is the same as what the concept "being-itself" endeavors to grasp. Without such a proposition to join the two realms, the symbolic and the conceptual would coexist as equally complete, equally total, and yet as totally opposed ways of thinking and modes of being. Barth, similarly, adopted from Anselm the basic proposition "God is that than which nothing greater can be thought," a definition that combines the name of God, as given to faith, with the rule of thinking contained in the phrase "than which nothing greater can be thought." Neither of these two formulations, however, expresses the unity of being and nonbeing which is the character of the freedom or grace of being and which is recognized in more recent interests in metaphor and analogy.[2] These interests in a being that is "being like" chart a direction to follow in order to arrive at a being that is "being . . . as."

By way of preparation, we might recall some remarks made by Picht about the nature of the metaphysical idea of God incorporated in Christian theology in the West. In this metaphysics, the synthesizing activity of thought is considered to be a positing, an activity that places an object within a whole of ordered relations so that true thought is determined by the necessity imposed upon thinking by how being presents itself in objects. Being, positivity, and affirmation go together. To judge "This is a tree" is to affirm it; to do something else—such as cut it into firewood—is to negate it. To this kind of positing thought, Picht contraposes, by following suggestions of Heidegger, a form of thinking that is a "thanking" or "marveling"; and he has contended that this latter is the kind of thinking theology requires. The difference between the two can be illustrated by the way in which the ontological question is answered. The "age of metaphysics," Picht writes, tried to answer the question by referring thinking to a final ground of being.[3] This ultimate ground was absolute being, which had to be thought of as be-ing, otherwise it could not sustain all other entities; and the concept that expressed the being of this *summum ens* was "substance." Metaphysics considered as true all those propositions which could be reduced to the truth of this absolute ground and which accordingly could show what it is that gives every entity its stability and inner consistency. But how else can we understand the sense of being, metaphysically, if not as positivity? Picht replies by calling attention to the "experience of thanking," an experience in which something is affirmed without being posited or held fast as so posited; in gratitude, we experience being not as "firmly grounded positivity" but as "groundless hovering in time."[4] Such thanking affirmations do not allow us to "assert" anything or ourselves with them, but they are affirmations.

This way of affirming, as Picht recounts it, has something in common with metaphorical and analogical thinking; for, as he adds, the "hermeneutics of the basic experience of thanking makes the opposition between doubt and faith disappear."[5] That is to say, it is a thinking of being in which there is a unity of the positive and the negative, a unity of what is otherwise understood as the opposition between being and not being. Doubt contradicts positivity and is always bothersome to thinking when thinking is positing. But for the assent which is expressed in thanks and which uncovers the wonder of creation, or the freedom of being, doubt is the very condition of its possibility.

What is involved here is the following contrast. To "posit" X as X is to place and to fix it on a basis; to "thank" X as X is to marvel at what shows itself in the midst of nothing or of other possibilities. Each of them is a way of thinking, that is, of presenting being to mind. In the context of sense perception, the judgment "This is a tree" is a matter of positing; but in the context of sport or, generally, of playing, an affirmation—for example, "That was a real game!"—is a matter of thanking or marveling. In the first case, being appears as a positive ground of what is there, the understanding (*substans*) unity of the perceptible and the cognizable in the object; in the second case, being appears as what shows itself despite the fact that things could just as well have worked out otherwise. Judging is a response to the positivity of being, whereas thanking (which may be expressed in what looks like a judgment) is a response to the grace of being. Positing suggests building on a foundation. To support judgments is to lead them back to their ground, to give a basis for them; and the ultimate basis is that of absolute substance, which just is. Marveling, or thanking, suggests letting something hover in midair. To support thankful affirmations is always to grant their improbability, to doubt them, but to point out that that is how, marvelously and nonetheless, things show themselves. If thinking is positing, then doubt is answered by referring to grounds or reasons; if thinking is thanking, then doubt is answered by referring to disclosures or events (in the etymological sense of e-vent). The pattern of positing is illustrated by "S is mortal because S is a man and all men are mortal," which cites a necessary and sufficient ground for the judgment. The pattern of thanking is illustrated by "S is mortal not for any hidden reason, such as the mortality of all human beings, but because—and 'because' is not strictly correct here—that is just how, luckily, he shows himself freely to be." Positing always has the character: "X is X because, given the ground or reason, it must be so and could not be otherwise," whereas thanking has the character "X is X though it need not be so and could always also have been otherwise." The being of X in the latter case appears as a fortunate coming together of the opposites that it unites (particular and universal, sensation and thought, activity and result). Its only basis is freedom or felicity; there is no necessary substance upon which it is founded.

I would take the formulations offered above to be in accord with the direction indicated by Picht's remarks. I would also understand those formulations—"God is God as other than God," "Thinking is thinking as other than thinking"—as being in accord with the intention of Tillich's method of correlation and of Barth's statement "God is who he is in the deed of his revelation"[6] as well as with the intention of the doctrine of analogy, even though the formulations involve a certain correction of the analogy—"God is God as other than God" instead of "God is like something (namely, man) that is other than God." The difference in wording has some bearing on how we understand the function of parables too. The parables of the kingdom of God, which do, of course, use the phrase "is like" (and not "is . . . as"), are cases in which the sense is, nonetheless, that the kingdom of God *is* the kingdom of God *as* what occurs in the parables. The difference between the two becomes clear if one contrasts the statement "Richard is Richard as Hamlet" (understood to mean that Richard comes to be himself in the role of Hamlet) with the statement "Richard is like Hamlet."[7]

From this point of view, I think I would have to disagree with part of what Jüngel says of the parables of the kingdom of God. He argues that they do not, in any case, say what the kingdom of God *is;* instead, they say that "mit der Gottesherrschaft *verhält es sich—wie mit* [e.g.] einem Schatz im Acker"—with the kingdom of God, matters are as they are with a treasure in a field.[8] It is not that the kingdom of God *is,* for example, a costly pearl or this treasure in a field; it is rather that, as things go with a pearl or a treasure in a field, so they go with the kingdom of God. Thereupon follows the telling of the story of how things do go. With a treasure in a field, it is so that a man, finding the treasure, sells everything he has and buys the field where he has found it (Mt 13:44 f.). The kingdom of God is of such character that the relation told of in the parable corresponds to it: "Die weltlich unbekannte und aus der Welt allein auch schlechterdings nicht erkennbare Gottesherrschaft (*x*) setzt sich von sich aus in ein Verhältnis zur Welt (*a*), das in der Welt dem entspricht, wie es sich mit der Geschichte vom Schatz im Acker verhält: x→a = b:c [the kingdom of God, unknown and unknowable from within the world, places itself in a relation to the world (x→a), a relation that, in the world, corresponds to how matters are with the treasure in the field (b:c)]."[9] But other remarks that Jüngel makes in this context come closer to what I am proposing here. For he also adds: "Und *während* diese Geschichte erzählt wird, wird der Hörende eingestellt auf die Pointe. . . . Und mit der Pointe *kommt* dann die Gottesherrschaft im Gleichnis selber beim Hörer *an,* wenn dieser sich auf das Gleichnis einläßt und sich durch dieses in dieses versammeln läßt [and *while* this story is told, the hearer is attuned to the point of it. . . . And when the point is reached, God's rulership in the parable *arrives at* the hearer's place, if the hearer is willing to listen and to be drawn into it]."[10] And, in all of this, he emphasizes that the first part of the analogy (a→b) means that God *comes* into language: "Gott *kommt* zur Sprache. Er *kommt* zum Wort."[11] Indeed, it is only the "analogical power" of the gospel that "even brings about" (rather than presupposes) "this special proximity of things which, in principle, are different [viz., God and world]."[12] Hence, a parable does "really [*eigentlich*] and in truth" speak of God even while it uses "the language of the world."[13]

The question in these latter remarks is only what formulation might best express that "proximity," or identity, of the different that is brought about in the effective presentation of a word, as in a parable. For this, again, it seems to me that the most accurate rendering is to say that God *is* God *as* . . . What follows the "as" then points out when, where, and as what, God is the deity God is.

In a literal sense, according to our judgment, the happening, the word, or the story that thus points out the being of God in the world is not God. This is so of the parables of the kingdom of Heaven, as it is of the existence and career of Jesus. The events in which a man sells all he has in order to buy a field where he has found a treasure are not of themselves the kingdom of God. But, at the right time, such events can become the place in the world at which the kingdom is what it in truth is. And when that happens, one can say, "The kingdom of God is the kingdom of God as what happens here." (As an incidental observation, it might be added that the tense of the declaration should perhaps always be the past—the kingdom of God *was* just there when this occurred, and it can come again; or: God *was* in Christ reconciling the world; and so on. Although this matter of tense is hardly negligible, it is a part of the theme from which I am ruthlessly prescinding.) The kingdom of God is what it is concretely as this particular occurrence. In this formulation, both the difference between God and non-God and their identity in time are asserted. The worldly entity or event is the concretion of the being of God, showing when, where, and as what God is really God. And in the whole thought and afterthought that it expresses, there is a combination of necessity and freedom (which Jüngel calls "nothing else than the essence of analogy"),[14] since the necessary thought of the entity or event as the entity or event it is, is combined with the afterthought of this entity or event in relation to the free existence of God—the being of God when God is other than God.

These considerations can be applied, now, to the identity between God and the crucified Jesus. The assertion that in the death of Jesus God shows himself as God is the assertion of the identity between God and the death of the man Jesus. It is, in Christian theology, the basic assertion of the way in which God is in the world and of the time when God was in the world. Abstractly viewed, the identity is an identity between God and not-God. The crucifixion of the man Jesus is the extreme opposite of the living God. The opposition is not only that between deity and humanity—an opposition pervading the biblical tradition, though not necessarily characteristic of other religious traditions, and an opposition that Spinoza expressed sharply in a letter in which he remarked that to speak of God as having taken on a human nature is as nonsensical as to speak of a circle as having taken on the nature of a square [15]—but also that between life and death, the living of deity and the suffering death of a man. If this assertion of identity is intended as the judgment or the thought "God is Jesus and Jesus is God," in which the predicate defines and interprets what the subject names and shows, then it is indeed as nonsensical as any assertion of a contradiction. It can make sense only if it is further interpreted to mean that there is a common basis, a ground, with reference to which one can see both the similarity and the difference between the being of God and the being of Jesus, just as we can make sense of such a contradiction as "An oak is a maple" (when to be a maple means to be not an oak) only by referring both terms to a concept of "tree" as their ground—an oak is a maple because both of them are trees although they are different trees. So, too, we might explain that God is Jesus in the sense that both are deity although they are different persons of the deity: "God" is deity as present to the mind in a word and an image (the first persona), and "Jesus" is deity as present in actual existence (the second persona).

The deficiency in such an interpretation is that it must overlook the sheer incompatibility between what the word and image "God" present to mind (for example, the meaning not-I, and the image of power and activity) and what the actual existence of Jesus is (the appearance of powerless suffering in one who is the "I am"). Christian theology has never really succeeded in showing how there can be an identity of the difference in a way other than the way that thinking must always follow—that is, through a reference to some ground of the difference and similarity. But this deficiency can be eliminated if we understand the identity of the living God with the having-died of Jesus as the point at which the freedom of thinking, executed in its turn to afterthinking, and the freedom of God, embodied in being other than God, correspond to each other. In its turn to afterthinking, it thinks of the death of Jesus as other than what it is; and in the freedom to be, God shows himself as other than God. In such a case, we understand the identity between God and Jesus to be the identity and difference expressed in the proposition

(C) "God is God as the man Jesus,"

a proposition that neither confers deity as a predicate upon Jesus nor denies the actual being of God in the world at a definite time and in a definite way.

3

THE BEING OF GOD WHEN

GOD IS NOT BEING GOD

Deconstructing the History

of Theism

Horruit creatura stupescens ac dicens: quidnam est hoc
novum mysterium? Iudex iudicatur et quietus est;
invisibilis videtur neque erubescit; incomprehensibilis
prehenditur neque indignatur; incommensurabilis
mensuratur neque repugnat; impassibilis patitur neque
ulciscitur; immortalis moritur neque respondet verbum.
—Melito of Sardis, Fragment 13

IN HIS lectures on Augustine and then, later, in his *Being and Time* (1927), Martin Heidegger proposed what he called a "destruction" (*Destruktion*) of the history of ontology, with the stated aim of retrieving the question of the meaning of being, which has been lost, or forgotten, in the metaphysical tradition. After him, there were some sporadic attempts to "destrue" (if one may coin a word parallel to "construe")—to destructure, or to deconstruct—the history of theism in a similar fashion. Dietrich Bonhoeffer's habilitation dissertation, entitled *Akt und Sein*, was discernibly influenced by the early Heidegger and is one of the first indications of how the attempt might be made;[1] but one can also understand the later Bonhoeffer's concern with secularity, together with his rejection of a metaphysical and religious deity, as indicating the same intention. Still, nothing has been done, with the theistic tradition, on the same daunting scale as Heidegger's continual re-readings, by taking apart and putting together again, of the history of ontology in the West. It has been argued that the theological counterpart of Heidegger in this respect may have been none other than Karl Barth, despite his own, "Barthian" reputation. It is not difficult to find the texts in Barth to support such an argument. Indeed, that Barth was never a theist in the traditional sense still seems clear; for, like Heidegger on the meaning of being, he placed the actuality of God prior to the division between theism and atheism and even prior to the logical form of contradiction. This is an aspect of Barth obscured by much of his own work, as well as by his more biblicistic followers. But it is unmistakable, among other places, in the famous controversy with Emil Brunner over whether there can be a natural theology and whether there is a point of contact, an *Anknüpfungspunkt,* in human being for the revelation of God. For among the reasons behind the sharp *Nein!* of his reply, with its "angry introduction," as he titled it, lay his warning that a concern with natural theology would inevitably reintroduce the division between believers and unbelievers, theists and atheists, that has caused mischief in theology for so many centuries. The new theology must reach back, instead, to a place anterior to such divisions, in order to start with the reality of a revelation that is unaffected by the differences between belief and unbelief, theism and atheism, being and nonbeing, optimism and pessimism, and all the rest. Amidst all this, however, Barth seemed never entirely willing to follow his own lead, as if the weight of Protestant biblicism was too much for him to cast off completely. In the end, his theology remained a mixture of an old theism with a new, "destructive" reading of the history of theism in the way it interpreted the theological tradition. The symptom of this is that Barth, like theistic thought otherwise, left the concept of being as such unthought while he directed his attention to the being *of* God or *of* the creature. Nothing shows this, in nuce, more clearly than his reconstruction of the being of God brought into view by the paradoxes—"the immortal dies and does not say a word in response"—formulated in the fragment from Melito of Sardis quoted as epigraph to this chapter.[2] Hence, the task of destruing the history of theism has remained, on the whole, unaccomplished.

Obviously, the present essay will not change that state of things. But, with the perspective of the intervening decades and with the advantage offered by the light of the many variations on the theme of destruction, one can perhaps see more clearly where the task lies.[3]

The Meaning of Destruction

The regressive analysis that is called "destruction," when it is applied to the history of thought, whether ontological or theological, is not something purely negative. To destroy, or destrue, is not the same as to do away with; it is, rather, to analyze the elements of the structure of thought and trace them back to their beginning—what that means needs still to be clarified—in order to discover the experience that is at the basis of the structure.[4] In *Sein und Zeit*, section 6, which is entitled "Die Aufgabe einer Destruktion der Geschichte der Ontologie" (The Task of a Destruction of the History of Ontology), Heidegger gave this account: "We understand this task [of loosening the hardened tradition and of dissolving its obscurities in order to make the question transparent in its own history] as that of the *destruction* of the traditional standing (*Bestand*) of ancient ontology, a destruction which is carried out *under the guidance of the question of being* and which works toward the original experiences in which the first and thenceforth the leading definitions or determinations of being were achieved."[5] This amounts to a kind of genealogy, as Heidegger indicated when he called it an "investigative issuing of a birth certificate"; and, more specifically, it is a genealogy of the ontological concept of temporality as the meaning of the being of human existence (Dasein). Out of what does this concept spring, of what "parents" was it born? Only by carrying out such a destruction of the tradition does the question of being become an actual question again; only such a destruction provides the proof that the question of the meaning of being is unavoidable and demonstrates what it means to "repeat" this question (p. 26).

From this description of the task, as Heidegger saw it, it is clear why the work of destruction is needed—it is the means for getting behind the self-evidentness of the tradition, behind the practice of taking its concepts as given. Because human being is itself historical—we always are what, in the past, we or someone else already has been—a tradition, as incorporating the past that is we, is capable of taking the self-responsibility that properly belongs to Dasein away from it. Traditional formulations then guide the way questions are put and offer the various standpoints of philosophizing as fixed "types" of question and answer, without ever freeing or obliging one to put the question of the meaning of being on one's own and as a question of one's own. This is how the obscuring, or the forgetting, takes place. For, without repeating the question as one's own, there cannot be any positive recourse to the past in the sense of a productive appropriation of it. The traditional formulations not only pass on an understanding of the meaning of being; they also hide it by displacing the questioner through letting the tradition be a substitute for the questioner's own self. Originally, the question of the meaning of being can be asked only in the first person singular—only "I" can ask it on "my" own. But one should not misunderstand this as implying an ultimate individualism—as though only the particular person that I am is affected by the question or concerned with its meaning. Instead, it implies that the very universality of being is appropriable not in the form of something common or general but in the form of the singular; inevitably, everyone asks the question of the meaning of being, but everyone must ask it as an "I."[6] A tradition of concepts can hide this universality because it offers the opportunity of reducing everything to a repetition of pregiven types—there are Platonists, Aristotelians, and so on—and of avoiding the question by saying it depends on whether one is Platonic or Aristotelian or Hegelian or of one of the many other types.

This singularity lies in the nature of the question and of human being as Dasein. The question of the meaning of being is ontological, that is, it is both a form of being and also an act of thinking. In asking it, one not only is directed toward "being" but is also carrying out the being that one is—one is be-ing as one asks about being. The answer to the question, similarly, involves ontological concepts, if "ontological" is taken to designate a concept that contains a self-understanding, a concept that, of itself, simultaneously defines being (as what one is) and also establishes a relation to being (as what one is thinking or asking about). To understand the self (e.g., to understand that "I" am "here") is simultaneously to exist in a certain way ("For me to be means to be in a world") and to relate oneself to being as the object of one's intention (through the thought of what being means). This is to say that the characteristic defining human being is just this: that Dasein is ontological—it is a thinking that is a being, and a being that is a thinking.

If the tradition not only transmits but also hides the question of the meaning of being (since we can treat the ontological concepts as things, without being concerned with what they are about) and if it takes the place of the self that asks the question (since we can treat the types of thought as pregiven forms for selfhood, into one or another of which we must fit, like it or not), then it is important to identify the structure of the traditional concepts in order to uncover what is behind them or what they are about. As it happens, the metaphysical tradition that begins with Greek philosophy is one that understands being on the basis of the world; concepts to grasp being are formed from thoughts of things in the world. There is a symptom of this already in the Greek definition of being as *parousia* ("being present, being before one's eyes"). To be is to be present, so that presence determines both the time and the place of being; being is before our eyes, and it is now. To get at the original experience of being that these definitions formulate, one must take apart their structure; they must be destrued, in a reversal of the process by which being was first construed as *parousia.*

Here it becomes clear why, despite the connotations of the word *destruction,* this regressive analysis is not intended to wipe out the tradition but to recall what it was about. It is a kind of unraveling, which aims to follow the thread back to the experience of being from which the texture of concepts comes. Destruing the tradition means finding the rule according to which the concepts were formed out of the experience, so that the motion of their genesis can be run backwards. Just as a "constructive definition" (of the kind employed for geometric figures) provides a rule according to which the defined object can be *produced* ("a circle is a line drawn so that the points of the line are equidistant from a single point, a center, which is not part of the line"), so a destructive interpretation or analysis provides a rule for reducing what has been produced, taking the ontological concepts back to the experience of being they formulate and doing so by finding the rule according to which they have been formed. Heidegger's work in *Sein und Zeit* and in the studies that followed it (especially the book on Kant and metaphysics) is an illustration of how this can be done. His guideline is the question of how time and being are put together in the history of ontology, if temporality is understood as the meaning of the being of Dasein—if to exist, to be there, means to be timed.

The first step back takes us to Kant, specifically to the "schematism" of the *Critique of Pure Reason* and to his concept of subjectivity.[7] From there one is led still farther back to Descartes, whose notion of subjectivity and time Kant assumed and then formulated precisely. At this second station back, Heidegger works out the unexpressed ontological foundations of the *cogito sum*, showing that Descartes failed to provide an adequate concept for his new beginning in philosophy because he took over the medieval ontology. The self-evident connection that he made between "I think, I am" and "I am *a thinking thing*" is the connection between his new point of departure—an understanding of being based not, as the Greek, on the objectivity of worldly being but upon subjectivity—and the inherited metaphysical concepts; the concepts turn a perception of how "I" am at all into a definition of what a human entity is, in contrast to other entities, namely, a thinking entity. But the significance of this formulation, which shifts categories in the move from "I am, thinking" to "What I am is a thinking thing," can be measured only by going back from the medieval metaphysical concepts to the ontology of ancient Greece, from which they are drawn. The Greek understanding represents, then, the final station along the way back.

How we recognize what is the last station, Heidegger does not explain. But the explanation is not hard to find. Greek thought is the place at which the language of everyday *understanding* is used, for the first time, for the conceptual *definition* of being. This is one way of explaining why the backward steps of Heidegger's destruction retreat to Greek ontology but no farther. For destruction takes the tradition back to earlier concepts—to Kant, to Descartes, to the Scholastics, and then to Aristotle and Plato—until it reaches the point where the concepts are first formed as concepts, that is, when everyday words, which, until that time, expressed an understanding of being and directly showed the world in its light, were enlisted in order to interpret and define the being so understood and shown. Their function of showing the world as it is understood is disrupted by the need to ask what they mean, a disruption that is illustrated when, for example, "The sky is blue" (to take an example from *Being and Time*) no longer simply shows the sky in a certain way, or says how the sky is, but prompts the question "What does 'is' mean? What does it mean that the sky 'is' blue?" Ontological concepts come into being when the words which normally say that things are something, and how and what they are, become objects of attention themselves—"is" not only says the sky in its blueness but becomes an object of attention itself.

Greek ontology did understand being on the basis of time; and, specifically, it understood the meaning of being as that of being present. Nevertheless, because it used concepts designating things in the world in order to characterize the being so understood, this ontology *conceived* of time not as the basis of being or as the meaning of being but as another entity, a thing in the world; time was something. This, we might say, is Heidegger's basic rule for destruing the metaphysical concepts—they contain an understanding of being, and of temporality as the meaning of human being, but they formulate that understanding in concepts that make of being and the meaning of being an entity among other entities. In these concepts, being and time appear as entities that, nonetheless, are not entities; they involve a contradiction in the concepts defining them because the difference between time and other entities, like the difference between being as such and entities, remained unthought.

To the first rule of destruction a second can be added, namely, that the structures of being were worked out in Greek ontology according to the way in which being appeared in talk ($\lambda\acute{\epsilon}\gamma\epsilon\iota\nu$). In popular as well as philosophical Greek understanding, Dasein was understood as the $\zeta\tilde{\omega}o\nu$ $\lambda\acute{o}\gamma o\nu$ $\acute{\epsilon}\chi o\nu$, the living thing that can talk. Hence, the capacity for $\lambda\acute{\epsilon}\gamma\epsilon\iota\nu$ became the guideline for articulating the structure of being. At first, this led to Plato's dialectic; but as the hermeneutics of $\lambda\acute{o}\gamma o\varsigma$ progressed, an ever more radical version of the problem became possible, so that, in Aristotle, not dialectic, but talking ($\lambda\acute{\epsilon}\gamma\epsilon\iota\nu$) or even $\nu o\epsilon\tilde{\iota}\nu$ ("thinking," in the sense of the simple perceiving of what is there at hand, "das schlichte Vernehmen von etwas Vorhandenem in seiner puren Vorhandenheit," p. 25) became the guideline. And since talking has the temporal structure of presenting something—when one talks about something, one presents it to mind—the being of entities is conceived of as presence: real entities are those that are perceptibly there, in front of our senses, especially our seeing, or of our mind, now.

It is not only in Greek thought, however, that there is a close connection of language—"language" in the sense that German, French, and English are languages but symbolic logic and computer codes are not[8]—with the being of human beings; for, like Dasein, a word is itself ontological, it is a perceptible thing that is also a meaning and a meaning that is also a perceptible thing. If the being of Dasein is care, or concern (*Sorge*), then the being of language is sign. Ontologically, language and Dasein are mirrors for each other: we can see what our acts of thinking-being are by their expression in language, and we can understand language by an awareness of our acts of thinking-being. Dasein is a thinking that is a being, as language is a thing that is a thought.

Destruing the Theistic Picture

Does the destruction of the history of ontology, as Heidegger envisaged it in *Being and Time,* involve any theological issues? In a way, of course, it must, since the history of ontology and the history of theology are intimate partners in Western thought. But we are looking, more specifically, for that formation in theology which, like the conception of being as being present, calls for an analysis of how it came to have the structure it has and which, in its traditional standing, hides what it originally signified. The elements in the work of destruction are, as the preceding section indicated: (1) that destruction reverses the construction, for it takes apart what has been put together in the history of thought; (2) that this dismantling serves the aim of regaining access to the experience that is at its basis by finding the rule of production of the concepts; and (3) that the original experience—whether that of being or of God or of the unity of the two—exceeds what can be grasped in everyday or cosmic concepts. By retrieving the original experience, one may be able to reformulate it in concepts that are more adequate to the experience itself than are the traditional ones.

For Heidegger, as he viewed the history of ontology, the basis lay in a revelation of being. That this revelation has been covered over by the metaphysical concepts, and the sciences derivative from them, is shown by the way in which the question of the meaning of being has been forgotten. For theology, we can ask whether, corresponding to the oblivion of the meaning of being, there is a forgetfulness of God, not only in the sense that Schleiermacher gave the term in section 11 of *The Christian Faith,* which describes the human condition as one of God-forgetfulness rather than of the denial of God, but, more specifically, as forgetting the *otherness* of God. The thesis I should like to propound here is that, in the theological tradition, the otherness of God (the being of God when God is not being God, or the freedom of God both to be and not to be) has remained unthought and conceptually forgotten in exactly the same manner as has the question of the meaning of being. The symbol of the otherness of God (incarnate deity, or existent deity) is subject to the same oblivion in the history of theology as the one that befalls the question of the meaning of being in the metaphysical tradition. Not God, and not being, are what is forgotten; but the *question of the meaning* of being and the *symbol of the otherness* of God. Hence, just as the symptom of having forgotten the meaning of being lies in our regarding the question "What does it mean for X to be what it is?" as nonsensical, so the symptom of having forgotten the otherness of God lies in our regarding as unintelligible the symbol of God (existent deity) which is the being of God when God is not being God.

To forget being, according to Heidegger's understanding, is to forget the question of the meaning of being, both in the sense of asking what the word *being* signifies and also in the sense of disregarding that being is the possibility most one's own. The symptom of such forgetfulness is that, instead of understanding being, we discuss the concept of being, and being is discussed not as something we can do, our own possibility, but as a concept, a view, a position, already given in the tradition to which we belong, or as a transempirical object about which one can hold different, though undecidable, views. Thus, for example, an analysis may distinguish between the singularity and the generality of a thing, or between how it is concretely perceived and how it is abstractly thought, but, in the process, what is left out is just the connection between the singular and the general, the concrete and the abstract, which is expressed by the word *is* and which represents the being of the thing. We distinguish, similarly, between the formal correctness (validity) and the truth of an argument, but we leave out of theoretical consideration the actual fusion of the formal with the material in any living thought. How to understand and to interpret just the connection between the formal and the nonformal is left to the vagaries of practice and prudence. As a consequence of forgetting being in this way, it is considered sensible and intelligible to ask what the meaning of a word is, or what someone means by a certain word, but it is considered to be nonsensical or unintelligible, or the result of confusion, to ask what it means for a thing to be the thing it is.

Theologically, this kind of question—what it means for a thing to be the thing it is—is answered, in one way, by the symbol of creation, which expresses that what it means to be an entity at all is to have been created, that is, to be the result of the work of a maker; it also expresses that to be an entity is to be something definite in the midst of the possibility of being other, for there is no necessity or reason about anything's being the thing it is, it could always also not have been anything at all or could be something else than what it actually is. The meaning of the being of anything, as expressed in this symbol, is that being there at all is an embodiment of a "can be" instead of a "must be," or of an actuality against the background of possibility. The meaning of creation is freedom rather than contingency.

But the doctrine of creation, which includes the concept of God as the uncreated being (*ens increatum*) in contrast to the creature as *ens creatum* and which carries with it the picture of "making" something, also leads directly into the theistic picture of God, self, and the world. For, according to the concept of finite being as *ens creatum*—where the idea of creating contains the picture of making—the difference between God and the world is thought of as the difference between one who makes something and the thing that is made, analogous to the difference between a sculptor and the sculpture or a painter and the painting. With this picture, there inevitably comes the accompanying thought that the whole of things is one in which there are two different kinds of entities, the Creator and the creature, and that the whole, called "being," comprises both. What cannot be thought, in the tradition of this picture, is that the world is itself a moment in the being of God; what cannot be thought is that the world is the being of God when God is not being deity, or the being of God in the time of not being. To reconstruct the picture of the relation between God and the world, after this destruction of the picture, requires rethinking the division between the uncreated and the created according to the idea of God's being God as God and God's being God as other than God. In effect, this would also take the doctrine of creation into the theological dogma of Trinity, if the trinitarian conceptualization is understood as one in which the very being of God incorporates its own otherness: to be God is both to be deity and to be other than deity. But it also takes time into the being of God, by distinguishing *when* God is not being God.

In the theistic picture, the negative is referred to God, the *un*created entity, only as the otherness of the creature—God is *not* creature. When this is put together with the other two aspects of the metaphysical concept, we have the three conceptions that mark the history of theology: God is being itself, God is supreme being, and God is uncreated being (the Creator). "Being itself" is understood without a clear distinction between the two senses of "being in general" and of "supreme being"; and uncreated being is a picture that encompasses both. What remains unthought, in the background, is being as such, as we shall see presently.

If to forget being is, in effect, to lose sight of the difference between being and entities (and the symptom of it is to think that the question of the meaning of being does not mean anything), the forgetfulness of God is to overlook the otherness of God—God's being God by being other than deity. Forgetting the symbol of the otherness of God is, in this way, a counterpart to forgetting the question of the meaning of being. About being, two questions can be asked: (1) What is this thing? (2) What does it mean for this thing to be what it is? The second question always implies that the thing, whatever it is, could also have been other than what it actually is; being, even as manifest in this entity, is different from this entity, as the background of otherness for the entity. Of God, similarly, there are two symbols: (1) The symbol of God as deity, of that in which one places unreserved trust, or of what embodies and elicits ultimate concern. This symbol of deity is the "I am" who delivers us from bondage. (2) The symbol of the otherness of God, which is the "I am" of Jesus in his worldly end, or of some other singular name in its worldly end. Just as the question of the meaning of being can be forgotten, so that we do not ask, "What does it mean for a thing to be what it is and not something else or not at all?" so too the symbol of the otherness of deity can be forgotten, so that we do not see that "I" may be other than the person who speaks and that God may be other than deity. Forgetting being shows up in not asking any longer what the meaning of being is; forgetting God shows up in not ascertaining that God is other than the "I" of "I am here" (Dasein), or that the God of "I am here" is God's being God when God is other than deity. One can confuse being with a supreme genus or the highest being; one can confuse deity with a supreme "I," or an unconditional subject.

The same observations can be stated more radically. To forget being itself is to lose sight of what comprises both being and not being, both the whole of being and nothing, both identity and difference. Similarly, to forget God is to lose sight of what comprises both the self and the not-self, the depth of the being of selfhood. The "I am here" of Dasein—the being of any human entity—is then not distinguished from the "I am here" of one who is other than the human subject. To symbolize the self in "I am here" as *other* than the speaking person can very easily appear to be as nonsensical as to ask what it means for a tree to be what it is and not something else or nothing. Who can "I" possibly be if not the one speaking or someone like it? Despite what analytical philosophers are wont to say, this question is not the result of confusing words with things, as though, knowing that we can ask about the meaning of words, we fall into the trap of thinking that we can ask about the meaning of beings and of being as well. Instead, to regard the question of the meaning of being as nonsensical or confused is itself attributable to having forgotten the meaning of being, that is, to having forgotten that an entity can signify (carry a meaning or a sense) just as can a word, because an entity not only is what it is but also embodies a possibility of being against a background of being other; it is what it is against the possibility that it might have been other or could become other than what it now is. Similarly, if we consider it self-evident that the "I" of "I am here" is the person of the one speaking—since pronouncing the word *I* is to make oneself an instance of what the word refers to—then to ask who the self of "I am" is, is as nonsensical as asking about the meaning of being; but this is only a symptom of having forgotten the otherness that God is. "Who am I other than the one here, or there, or at another place?" is thought to be as pointless as asking "What does it mean for *X* to be *X?*" But this is a pointlessness that vanishes when the depth in which both I and not-I have their origin is uncovered or recalled. To forget the otherness, the negation, in God means being oblivious both of the difference that is in the "I" of "I am here"—the difference between Dasein and deity—and also of the difference that is in God and that makes it possible for God to be God as other than deity.

There is, to be sure, an experience of the otherness of God contained in the theistic picture, which is indicated by the placing of God outside the whole world and the human race. But the picture is a picture *of* being as a whole—of the whole of being, in which God, world, and Dasein are three kinds of being. In the theistic conception, which this picture portrays, the concept of being is all-encompassing; there is divine being, human being, and cosmic being, but all are subsumable under the heading of "being." The mode in which they are what they are differs, but "to be" is common to all of them.

One of the major problems arising from this conception is not knowing how to think of the relation between finite and infinite being, if finitude belongs to Dasein and world, and infinity is the being of God. This involves two questions, both of which offer a first indication of why being as such remains unthought in the theistic picture: first, the relation of entities to being, and, second, the relation of finite to infinite. Aristotle already rejected the idea that being is the universal genus to which entities and kinds are related as species. A genus is that universal with reference to which species can be both compared and contrasted—maple and oak are both trees, but they are different trees. But the generic concept, in turn, can be definite because it is distinguished from other generic concepts by reference to a still more common genus, the ground of the similarity and the difference. The concept of being, however, allows of no such definition because there is nothing with which it can be contrasted. Since it lacks the determination necessary for a generic concept, its relation to entities cannot be that of a genus to species or a species to particulars. Instead, Aristotle spoke of the "analogy" of being. Though the being that appears in all entities cannot be defined, since the condition for definition is missing, it can be understood, or intuited, because of how it appears in all entities.

This line of thought has been incorporated into the theistic picture, since the relation of creatures to the Creator can be understood as the relation of entities to being—but only on condition that God is equated with being itself, *Deus est ipsum esse*. What is pictured as the uncreated entity is understood as being itself, and what is pictured as the created entity is understood as the entity in which, by analogy, being appears. Every creature participates in the Creator in the way that every entity participates in being. As being appears in all entities according to the measure, or "collection" (*analogia*), of each, God is the creativity that appears, according to measure, in each of the creatures. When used in theology, this doctrine of the analogy of being did not serve, originally, to give intellectual control over deity, as though our knowledge of being could be used to determine what God is and must be. One might read Barth's rejection of the *analogia entis*— which he once called *the* invention of the Antichrist and the reason, next to which other reasons were shortsighted and frivolous, for not becoming Catholic—in this fashion;[9] but, as Eberhard Jüngel has argued, Barth's objection was based not on the idea that the analogy of being makes God accessible but on the way it makes one overlook the nearness of God.[10] The doctrine of the analogy of being arises out of a motive different from that of finding a criterion for judging deity; it arises not from the motive of the fullness and definiteness of our knowledge of being through its appearances in entities but from the indefiniteness that results from the inability, in principle, to define and delimit or demonstrate the concept of being as we can other concepts. What is known by analogy remains undefinable and ungraspable.

The point at which this doctrine calls for destruction is not, then, its purported claim to control what deity can and cannot be but, instead, the matter in it that remains unthought, namely, the unthought difference between God and being, and between the general and the supreme, which is a part of not thinking of being as such. The difference between the general and the supreme (between overall being and being over all) can also be called the difference between the one and the one: "one" in the sense of anyone at all ("One does not do that") and one in the sense of The One, the supreme and only one, the one next to whom there is no equal ("I, the Lord your God, am One"). True, that difference is acknowledged in the idea that God utterly transcends the creatures. But it is not incorporated into the theistic conception. This is shown, for example, by the way the scholastic term "first cause" can mean, indiscriminately, the "absolute beginning," the first of a series, and the "causality" that is the quality expressed by all causes, as being is expressed in all beings, analogously. Similarly, *qui est* ("one who is") as the name of God is not distinguished from the same phrase as applicable to anyone who is. Alongside the identity between God and being, formulated in the proposition that God is being itself, there is, accordingly, always the difference, unthought, between the two. God is not being itself, if for no other reason than that participation in being is not the same as participation in deity. Nongodly being is outside God; it is not God, and it is what God is not.

With this we are brought to the heart of the theistic problem. If, for the history of ontology, as Heidegger destrues it, the question is that of being and time, then, for the history of theism, the question is that of God and the time of negation. What is the connection of God with time and with "not"? The theistic picture does not depict the experience of the time of negation—namely, that worldly being (the being of what is not God and what God is not) is the being of God when God is not being God; it does not depict the phenomenon of the world as a moment of time in the being of God. Nor does it contain the difference in the negative itself, the difference between the negative stated in the proposition that a subject is not an object (and conversely) and the negative stated in the proposition that the infinite is not the finite. In the speculative idealism of the nineteenth century, this difference—between negation and the negation of negation—became the focus of the dialectical concept of God. What Hegel distinguished as the bad infinite, which is the endlessness or interminability of something, from the good infinite, which is the "reconciliation" of the opposites constituting finitude, introduces the thought of that difference into the concept of the infinite. For, if one thinks of the infinite as the nondialectical opposite of the finite, then it is limited by the finite, as the positive is limited by the negative, the subjective by the objective, and so on; but if the infinite is limited, then it is not infinite, hence, the infinite that is conceived of as the simple opposite of the finite is not truly infinite but, in its own turn, finite. This is to say that to define the infinite by setting it over against the finite is to deny the infinity of the infinite.

In contrast to this spurious infinite, the dialectical concept thinks of the infinite as the opposite *of the opposition* that is the definition of finitude itself. Finitude is constituted by the limitation of subject upon object, self upon world, destiny upon freedom, and so on; each is defined by, and dependent upon, the other to be what it is. In that sense, finitude is negation—each is what the other is not. The infinite is the negation of this negation—it is different from the difference between a subject and an object or a positive and a negative because it is both of them. It is the opposite of the opposition, and, in being that opposite, it is also the unity or reconciliation of the opposite members.

But even speculative idealism, which did thus distinguish the difference in negation and see through the illusory concept of infinite, did not think the difference between God and the infinite.

These unthought differences become clear when analyzing Anselm's formulation of the name of God as "that than which something greater cannot be thought." Even Barth, however, who made much use of this definition in laying the foundation of his *Church Dogmatics* and whose *Fides quaerens intellectum* provides one of the most acute and comprehensive analyses of it, seems to have missed these differences. The otherness of God is formulated, in Anselm, in a way that connects it with an existential possibility—God is that than which we "cannot think" a greater. But the incompatibility of this formulation with the theistic picture of God, self, and world in the whole of being is almost immediately obvious. For if being comprises both God and the world, both divine and nondivine being, then there is something greater than God—the whole of being; and to think being is, accordingly, to think what is greater than God. Implicitly, Anselm's definition contains a prohibition against the very metaphysics, the thought of being as being, that he helped to bring into alliance with theology. Would it be too farfetched to conjecture that the voluntarism of the late Middle Ages as well as the antimetaphysical strand in such Protestant dogmatics as those of Schleiermacher and Barth are a reflection of this same connection between the name of God and the prohibition against the thinking of being as such? However that may be, "being," in the theistic picture, comprises both God and what is not God. At least in quantitative terms, therefore, the whole of being is greater than God. There is something outside God, and when one adds that to the thought of God, the sum is more than God alone. Yet, if God is to be understood as that than which a greater thing cannot be thought, then, in the theistic picture, either being is God and God is not truly God or, in anxiety before this prospect, one must desist from thinking being at all, one must forget being in order to save the God of the theistic picture.

Destruing the theistic picture is one way of showing why the deity of the God than whom a greater cannot be thought transgresses the affirmations of theism and embraces atheistic negations as well. It also shows another way of recognizing when the destruction has reached the beginning. Historically, as Heidegger's train to Greek ontology shows, the beginning is found at that point where everyday language, instead of being used to show the world, is used to define the being of what is shown. But, in subject matter, the origin is found at the place where the concepts are self-contradictory—where it appears that the entity time is no entity or that the God of theism is not deity. This is the point at which the concepts are purely open to the reality they are to grasp. The same is so even in the relation between concepts and things in the world. We cannot think the exact appearance of a color, for example, without starting from the thought that X is and is not that color. Subsequently we can determine in what respects X is, and in what respects it is not, the given color. But the condition for being able to make this further determination is the pure openness of mind to reality that is contained in the combination of being and not being, the thought that X is and is not.

Anselm's own interest, of course, lay elsewhere than in the question of the name of that whole which includes God and non-God; it lay, rather, in determining whether the God so named and defined can be merely a thought-entity without also being a real entity. Yet the name that prevents thinking God as only a thought-entity (because what is only a thought-entity cannot be "that than which a greater cannot be thought") also prevents thinking God as part of a whole of being, even as the supreme being in that whole; for as one member of the whole, such a deity is less than the whole. Only if God is being itself, divine as well as nondivine, is this conclusion avoidable; only if God includes a theism as well as an atheism with respect to the theistic picture is God one than whom something greater cannot be thought.

In Anselm, this difference between God and the whole of being remained unthought, as did the difference in the negative, which emerges when we reword the name to say God is that than which "nothing greater" can be thought. For this latter can mean either: (1) given X, if X can be thought to be greater, then the one called God is not God, or (2) nothing *can* be thought to be greater than God, that is to say, we can think the thought of nothing and, when we do so, we are thinking of what is greater than God, when God is identical with being. In the thought of nothing, we are confronted with what is greater than deity. This second interpretation of "nothing can be thought to be greater" associates freedom with nihilism and order with theism, and it is the thought behind contemporary nihilism. To pose the issue, theologically, as the decision between God and nothing—"Either God or nothing!" "Either theism or nihilism!"—is to miss the God who, even in the time of nothing, is God, the God who is God even when not being deity.

The oblivion of which we are speaking has, then, as its symptoms that we consider to be nonsensical something that makes no sense only because we have forgotten what it is about. Such is the case with the question of the meaning of being ("What does it mean for X to be what it is?") and the symbol of the otherness of God (the symbol "God" as the self that is other than the I of the person speaking the "I am," and the symbol that is existent deity when God is other than deity, both symbols concentrated in the "I am" of Jesus in his worldliness). But this same symptom can appear in the guise of differences that, in the tradition, have not yet been made the object of thought. Such are the differences between the general and the supreme (the thought that the most general is not the same as the highest), between God and being (the thought that God is not identical with being), between nothing and nothing (nothing as no thing and nothing as "not," the sheer otherness of being), and between the negativity of finitude (the self is not the world, and conversely) and infinite negativity (the negation of that negation).

The Question of Reference

Destruction analyzes the history of thought in order to discover what the thought is about by getting back to its origins, which appear at the point of self-contradiction in the thought. What is the referent of the theistic picture? What is it a picture of? Is it about being as a whole, constituted by the interplay of God, who is only God, and the entities that are not God? This question can be evaded or, again, forgotten; for a picture which, like the theistic picture, shows the meaning of a metaphysical tradition of thought takes on an independent existence once it is formed. Like a photograph, it can be contemplated, retouched, and reproduced without regard to whether it is a picture of anything at all; or it can be treated as a photographic likeness of something that, of itself, is never seen. The picture can become the object, signifying only itself; other pictures can be made of it, but there is nothing it is a picture of. Indeed, it *can* mean and signify only itself if what it depicts is something that, in principle, can never be seen at all—a view of the whole of things from outside the whole.

But the question of referent takes a turn that should not be disregarded. It is one thing to say that a picture has no referent because it is not a photographic likeness of anything; it is another thing to say that a picture is about something, and therefore has a referent, even though it is not a likeness of anything. The question of referent is not necessarily whether there is something in reality that looks the same as what is described or imagined in a picture. This is evident even in the normal relation between meaning (or sense) and referent. A meaning is what we understand in a word or a sign; and a referent is that to which the meaning points. When we hear the statement "The leaf is green," we may picture what we understand through a mental image of a green leaf. We say the statement has a referent if there is something that is a leaf and is green. In objective terms, we do not make a distinction between the referent as the green leaf and the referent as the being green that the leaf represents; and this is so, in part, because we make no difference generally between the picture of a thing and the picture of the being of that same thing. Even in this everyday case, however, the relation between the words that bear the meaning (the visual or acoustic figure "green leaf") and the mental picture that is formed of the meaning is not one of likeness; for the words do not look anything like the leaf they mean and signify. In principle, the same holds for the relation between the meaning and the referent too. There can be a referent for a meaning even though the meaning does not yield a picture that looks anything like something real. The world about which a poem is written may not look like anything in the physical world, but it is still a referent of the words of the poem.

What, then, is the referent of the theistic picture? Theologically, this question is complicated by the fact that, in the biblical tradition and the theology shaped by it, there is a sense in which the very word *God* is what the word *God* is about. That is to say, there is an identity between God and the word *God*, and between the being of God and the being of language, that is part of the same tradition as that to which the theistic picture belongs. This identity is rooted in the way the word *God* embodies the meaning of any word as a word—its function is to be a sign-of. A word, in contrast to an empty sound, is characterized by its carrying a meaning; it is a sign, a perceptible figure that serves not to call attention to itself but to lead the mind to the meaning it carries. When we understand a language, we do not pay attention to the sound and sight of the words themselves, but we grasp the meaning the words carry. In that sense, every word is a sign, a pointer-to. It points to the meaning it carries, and that meaning, in turn, points to the referent that is signified. So, for example, when we hear the word *tree* (in the context of an intelligible discourse), we understand that the word, though it is different from the object, is *of* the object. This "being of" while "not being" is the structure of a sign (or of what, today, is usually called a "symbol" in theology). It links words with things without eliminating the difference between the two. The reality of the perceptible and intelligible world of everyday depends upon upholding the difference between meaning and referent, between what something says and what it is about; for without the distinction, the reality of the world out there disappears or becomes confused with subjective states.

Theologically, however, the matter is complicated, not because "God" and theological discourse have no referent, but because there is a sense in which the word *God* refers to the word *word*, and the word *word* refers to the word *God*—so that language is the reality to which the meaning of the word *God* refers and the word *God* is the reality to which the meaning of language points; God is what language *means*, and language is what "God" means. The word, which normally is not the referent but about the referent, is here the referent, though without eliminating the difference between the word and the object. I think, if I read him cor-

rectly, Karl Daub was the first to point out that the word *God* is
the reality to which the sign character of language points, or to
which it refers through its meaning as sign-of, and that the phenomenon of language (or the single word *word*) is, in turn, the reality to which the word *God* refers, since the word *God* means
"sign-of" or "pointer-to."

In what way does "God" mean sign-of or pointer-to? It has the
sense of "not-I" and "not-this," the one that "I" and "this" are not
and that is not "I" or "this." "God" means the negative that can
be instantiated upon any object and any subject by the saying of
the word. The word instantiates the negation—that is to say, it
turns the subject by which it is spoken or the object to which it is
applied into a sign of the subject's or object's own otherness. God
appears as the otherness that can be at the place where any subject or any object is. Like the words *I, this, here,* and similar ones,
the word *God* always has a referent because the very naming
of the word creates a referent out of the thing upon which the
"not," the intended otherness, is made manifest. In actual talk,
one cannot say the word *I* without becoming the one so named,
and one cannot say the word *this* without making something the
object referred to. Similarly, one cannot say "God" without becoming or indicating the otherness that appears in the negation of
the subject or the object or both. "God" refers to the otherness
that is manifested upon the speaking subject or the object spoken
of or both. In this way, the word *God* is the reality of God, just as
the words *I* and *this* are the realities of the subject and the object.
But they are those realities potentially—the word *I*, because of
the meaning it bears, makes it *possible* for a subject to come to be
at all, as the word *this* does for an object. So the word *God* makes
it possible for a subject or an object to be the sign-reality that is
God's presence, the otherness that is there in the naming. This is
not the same as saying that the word has no referent outside itself
or that it refers only to itself or that there is no difference between
the meaning and the referent of the word. But it is to recognize
that, unlike the relation between the word *tree* and the object it
names, the meaning and the referent are so intimately fused that
the meaning makes the referent and the referent appears only
with the meaning. Thus, in the theistic picture, it is the word
God itself to which the contradiction in the picture refers, and it
is this word that makes the picture significant.

To complicate matters still more, the peculiarity of this refer-
ential relation in theology is that the referent of the word *God* is

given twice over. It is given, first, through what is instantiated with the pronouncing of the word—the subject or object as a sign of what is other than any subject or object and other than the otherness between subjects and objects. And it is given, second, in the phenomenon of language or, by concentration, in the word *word* itself. Thus, there is a double answer to the question of the referent of the word *God*. It refers to the "I" or the "this" upon which, or at which, otherness appears, and it refers to the other word (namely, the word *word*) for the word *God*, or to that as what God is God. "God is God as the word" asserts that "word" (or language) is the way in which God is the deity God is (namely, as not being God, that is, as other than the word *God*). God is God, then, as what is other than God doubly (as the word *word* and also as the word *God*); for the otherness that appears upon a word, which is always a pointer-to, is the same as the otherness as which God exists.

In view of this relation, the question of the extralinguistic referent of theological discourse is, in one sense, not important, since the referent of theological meaning is given in and as language. We do not need to know to what historical and biographical events or to what chemical and physical processes the narrative of Moses and the burning bush—to take this as an example—actually refers in order to understand what it is about. And we do not need to know to what metaphysical entity the theistic picture refers. But, in another sense, the question of referent is indeed important, and to deny the importance of a certain kind of referent is not the same as saying that the narrative has no referent; for what it is about is not an odd bush or an odd biographical episode, as such, but the otherness that Moses met in the bush. A bush that burns without burning up is certainly "other than" a bush of the world; it "is not" the bush it generically "is." This depiction of the unity of being and not being in the bush is the way in which the narrative speaks of the otherness that is the real referent, as otherness that appears in the theistic picture in the God who is not deity when one thinks being as such.

To destrue the story of the bush does not mean to confine ourselves to such elements of the narrative as the combination of images, the play of sounds and rhythms, the rhetorical figures, instead of ascertaining the referent; it does mean, rather, rediscovering the experience of otherness that is being told in the narrative. What was it that happened to Moses? What would it mean for someone today (for "me") to come face to face with the other voice of "I am"? Or is it the intention of the Mosaic narrative to say that what happened there happened only there and will not happen again? that it can be remembered and recalled but not experienced again, for, having given itself a name, this deity no longer can be encountered in its deity? If so, we cannot ourselves ever expect to encounter the otherness that addressed Moses, but we can understand it, that is to say, we can understand what it was that he heard, even though we cannot hear it for ourselves. It is possible that deity never appears twice in the same way; once the name has been given and heard, it cannot be heard again, though it can be understood, remembered, and recalled. In such a case, God is around only as the absence to which the divine name testifies, though this absence is not like that of what never was and never could be there but like the absence of one who was there and who now has gone for a good reason. Once and only once did the reality appear and leave its name ("I am the one I am"), so that, henceforth, there is no appearance of it except in the name, in every repetition of the words *I am* by anyone. Then it is so that, any time anyone thinks or says what is meant by the words *I am* or *I am I* or *I am the one I am*, this repetition presents God who, for good reason, has gone. The unity of absence and presence that is intended by this name can be paraphrased, perhaps, by the notion of one who has gone away, for a good reason, in order to return after a while, one whose being away is not to be lamented because the "good reason" is the one named by "freedom." So it is also possible that the God of the theistic picture, who now appears not to be God, is, at the end of the era of theism, the annunciation of a real otherness that can be seen after the Enlightenment.

Conclusion

The theistic picture presents the choice of thinking God and forgetting being or of thinking being and denying God because what is in the theistic picture, at its origin, is God who is not being God. To uncover this by a destruction of the picture, however, is to provide the opportunity to think in a different way what cannot be thought there; and that is to think of the relation between God and being by incorporating time and negation into deity. The end of destruction is the beginning of a retrieval of the symbol of existent deity, lost in theism, and of its attendant conception of the being of God when God is not being God. Destruing the theistic picture shows the way in which time and negation remain un-thought in the tradition. To think what is unthought is to grasp anew what appears in the picture but is now hidden by the picture itself, and what appears in it at the point of the contradiction sus-tained by the word *God*—that the theistic God is not deity be-cause something greater can be thought.

In comparing his own reading of the history of thought with that of Hegel, Heidegger drew the following contrast: For Hegel, a conversation with the history of philosophy involved entering into the power and the milieu of what had been thought by earlier thinkers and taking it into one's own thought. For Heidegger, by contrast, the power of earlier thought is not in what past thinkers have already thought but in what they left unthought, the un-thought condition of their thinking as they did think, from which what they did think gets the room essential for it to be what it is.[11] One could apply a similar description to the destruction of the theistic picture. The intention is guided by the belief that the vitality of theistic thought lies just in what is unthought in the tradition; for God, understood as that than which something greater cannot be thought at all, can be identified with supreme being as long as one does *not* think of being as such but only of infinite or uncreated or divine being in contrast to finite or cre-ated or human and cosmic being. In view of the history of meta-physics, Heidegger's program implied that it is possible to carry on traditional metaphysics only as long as one does not think the "ontological difference," the difference between being and en-tities, that is to say, as long as one does not think the thought that being is *not* any entity.[12]

But perhaps—at least, so it seems to me—what is unthought in metaphysics should be stated differently; for the unthought con-dition of metaphysics is not so much the difference between being and entities as it is the difference between the necessity of thinking that is imposed by the laws of thinking itself, and con-tained summarily in the law of identity (*A* is *A*), and the constraint upon thinking that is effected by how things actually appear to thought. Only as long as one does not think of the difference be-tween that necessity and this constraint is it possible to carry on metaphysics as a working out of those ideas that are necessary to make experience intelligible on the basis of an ideal world behind the appearing world.

But when the unthought gets to be thought, then something must be done besides rethinking the tradition. A deconstruction of the theistic picture, therefore, obliges one to rethink that origin which appears in the picture, as in the metaphysical tradition, at the point where the contradiction is uncovered—the point where it happens that, if we think of being as such, then God is not God. I have suggested that the formula for reconstructing that appearance is "the being of God when God is not being God," a formula that includes time and negation in the being of God and that opens thought to deity existing not as a transtemporal or metaphysical entity but as an actuality in life and history.

4

BEING "AS NOT"

Overturning the Ontological

THE OVERARCHING theme for this essay is the relation of religious language to ontology. That theme leaves some matters to be defined more specifically. Is ontology itself a kind of language, so that the comparison is between religious language and this other language? Again, is there a contrast between language and concepts as well as between religion and being so as to result in a double comparison—of religion in language on one side with ontology in concepts on the other? Finally, is "religious" to be equated with "theological" in this context? All of these possibilities are legitimate understandings of the theme, but it will simplify matters if, for present purposes, we adopt one or another of the possibilities. I shall do so presently, by setting up some definitions at the beginning, and I shall also introduce "theological" as a third term, not identical with "religious." In order to keep the whole from being only an exercise in definitions, I shall take as a guiding question this one: "What is the kingdom of heaven if the term 'kingdom of heaven' refers to a theological entity that is not the same as either an ontological or a religious entity?"

I propose the thesis that, in defining the relations among the ontological, religious, and theological worlds (or among those three kinds of texts), one needs to take account of a certain overturning of the ontological and religious that is effected by the theological. This can be taken, then, as a commentary and elaboration upon an observation that Ricoeur makes in his essay "Philosophische und theologische Hermeneutik."[1] There he writes:

My interest is directed to the double meaning of the relation of philosophical to theological hermeneutics. On the one hand, theological hermeneutics seems to be a special case of philosophical hermeneutics, inasmuch as its most important categories, those of discourse, writing, explanation, interpretation, alienation, appropriation, and so on, reappear there; their reciprocal relation is thus that of a general hermeneutics to one of its divisions. On the other hand, theological hermeneutics possesses specific characteristics which place into question the universal claim of philosophical hermeneutics, as the latter is formulated, for example, by Hans-Georg Gadamer. Here the relation of the two hermeneutics appears reversed: the philosophical becomes an organon of the theological hermeneutics.

What is implied about the connection between ontology and theology if the relation of the special to the general can be thus inverted—if, on one side, theological hermeneutics is a special case of general hermeneutics and, on the other side, philosophical hermeneutics turns into an organon of theological hermeneutics?

Some Definitions

Terms like "religion" and "ontology" do not refer to things, like trees and animals, that can be defined by genus and specific differences. They are not given objects. Hence, they require constructive definitions, which formulate the rule for constituting a thing as religious or ontological or theological. When defining things like plants and animals, we have definite entities in view, even before and without the definition, and we ask what their characteristics are—what, for example, are the features that distinguish a dog from a cat or a Persian cat from an Angora cat? In the case of terms like "religion" and "ontology," the perceptible features of a thing do not serve to distinguish the one from the other. Any object can serve as a potential illustration of the terms; for the definition lies in the way the entity is constituted. That is to say, constructive definitions take account not only of what a thing is on its own but of what it is in the framework of a certain kind of relation to it. Thus, what distinguishes a certain figure—say, a sculpture of a man on a horse—as an aesthetic object, a work of art, from a physical object is the way in which the object is constituted in relation to the one making or viewing it.

The constructive definitions of the terms "ontological," "religious," and "theological" that I offer here will make use of the elements of meaning (or sense) and reference (or significance, or world) in order to show the nature of their constitution: an entity (or word or text) is ontological (religious, theological) if meaning and reference are connected in certain ways. "Sense" refers to what we understand to be carried by a sign (whether a word or an entity); "reference" is what the sense in the sign signifies, or what it is about. Thus, the sense of a proposition is what it *says*, and the reference of that same proposition is what it says it *about*. It does raise problems, admittedly, if we too easily shift from the sense of a word to the sense, or meaning, of a thing. But, on the assumption that the shift can be made, the sense of an entity is defined as what we can understand it to say, and the reference is what that meaning is about. A tree in autumn may convey the sense of mortality ("You too are mortal!"), when that is what we understand the browning and falling of its leaves to be saying. The referent of that meaning is the life process of nature as a whole, including our bodily existence, or, at least, of that part of nature to which the tree belongs and which it can signify.

By the different ways in which sense and referent are put together, we can make the following distinctions:

An *ontological* entity (be it a word or a thing or a person) is one in which sense and reference are always given together. The two main examples of ontological entities are *human being* (Dasein, understood as a thinking that is also a being—how we think and how we are are one and the same) and *language* (for a word, in distinction from a mere sound or a mute entity, is a thing—a perceptible sound or sight—that is also a meaning). A human being is a meaning that is a thing, and a word is a thing that is a meaning; both are ontological. Take away either the meaning or the thing, and what is left is not a human being or a word but an animal of a certain kind, or a sound or sight of a certain kind.

A *religious* entity can be, and often is, understood to be identical with an ontological one as just described. But if we make a distinction between the two terms, we can say that a religious thing differs from an ontological one in its embodying a unity of sense and referent when the sense is not a thought-content but an image. Words that bear thoughts (concepts) are different from words that bear images, but both can signify a referent. A word is religious when the image and the referent are given together.

A *theological* entity, as distinct from both an ontological and a religious one, is an entity in which being is overturned. Since this is the matter that I want to explicate further in the following paragraphs, I shall add here only that the formula underlying this conception of the theological is not the identity between God and being expressed in the proposition "God is being" but rather the identity and difference expressed in the proposition "God is God as not God," which has to do with the being of God in the time of not being, or with the being of God when God is not being God. A corollary of this formulation is that worldly existence will also be understood not as "finite being"—being limited by nonbeing—but as being in the time of not being.

In summary form, then, an "ontological" text is a text that both carries a thought-sense and also is the world that that sense signifies; a "religious" text is that same unity of meaning and signified except that the meaning is an image instead of a thought; and a "theological" text is—in a way still to be elaborated—a religious or ontological text that is overturned so as not to be what it is or to be what it is not.

To explicate these definitions, it will be helpful to introduce an additional term, besides those of sense and reference. Ricoeur generally follows Frege's essay "Über Sinn und Bedeutung" in describing the relation of language to reality by making the two aspects those of sense and reference. In a statement like "The leaf is green," the sense is what the statement says, and the reference (or significance) is what it is about. But we can notice an additional aspect—there is a difference between the leaf that the statement is about and the being of the leaf that the statement is also about. Usually this difference plays no role at all, and, certainly, in our dealing with things in the world nothing much hinges on our being able to distinguish between a thing and the being of that same thing, between the leaf and the being of the leaf. In hermeneutics, however, when one tries to understand what we routinely understand, or to interpret what is understood, we need to pay attention to this distinction. In order to mark it, let me propose that we speak, threefoldly, of what a statement *says* (that the leaf is green), what it is *about* (the leaf), and what it is *all about* (that the leaf is the leaf it is as the green thing there). This provides a first introduction to the way in which the concept of "being . . . as" comes into interpretation theory.

This triple distinction can be found not only in statements about physical things but also in references to Dasein. The basic assertion of the presence of Dasein is "I am here," or "I am this one here." What it *says* is a unity between the subject "I" and the place "here." What it is *about* is the very person making the statement (though one can abstract from that reference artificially in discussions, when "I" means not much more than "one" or "some person"). And what the assertion is *all about* is the mode of being expressed in the statement that I am myself *as* what is here—I am I *as* "here."

For purposes of theological interpretation, and also for purposes of understanding the relation among the religious, ontological, and theological, a key phrase is, then, that of "being . . . as," which has to do with what texts or propositions may be all about in addition to what they say and what they are about.

Being Like and Being As

The phrase that Ricoeur has used in order to designate the unity of being and nonbeing involved in the metaphorical process is the phrase "being like." "Metaphor is the rhetorical process by which discourse unleashes the power that certain fictions have to redescribe reality." The place of metaphor is not the noun or the sentence or the discouse as such but the copula of the verb "to be": "The metaphorical 'is' at once signifies both 'is not' and 'is like.'"[2]

But this phrase occasions certain difficulties when applied to parables about the kingdom of God. Normally, in making comparisons by using the phrase "being like" ("*N* is like *X*"), one has to assume that the subject of the metaphorical predication can be shown for what it is before it can be shown as like something else; it must designate something, so that we know what we are talking about and what we are comparing to something else. But the name "kingdom of God," or "kingdom of heaven," does not designate a kingdom which can first be pointed out and then, through the parable, be shown to be like something else. With this name we do not know, initially, what we are talking about; the name does not designate in the same way as does "the kingdom of Prussia." For similar reasons, Gadamer has indicated hesitation about using the concept of "metaphor" for the process that is at work in poetic literature. So the question is whether there is not a more accurate way of describing the unity of being and not being which is characteristic of poetic worlds as well as of the world designated "the kingdom of God." I think the answer lies in the difference between "being like" and "being . . . as"; indeed, it seems to

me that the being characteristic of such worlds as the kingdom of
God is a unity of being and not being that can be exactly formulated with the phrase "being . . . as not." The intention of this
wording is, I think, the same as Ricoeur's when, for example, he
speaks of the kingdom of God as the "extraordinary" that "is
like" the ordinary.[3] But there is a difference in what the two word-
ings can say.

A simple example will show the difference almost immediately. If we say, "Richard is like Hamlet," we draw a comparison
between a Richard who can be named and known independently
of the comparison being drawn and Hamlet. Richard is the person
we have known for years, have conversed with, played games
with, gone to school with, and so on; and we can make non-
metaphorical predications of him. But then something happens
that occasions the thought "Richard is like Hamlet," in which the
biographic and the dramaturgic worlds converge to show a new
world. This is—if I understand him rightly—the way in which
Ricoeur conceives of metaphor, or the metaphorical process. Before the expression of this thought, there existed the biographic
discourse in which we could speak of Richard—his friendship, his
schoolwork, his character, his physical features—and, next to it,
the dramaturgic discourse connected with Shakespeare's play
Hamlet. What we said about Hamlet (such as: "He was played
well by *N*") and what we said about Richard referred to different
worlds. Richard was an actual person in our circle of acquaint-
ances; Hamlet was a dramatic figure played by different actors
over time in different places and not identical with any one performance or actor. But when something happens to make us see a
connection between the biographic and the dramaturgic, a new horizon likens the two in the metaphor that Richard is like Hamlet.

This does not mean that Richard has become an actor and is
playing the role of Hamlet; but it does mean that an identity between two orders of personhood (a biographic and a dramaturgic)
is opened up and an identity in difference is now expressed in the
metaphor. We are not comparing Richard with Hamlet by finding
features common to them. We are not saying, for example, that
Richard hesitates before decisions and cannot resolve to do what
he has decided he should do, just as Hamlet hesitates before the
prospect of being or not being and of killing or not killing his step-
father. Instead, the intention of the metaphor is to say that Richard
"is" Hamlet in a context of being at which the biographic and dramaturgic coalesce. Once the identification between the two is

made, a whole range of predicates can accrue to Richard, from the world of Hamlet, that did not accrue to him before. With the metaphor, a kind of new being is manifested upon the being of Richard as Richard. It is new in comparison both to the biographic world of Richard and the dramaturgic world of Shakespeare's *Hamlet*.

It is not difficult to see a difference between the sense of "Richard is (like) Hamlet" and the sense of a second proposition: "Richard is Richard as Hamlet." The latter proposition, too, combines being and not being and transgresses the biographic world associated with the person of Richard. What it intends to say is, again, not that there are points of comparison between the figure of Richard and the dramatis persona of Hamlet but something else. It intends to say that Richard becomes who he is in playing the role of Hamlet, which implies that, in ordinary biographic terms, the one we know as and name Richard falls short of being who he really is. Now, I do not wish to go into the question of whether such a situation is ever literally possible (though one is reminded of Peter Sellers's thoroughgoing identification of himself with his various roles so that, at the end, he was not sure who, if anyone, he was on his own, biographically). If one were to pursue the matter, one would have to take up such questions as how we recognize that a person is not who he really is. But I think the kind of situation referred to is familiar enough that these further questions do not provide a hindrance. We all know an instance or two, I should think, where it has been said that someone is really himself when playing a certain role. The similarity in difference that is noted in such observations is not that of likeness but that of the way, or the time, in which a person becomes the self he or she essentially is.

"Being as," in this sense, seems to come closer to the kind of unity of being and nonbeing that the metaphorical character of parables involves. But one more consideration must be brought in.

Being . . . As Not

The difference between "Richard is like Hamlet" and "Richard is Richard as Hamlet" does not yet take us to the overturning that the theological world effects upon the ontological. Richard, even if he comes into his own in the role of Hamlet, still exists apart from that role; the name of Richard designates, or shows, a subject apart from its identification with Hamlet's role. Hence, we do not need to overturn the identity between Richard and himself, what he is biographically and what he is essentially, in order to say that he comes to himself in the role of Hamlet.

Even in this example, however, there is a hint of the change because what Richard biographically is is not what Hamlet dramaturgically is. The complete overturning comes about with the naming of a different kind of subject, one that is not shown except through what constitutes the material of the predicate. This is the case with such a term as "the kingdom of heaven" (though one will need to specify more exactly how it is not shown by its name). Unlike Richard, who is a person among persons in a biographical world, the kingdom of heaven is not a kingdom among the kingdoms of the political world. The very title "kingdom of heaven" introduces a negation of the existence of the subject. To refer to the kingdom of heaven is to refer to a kingdom that is not before us as are the other kingdoms. Hence, we cannot construe a parable about the kingdom of heaven as a comparison between an identifiable subject and some other thing with which it has certain likenesses. The kingdom of heaven does not exist at all *except as* what is shown through that to which, in the biblical parables, it is being likened. This is a way of saying that the kingdom of heaven *is* what it is as what is shown in the parable—the kingdom of heaven is the kingdom of heaven as the man who finds a treasure in a field and sells all he has to buy the field. (Mt 13:44: "The kingdom of heaven is like treasure hidden in a field, which a man found and covered up; then in his joy he goes and sells all that he has and buys that field.")

In the case of such titles as "the kingdom of heaven," therefore, we have to attend closely to how being and not being are intertwined:

1. "The kingdom of heaven" contains a negation of the concept or name "kingdom." To speak of the kingdom of heaven is to speak of a kingdom that does not exist. It is a kingdom that, strictly, is not a kingdom at all. Like the term "God," which instantiates the negation of the "I" upon which it is shown, the term "kingdom of heaven" instantiates the negation of the world that is designated by the term "kingdom."[4] The kingdom of heaven is, in any case, not the kingdom of Israel, or of Egypt, or of Prussia, or of any other nation. Ricoeur adopts the characterizations "enigmatic" and "limiting" for such names. But those terms do not indicate that, in "kingdom of heaven," there is a combination of a *denominator* and an *alienator*. "Kingdom" denominates, and "of heaven" alienates.

2. Hence, to begin a parable by reference to the kingdom of heaven ("The kingdom of heaven is like . . .") is to begin by reference to something that appears only as the negation of kingdoms or, to put it differently, as the otherness that is shown upon any kingdom or a given kingdom; showing the otherness is the function of the alienator, which it performs in conjunction with the denominator.

3. What is designated thus by a negation of some real entity— the kingdom of heaven is the "not" or the otherness that appears upon some kingdom and is actualized there—is, in the course of the parable, shown *as* something else. What is that kingdom, which is other than kingdoms, like? How does it appear besides as the "not" of any actual kingdom? It appears as the event that is narrated in the parable—as, for example, the man who sold all to buy the field in which he had found a treasure. (We can leave aside the question of whether the happening is the event narrated in the parable or the very telling of the parable. In either case, the relations described will be the same.)

4. Of itself, the event of a man's buying a field is not the kingdom of heaven any more than is one of the existing kingdoms. Hence, to say that the kingdom *is* the kingdom of heaven as the occurrence in that parable is to say that the kingdom of heaven is what it is as something that it is not.

I would propose formulating this relation of being and not being in the showing of the kingdom of heaven by saying: "The kingdom of heaven *is* this occurrence *when* the kingdom of heaven is *not* being the kingdom of heaven." And this is the sense of the "being as not" which I have designated as the overturning of the ontological by the theological. The ontological refers to an identity between the meaning and the reality. In that sense, the ontological dimension of the phrase "the kingdom of heaven" has to do with the extent to which the very meaning shows the negation, the otherness, to which it refers. If, in the telling of the parable, the otherness meant is at hand, the parable itself is ontological. To understand the meaning of the parable is, in such a case, simultaneously to be in the kingdom to which the meaning refers. That occurrence *is* what the kingdom of heaven is. Yet this is not simply an ontological relation, but a relation in which the ontological is overturned, just because the reality to which the meaning refers is the reality of the kingdom of heaven when that kingdom is not the kingdom it is; it is the kingdom of heaven in the time when the kingdom of heaven is not being the kingdom of heaven. To understand the parable is to understand that what shows the kingdom is not the kingdom, and to be in this kingdom (while understanding the parable) is to be in the world that is not the kingdom of heaven. Hence, the summary phrase for the being of the parable and its referent is "being . . . as not." The kingdom of heaven is the kingdom of heaven as what is not the kingdom of heaven.

An Illustration

I should like to illustrate as well as test the preceding by reference to a text which makes no mention of the kingdom of heaven but which will show the ontological, religious, and theological worlds. (Implicitly, it will also show the difference in giving ontological, religious, or theological *interpretations* of a text.) The text I have in mind is Robert Lowell's poem entitled "Skunk Hour." It is helpful for illuminating the relations and for disabusing ourselves of the notion that a religious text has to be one found in a sacred book, or must mention the subjects that sacred books mention, and that an ontological text must be found—to exaggerate the point—in a work by Heidegger or one of his followers. The pertinent lines from the poem are these:

> I myself am hell;
> nobody's here—
>
> only skunks, that search
> in the moonlight for a bite to eat.

and the concluding lines:

> I stand on top
> of our back steps and breathe the rich air—
> a mother skunk with her column of kittens swills the garbage pail.
> She jabs her wedge-head in a cup
> of sour cream, drops her ostrich tail,
> and will not scare.

What are the ontological, religious, and theological references in these lines (as they form part of the whole poem)? To approach this question, I shall follow Ricoeur in distinguishing the first and second senses of the lines. The first sense is what we understand as borne by the words, what they directly say. This sense of the four lines does not present any problem, except perhaps in the first line. "Nobody's here—only skunks, that search in the moonlight for a bite to eat" is readily intelligible. "I myself am hell" is somewhat different, since "hell" is not a usual predicate for the self. Let me offer the interpretation that "I myself am hell" says that the self is in a state of internal contradiction. One can support this interpretation by the concept of hell (absolute self-contradiction) as well as by reading "I am hell" as the appearance in meaning of "I am (ill, not w)ell," a reading which, obviously, involves more conjecture.

In addition to this first, plain meaning of the words, there is a second meaning, provided by the structure of the verse (not by the sense of the words themselves). Significant for our purposes is the structure of "existential interruption," if I may term it so, in the four lines. Consider that the formulation of the being of Dasein is given in the words "I am here" and that the "I am here" presented in the lines is interrupted by the incursion of the *Nichts* (hell; nobody): "I myself *am* hell; nobody's *here.*" And what follows this interrupted existential assertion is an opening, marked by the dash after "here," a sign of the openness of existence qua existence: I am here—("Where?" "In the world"). What appears there, to show the in-the-worldiness of Dasein is "skunks, searching in the moonlight for a bite to eat."

This second meaning—the meaning of the being of Dasein—is drawn from the structure of the poetic lines. Whereas the "I" of the first sense is read autobiographically, the "I" of the second sense is universal—it is the self of any existent, and the disruption by contradiction is the background of the *Nichts* against which existence stands out.

The two meanings correspond to two different referents, or worlds. The referent of the first meaning is the self of the poet or the speaker and possibly the reader of the poem. Conceivably, it could be anyone who has found himself or herself on Nautilus Island in the scene the whole poem portrays. The second referent (which Ricoeur calls the "world of the text," made possible by the poem's being able to "redescribe reality") is the being of Dasein, as the self's being the self it is in the midst of Nothing.

Given this interpretation of the lines, brief as it is, we can identify the ontological in the text as the place (or, perhaps better, the time) where what it means and what it is converge. That is to say, the lines are ontological when in the very reading or hearing of the verse, I am the self I am—not only does the structure of "I myself *am* hell; nobody's *here*—" show the being of Dasein but it makes it possible for "me," any reader, to be a self in the reading-thinking of those lines. If I cannot read the lines without becoming disrupted and established in doing so, they are ontological—meaning and reality at once. Normally, these lines may not function ontologically in that sense; but they have the potential for doing so, and, indeed, they may have done so for Lowell himself.

Similarly, the lines are religious if the meaning that the structure signifies is the imagery itself (hell; nobody; skunks) and if this imagery *is* the very world it imagines. Again, this potential lies in the lines, even if it is not normally actualized in the reading or hearing.

The ontological and religious referents appear in correlation with the second meaning; the first meaning is about the everyday (a scene on Nautilus Island). What of the theological, if the theological is to overturn the ontological and religious? It seems to be absent; the poem contains no alienators in denominators (not even in the "Trinitarian Church" under whose spire the skunks, in a line not quoted here, "march on their soles up Main Street"). But to show the theological upon the material of the poem, through its ontological and religious meanings and worlds, we might fashion a short parable for the poem's readers, taking "island" as a denominator and "Utopia" as an alienator: "The Island of Utopia is like a man who breathes the 'rich air' of a column of skunks but does not flee or chase them away."

5

DOES SAYING MAKE IT SO?

The Language Of Instantiation

In Buber's *I And Thou*

IT IS a fairly common notion that what is meant by the word or name "God" is finally ineffable. There is a kinship, in this respect, between the words *God* and *nothing*—both of them have a meaning that is contradicted by the existence of a word for it, and both of them are, for that reason, a source of the dialectical power of active thought. The chief difference between them is that the meaning of "God" contains, as it were, an additional negative, since God is not only not this or that or any other thing but is also not nothing either. But, as treatises on the divine names always tried to show, one cannot draw from this only a negative conclusion, because the other side of the picture is that language is also the medium in which anything real is what it is. This function of language is dependent upon its capacity to "show" the reality it means through its "names." But among these names, in turn, a distinction must be made between those that have "intentionality" and those that have not merely intentionality but also "instantaneity," or instantiating capacity.

In this chapter I use Martin Buber's treatise of 1923, *I and Thou,* for some reflections on the way in which language and reality coincide in the event of instantiation. That treatise is widely known for its having worked out the category of the "thou" in contrast to that of the "it" and is certainly one of the more influential documents in the history of philosophical and theological thought in the twentieth century. But it is usually regarded from the point of view of the category defined rather than from the point of view of the power of language that is contained in such *Grundworte* as I-thou and I-it—that is to say, the power by which language brings about, rather than reflects or clarifies, reality, especially, in Buber's case, the reality of a relation between the self and its other.

Hence, I should like here to direct attention to just this aspect of the treatise and, at the end, to raise a question about the role of the word *God* in the context of instantiating language.

Instantiation here refers to a relation between language and reality different from intentionality. Words that are names of physical objects have intentionality in the sense that when we hear or read the words, we are directed toward that of which they are the name while at the same time we recognize that the word is not the same as the thing. The word *dog* is a name *of* the animal to which it refers; but the word is not the same as the animal. That we recognize both aspects—it is of the thing but not the thing—is our understanding of the intentionality of language. Other words, however, have more than intentionality because their meaning is such that we cannot think it without simultaneously bringing about the reality they name. The word *I*, for example, is one whose meaning we cannot think without becoming the very one meant by the word. This kind of word has not only intentionality but also instantiating capacity. Buber's term for such instantiating words was "basic word [*Grundwort*]"; and in his treatise *I and Thou* he developed the instantiation of "I" in two directions, as correlative with "thou" and as correlative with "it." Buber did not claim to be the first to have discovered the category of thou. Indeed, in the epilogue to *Schriften über das dialogische Prinzip*, he showed how his own work fit into a considerably longer history including such names as Ferdinand Ebner, Søren Kierkegaard, and even Ludwig Feuerbach. It is safe to say, however, that more than the work of the others whom Buber mentions the treatise *I and Thou* is the one to which most people owe their recognition of the fundamental distinction between the two categories. The linguistic, rather than the categorical, aspect of it is, similarly, not unique to Buber but can be found, among other places, in the work of the Patmos group, which counted among its contributors not only Buber but such other figures as Franz Rosenzweig, Eugen Rosenstock-Huessy, and Karl Barth.

Here I shall offer some reflections on the treatise under three headings: (1) its importance for the theory of language; (2) its importance for epistemology; and (3) its importance for philosophical theology. The reflections are guided by the question of linguistic instantiation, or of how saying can make it so.

Theory of Language

The importance of Buber's treatise for theory of language lies doubtless in the understanding of the relation between language (either as spoken or as written, though, in Buber's case, the emphasis is clearly on the spoken) and reality. What is important in the I-thou and the I-it relation is not only that a different category is involved in each case but also that the very words bring about a relation at all. Without saying or thinking the words there is no relation; and where the words are spoken, the relation comes about through the speaking.

According to Buber, the world is twofold, and one dwells in it in a twofold way, with a twofold attitude (*Haltung*) depending upon whether one speaks the basic words I-it or I-thou. That the basic words effect what they name means one cannot say "I" without thereby being an I, and one cannot say "thou" or "it" without thereby making the other into a thou or an it and without, at the same time, speaking and being "I" as well. The relation that is meant by each basic word "enters into the word and stands in it [*tritt in das Wort ein and steht darin*]."[1] This entering and standing in the word, as Buber calls it, is what we can designate as "instantiation." It is, then, the instantiating capacity of language to which Buber refers with the term *Grundwort*.

The instantiating of language is the power of language to bring about the reality it names or to actualize the relation it means. It would correspond to what Hegel in his *Logic* spoke of as the "existing concept [*daseiender Begriff*]"—a concept which does not serve only to grasp the being that is given but which, as a concept, is not only thought but also something present. Thus, the concept "I" is, by contrast to object-related concepts like "tree" and "dog," one that is realized as soon as it is thought or said. It is possible to think of a tree and to say the word *tree* without making something into a tree actually, or without realizing a tree. But one cannot say or think "I" without becoming a thinking subject; I become such by that thinking or saying. This is something that may be more obvious in vigorous controversy when one person feels obliged to say to another: "That's what *you* say; but *I* say . . ." For at such times it becomes clear how one becomes a self-conscious subject through the saying of the word. In contrast to Buber's account, one would have to add that this takes place not only in the speaking but already in the thinking of the content of the word. To think "I" and to be a self-conscious subject are, in this sense, the same. It is only in relation to others that speaking, in contrast to thinking, comes into play; the relation between I and thou is established through the speaking. Only in speaking, as actually done, and only in the power of language, as a possibility, does this relation of the one to the other become actual. A basic word that, in this way, brings about, or establishes, a relation differs from other words and concepts because meaning and reality converge in such a word.

From these remarks it is clear that the I-thou relation, as Buber set it forth, is not identical with the relation of person to person. In that sense, Buber is not classifiable simply as a philosophical personalist. This is evident even in the example that he uses to illustrate the I-thou relation. For one example that serves both the I-thou and the I-it relation is a tree. In other words, for both the I-thou and the I-it, what is involved is not the question of whether the other is a person or an object but the question of how, in respect to the other, one enters the relation that is made actual by the basic words. A spiritual entity, as in a work of art, another human being, and even a natural object can all be encountered as "thou." Thus, Buber initially adduces the example of a tree and explains that one can take up several different stances toward it. One can perceive it as a picture or image; one can sense a movement in it; one can assign it to a genus and view it as an example; or one can, finally, "volatilize and eternalize" it as an expression of a law or a mathematical formula. In all these cases, the tree is an it. But it can happen—out of will and grace together—that, while viewing the tree, I am taken into relation to it, as its "power of exclusiveness" grasps me. Then it is no longer an it, but a you. When that happens, one does not suddenly give up all observation of one's own; rather, it happens in the very midst of one's scrutiny of the object (p. 81). The same thing can happen when dealing with other persons: "If I am over against someone as my thou, if I speak the basic word I-thou to him, he is no thing among things and does not consist of things" (p. 83). Finally, the same can happen with respect to a work of art: "It is the eternal origin of art that a figure emerges over against oneself and desires through oneself to become a work. . . . If with one's whole essence one speaks the basic word to the appearing figure, then the effective power streams in, the work arises. . . . Objectively the figure is not 'there' at all; yet what is more present than it is? And it is a real relation in which I stand toward it: it affects me as I affect it" (pp. 83–84).

Buber calls this an "immediate" relation because it is not mediated through any concepts. Hence, it is not possible to say *what* the other is as thou; for the thou meets one as a whole, not as a divisible unity. A tree as a thing can be divided into its perceptible and cognizable elements, its singular and general aspects. A tree as a thou cannot be so divided; for it is not there as an object but as a presence. This is not, however, the same as saying that the encounter with a thou is wordless or silent. Rather, it is language that actualizes the relation. The sphere of immediacy is for Buber—as it was also for Hegel in his *Logic*—the sphere of language. To exist immediately means to exist in the word that names the thing or presence. If a tree is "immediately" there, it is there in such a manner that the name "tree" is not reflectively separated from the object-tree. There is, to be sure, a difference between a tree and a person in the I-thou relation; but it is not a categorical difference between things and persons. It is, rather, a distinction derived from the three spheres in which relation is actualized: the spheres of nature, of human being, and of spiritual entities. In life with nature, the I-thou relation "hovers in the dark and is sublinguistic"; in life with other human beings, it is "manifest and in the form of language"; in life with spiritual entities, it "reveals itself, is without speech but gives birth to speech" (p. 81). This contrast in the three spheres, as Buber drew it, is thus a contrast with respect to language—the difference depends on whether, in a given case, life is carried on with the sublinguistic, the linguistic, or, finally, the speechless-but-speech-bearing aspect.

From the point of view of the philosophy of language, this is probably Buber's most important principle. Language as a power that effects a real relation, language as the realm of immediacy that can be reflectively mediated—that is how one might formulate the content of the phenomenon of Buber's conception of "basic words" or of what here is being called "instantiation." One might see in this an effect of his work with the Patmos group in the period after the First World War; for the notion that language was the sphere of the immediate and also of the creative was one of that group's basic insights. It is true that the insight was not formulated in just those terms; but one can recognize it in the way that Buber treats the basic word *thou* as a word through which an immediate relation is brought about. The principle also makes clear how it is possible to enter an I-thou relation with a thing—such as a tree—despite there being no consciousness or soul or selfhood to such objects. Buber himself puts the question: "Does this mean that the tree has a consciousness like ours?" And he answers: "I have no experience of such a thing. . . . What I encounter is no soul of the tree, no dryad, but the tree itself" (p. 82). It is the tree itself that we meet when saying "thou" to it.

Epistemology

To this basic insight one can add some observations concerning the epistemological significance of this way of approaching the dualism in the self-world relation. Buber was one of those who, in the first decades of the century, sought to overcome what has been called the Cartesian split between subject and object. He does so both through his understanding of the relation that is actualized through the basic word of I-thou and also through his understanding of the way in which knowledge is achieved in the relation. An indication of this is given by the formulation that one has to speak the I-thou with one's whole essence.

Since about the beginning of the century, Descartes has more or less been the scapegoat for what is wrong in modern epistemology, if not in human self-understanding. The subject-object split attributed to his philosophy divides reality into two different kinds of things—thinking things, or subjects, and extended things, or objects. With that division, it is always problematic how a bridge is to be built from one side to the other. Built from one side alone, it implies either idealism or realism (criticism or dogmatism). Built from two sides, it implies an unsolved dualism. Not only that: even by giving attention to such questions, by trying to find a theory to explain how there can be a bridge between subjects and objects, epistemological theory has become increasingly removed from everyday thinking, which is always, from the start, a thinking involved with the world in its very existence (as Heidegger set forth in his *Being and Time*). To exist is to be in the world; it is, from the start, to be involved already with so-called objects. Over against this kind of everyday understanding of the self and its world, epistemological theories seem abstract and inconsequential. They have no importance both because they seem to contradict, in an artificial way, what everyone always already

knows (that there are real things out there) and have nothing to do
with what are real concerns of existence and also because the validity of the one or the other theory seems undecidable. The consequent isolation of theory from actual life and from a concern for
truth can then be viewed as a result of the Cartesian epistemology.

One cannot, of course, simply undo the whole philosophical development from Descartes on, and Buber did not attempt to do so.
Rather, one must understand what Descartes's concern was, why
he was misled, as it were, into separating subjects and objects, and
how one might better bring out the element of truth that lay in
this separation. Buber declares in the first sentence of his essay:
"The world is twofold, depending upon the twofold attitude toward it" (p. 79). That is to say, it is not two metaphysically distinct realities with which we have to do but rather two different
kinds of attitude, or relation, to the actual world. The attitude is
twofold, moreover, "according to the twofoldness of the basic
words that one can speak" (p. 79). With this description, Buber re-
tains something that Descartes had not held—the immediacy of
language. What, in Descartes, is two different spheres of reality is,
in Buber, two possible relationships to the one reality of the
world. And what Descartes understood as two separately existing
kinds of things, the *res cogitans* and the *res extensa,* Buber understands as two attitudes (*Haltungen:* attitudes, bearings, postures,
positions), which are established by the basic word pairs. That the
attitude has, from the start, two possible explications brings with
it the consequence that the instantiating word is not a single one
but a word pair—either the pair "I-it" or the pair "I-thou." There
is no I as such without a reference to either thou or it; and no thou
or it without I.

The second thing that distinguishes Buber from Descartes in
their epistemology lies in Buber's assertion that the basic words
must be spoken with one's "whole essence." This assertion does
raise a difficulty as soon as one tries to explain what it means to
speak a word with one's whole essence. Negatively, such a speaking is set off against the kind of neutralized subject that is characteristic of scientific statements. That much is clear. For a scientist who discovers or ascertains something about an object of
investigation does not need to make his or her discovery or ascer-
tainment with his whole essence. What is discovered may be important or unimportant; but, in either case, it does not demand
that a scientist set it forth with his whole essence. In this sense, it
is not difficult to say what speaking with one's whole essence

means: it means speaking in such a way that the speaker's understanding, will, feeling, and sensibility are activated together. But in another sense, it is difficult to determine what this possibility is. More than once, Buber emphasizes that he is not speaking of something supranatural or extraordinary but of everyday actuality. But one does at least wonder whether it is ever possible to speak in such a way that one's whole essence is brought to bear in the speaking itself.

Perhaps it is never possible to do so while being conscious of it. If that is so, it points to something to which Buber alludes but does not explicate here: such "essential" speaking may be apprehensible only retrospectively, after it has passed. In such a case, we are aware of those realities always in the past tense, as moments that we can remember but not be conscious of as such when they occur. Even so, this would not alter the phenomenon; for whether or not something is real does not depend on whether one can be conscious of it in the present tense. That is illustrated by an example that Buber uses in the English translation of his essay "What Is Man?" (The illustration does not appear in the German text in the three-volume *Schriften*.) In that essay, he uses a kind of phenomenological observation for which the actuality of human activity can be made an object of thought only through a reflective recollection of the occurrence. The example used is that of anger. Anger as a movement of the whole self cannot be ascertained through external observation of another's behavior or through introspection of one's own states of mind; rather, it can be made an object of reflection only through being able to recall the moment in which, with one's whole being, one did respond to something angrily. Having-been-in-anger is the mode in which the phenomenon as a whole can come into view, without its being reduced to an externally observable pattern of behavior or to an introspected state of mind. Indeed, Buber maintained that only through this kind of holistic method could one set forth a philosophical anthropology differing by its holistic character from that of the particular sciences. Such a method does not abstract from the totality of actual life; but it does acknowledge that this totality, this life as a whole and each of its acts as a whole, is accessible to reflection only retrospectively, when one self-consciously recalls the act in its very unself-conscious vitality. This example might be, then, a clue to what Buber means by a speaking that is done with one's whole being. Such a speaking is one in which, in formal terms, understanding, will, feeling, and sensibility are all involved in the actual performance; but what that means existentially or really can be known only through recalling an instance in which such speaking actually, prereflectively, took place, and language is the medium that makes the recollection possible.

A third question connected with these epistemological concerns leads to the matter that is of most importance from the point of view of philosophical theology. If the word *thou* is what instantiates, then how, on the one hand, are the many thou's distinguishable from the one thou, and, on the other hand, how is the eternal thou, who is God, related to the presence of thou as such?

Philosophical Theology

God is the one thou that encounters us in all particular presences. This implies that one cannot abstract from the human thou in order to encounter the divine; for one encounters God not in an independent relation but in the midst of other relations. But asserting this raises the question of how the divine and human are differentiated in the encounter with thou at all. If, in the end, one has to do only with a single thou, the thou that meets us in all particular thou's, does this impugn the real presence of the other thou's? Are they mere ciphers, through which we are to meet the one but which have no standing of their own? Buber himself raised this question, and it is easy to see how it occupied his thinking. His reply seems to me to be, despite his efforts, insufficient; and the reason for the insufficiency appears to lie in his not taking account of the way in which the word *God*, too, has instantiating power.[2] That leads to the thesis that I would propose concerning the distinction between the many presences of thou and the one thou in all of them; namely, it is possible to distinguish between them only if both the word *thou* and the word *God*, like the word *I*, have instantiating capacity. Before developing this thesis, we may take a look at how Buber himself endeavored to make the distinction.

Buber sees four marks by which, in principle, one could distinguish the eternal from the temporal thou. With every other thou, one cannot avoid also making it into an it; by contrast, God is the thou that can never become an it. That is the first mark. The second is that God is the eternal thou implied in every you; every relation to you is, on that account, of itself a relation to God.

Seeking for God is thus as impossible as it is unnecessary, because God is always already there in the encounter. Third, the relation to the eternal thou is distinguished by its being not only exclusive, as is every thou-relation, but also inclusive. It is to be noted here, parenthetically, that Buber does not say the eternal relation is inclusive *instead of* exclusive, but inclusive *as well as* exclusive. Conceptually, that is a much more difficult thought. It leads to the fourth mark: the eternal relation is purely paradoxical, including in itself a contradiction that cannot be resolved but can only be lived.

In all of the marks, no reference is made to a particular role played by the word *God*. Rather, this word is referred to the basic word *thou*. As Buber puts it in the third part of his *I and Thou:* "People have addressed their eternal thou with many names. When they sang of the one so named, they always meant thou: the first myths were songs of praise." Then Buber puts the question: "Of what importance is all the errant talk [*Irr-rede*] about God's essence and works . . . compared to the one truth that all people who have addressed God have meant him? For anyone who speaks the word 'God' and really has 'thou' in mind, whatever be his illusions otherwise, addresses the true thou of his life which cannot be restricted by any other one and to which he stands in a relation that excludes all others" (p. 128). From these quotations it is easy to see that Buber here regards the word *God* as a designation that can differ among peoples and that serves, as it were, as a representative of the basic word *thou*. "Whoever speaks the word 'God' *and really has 'thou' in mind*, addresses . . . the true thou of his life." That is to say, one can use the word *God* as well as other words in order to address the eternal thou. But what counts is whether the speaker has "thou" in mind while doing so; for if he does so, then he or she enters a relation to the eternal thou. This same point could be documented by other passages in Buber's writings. What they make clear is that Buber considered the word *God* to be dependent on the word *thou*. The word *God* does not set up a relation, as do the basic words, by the very instantiating that takes place through the figure and meaning of the word; rather, it gets its meaning from its connection to, and from its being a bearer of, the word *thou*.

In a certain way, then, the name "God" is related to the word *thou* much as each thou is related to the eternal thou. The many have a certain transparency to the one, which Buber formulates by reference to a geometric figure: "The extended lines of the relations intersect in the eternal thou. Each thou is a window [*Durch-blick*] to it. It is from this mediating role of the thou of all beings that the satisfaction [*Erfülltheit*] of relations to them comes, and also their dissatisfaction. The inborn thou is actualized in every relation and is completed in none of them. It is completed only in the immediate relation to the thou that, by its essence, cannot become an it" (p. 128). In thus identifying God with the eternal thou, always in real relation to the I, Buber consciously took a position against every notion, mystical or other, in which the I is ultimately absorbed in or identical with God. "The Father and the Son—the two who are essentially alike—or, we can say, God and man, are the irreducibly real two, the two bearers of the original relation," he said of Jesus' words "I and the Father are one" in the Gospel of John. "[This relation], from God to man, has the form of mission and command and, from man to God, that of seeing and perceiving and, between both, that of knowledge and love. . . . All modern attempts to reinterpret this original reality of dialogue into a relation of the I to itself, or such things, that is, into a process enclosed in the self-sufficiency of human interiority, are in vain" (p. 135). But Buber does not seem to have been quite so clear on the relation between one thou and another thou.

The third mark of the relation to the eternal thou is that this relation is both exclusive and inclusive. "Every actual relation to a being [*Wesen*] or to a presence [*Wesenheit*] in the world is exclusive" because everything else lives in the light of that being (p. 130). Not that there is nothing but thou there. Rather, everything that is there is seen as having its life in the light of the thou. The light lasts as long as the presence of the relation lasts. "As soon as a thou becomes an it, the cosmic reach of the relation appears to be in the wrong in the world, its exclusiveness appears as an exclusion of the totality" (p. 130). That is true of every actual thou. However, in the relation to the eternal thou who God is, the unconditional exclusiveness and unconditional inclusiveness are one and the same. Although the nature of this paradox would need some further exploration, we can leave it with Buber's statement, in order to move to the last mark of this relation, its antinomy.

This antinomy lies in the religious situation of human beings (p. 142). Human existence in the presence of the eternal is marked by "its essential and insoluble antinomy." It is a different antinomy from the philosophical one that Kant explicated in his critique of reason, for the two sides of the contradiction cannot be ascribed to two different spheres, as can the Kantian freedom and necessity. "If I have in mind necessity and freedom not in the world of thought but in the actual reality of standing in the presence of God; if I know, 'I am in the hands of another,' and simultaneously know, 'It all depends on me,' then I cannot try to evade the paradox, which I have to live out, by ascribing the incompatible propositions to two separate spheres of validity, and I cannot make a conceptual resolution by an artificial, theological concept; rather, I must take it upon myself to live out both sides in one, and when lived they are one" (p. 143).

One and Many

What Buber intended with this kind of phrasing is clear. In distinction from an accent that he found not only in Kierkegaard but also in Ferdinand Ebner, two predecessors in the same concern, he wanted to insist that the human thou in its temporal concreteness is a real other for the I; it is not an indifferent and ultimately inessential cipher for the divine thou as the only real other of the I. So he had a double opposition in mind: first, against a mystical identification of I and God, and, second, against a Docetic view of the temporal thou. To see the extent to which Buber may or may not have succeeded in distinguishing thou and thou, it will be helpful initially just to make a list of the ways in which anything is distinguishable from something else. Thereafter, it will be clearer how one might maintain, conceptually or otherwise, the distinction between the eternal and the temporal thou (and with that also the distinction between I and thou).

The first possible way of making a distinction is the formal one. For example, we can distinguish between a tree's being a tree and its being a giver of shade; or we can distinguish between the tree as it is actually there before us and the tree as it might be made into furniture. What is materially one and the same thing can be viewed from a number of different formal possibilities. Second, we can distinguish things materially. We can thus make a distinction between one tree and another tree. Formally, they are both the same, as a tree; but materially they are different trees. Third, there is a personal distinction, which is neither formal nor material but historical (or "spiritual," if the word is rightly understood). What distinguishes one person as a personality from another is not the material difference (although there is a material difference present) nor a formal difference (that may also be present) but the historicality of the person (the particular set of memories, occurrences, encounters, and the like that have made the person an individual personality or a unique subject).

Fourth, one can distinguish one thing from another thing temporally. With respect to the appearances of the thou, this is the kind of distinction that initially is employed. Thus, the difference between the thou that is actualized in a tree and the thou that is actualized in another person is neither material nor formal nor personal but temporal. The time of the one and the time of the other are distinct. Since the thou essentially lets everything appear in its light, the thou of one encounter can be distinguished from that of another only in this temporal way. If there were no difference in time, there would also be no possibility of distinguishing the one thou from the other. "Who" the thou is of a given encounter can be recognized and named only by reference to the time of the appearance; the material and formal differences, which are, of course, also there, are not essential. Materially we can distinguish between several examples of one genus or species; formally we can distinguish between different possibilities of development or formation of a given material content. But neither the one nor the other of these two distinctions is the same as the distinction between the one and the other thou. What becomes named as a thou is time.

In the fifth place is the distinction between the two basic words. The I of the I-it relation is not the I of the I-thou relation just because the relations that are established by the words are different. Finally, there is the difference of the infinite from the finite, which can be grasped only dialectically, not in linear concepts, because the infinite is not the simple opposite of the finite (otherwise it would be limited by the finite and would not be infinite) but is rather the opposite of the opposition that constitutes the finite—what limits something finite is something else that is finite. This distinction is neither formal nor material but speculative; it is not a distinction that is given but one that arises and shows the emergence of any given thing; it does not distinguish some things from other things but represents the coming-to-be of anything at all.

This brief and rather unsystematic enumeration of the possibilities makes clear how difficult it can be to make a distinction between a temporal thou and the eternal thou. For, according to the distinctiveness of the basic words, we can distinguish between thou and it but not between thou and thou or between a temporal and an eternal thou. If, moreover, the distinction is speculative, so that every you and every it bear the eternal thou in themselves as their origin or their coming-to-be at all, then the eternal thou is not a genuine thou whom we encounter but, as it were, the framework in which the relation to thou or it takes place at all. That, clearly, would not fit Buber's intention, precisely because he was concerned to maintain the genuine dialogical relation between the human I and the divine thou. It is a concern that, he reported, had occupied him from early youth and that made the dialogical principle so important for him (p. 297). Still, it is not clear how that dialogical principle can be maintained if one cannot show how, conceptually or otherwise, the difference between the many and the one of the encountered thou is to be understood.

It appears to me that the one recourse which Buber did not take, but which seems to suggest itself, is that of the instantiation brought about by the word *God*. For if this very word instantiates what it means, then the difference between the temporal and the eternal thou hinges upon the difference between these two words, and the problem of the distinction is solved. If one wanted to take a biblical verse as a guideline, it might be the words with which the Doubting Thomas acknowledged the risen Jesus: "My lord and my God" (Jn 20:28). For this expression indicates that what came about was not only the relation of I-thou ("my lord") but also that of I-God ("my God"), the temporal and the eternal presence. I-thou and I-God together maintain both the identity and difference in the presence. It is a real difference only if the instantiating capacity of the one word is equal to that of the other; it is a real identity, because it is one and the same physical figure, and one and the same time, that evokes the two words. If that is the case, then one can say that the saying of "it" (with which there always goes a corresponding "I") is what establishes the world of objectivity; the saying of "thou" (with its corresponding "I") is what establishes the world of exclusive relation; and the saying of "God" (which can accompany either or both the saying of "it" and of "thou") establishes the world of the eternal. Through the saying of the word *God*, what is shown is the "not" of every it and every thou, as well as of I—God is not this or that or any other one, and not I either. But, at the same time, God is not nothing either, so that the presence of the eternal is not only the negative that is shown upon any it, thou, or I but also the negative of that negation in turn.

6

HEGEL AND

THEOLOGY TODAY

HEGEL HAS survived his several burials quite well. He was, no doubt, the last of the great systematic thinkers still to be able to assume the truth of Christian theology (although his contemporaries did not all see that) and to make his life's task a matter of thinking it through and of comprehending it in the concepts of a philosophical theology. After him the truth of the Christian religion and the civilization founded on it became contestable in a different way, so that the question was not one of understanding and grasping the truth that it bore but one of ascertaining whether it was even true, with the possibility of arriving at a negative answer. Yet Hegel's philosophy and theology have continued to draw interest, despite Marxists, positivists, and analysts, not merely as a historical phenomenon but also as a living voice in the philosophical and theological discussion. Of course, that is true of other thinkers besides Hegel; their thought lives on beyond the time of their own death. But, for whatever reasons, Hegel seems to have created in his successors a more intense wish for that not to be true in his case than have other thinkers. Perhaps the reason lies in a caution that Karl Barth gave in 1932: those who think they have refuted Hegel might very well find that their refutations have already been anticipated by Hegel and already rebutted; the very possibility that that might be so is enough to arouse apprehension. The same Barth went on to observe that it "may be that the dawn of the true age of Hegel is still something that will take place in the future."[1]

One need not decide, however, whether or not such an era

of Hegel will, or ought to, come in order to recognize the influence of his thinking in theology today, particularly in two interrelated matters, an influence that indicates the extent to which
his thought still offers conceptual tools for theology that are overlooked only at theology's peril: the trinitarian concept of God, and
the overcoming of nihilism in a theology of the death of God.
Both of them are indicated in this quotation from Hegel's *Lectures on the Philosophy of Religion:*

> "God Himself is dead," as is said in that Lutheran hymn; this con-
> sciousness expresses that the human, the finite, the frail, the weak,
> the negative is itself a divine moment, is in God Himself; that
> being-other, the finite, the negative, is not outside of God and
> as otherness does not disrupt the unity of God. . . . The highest
> knowledge of the nature of the Idea of Spirit is contained in this
> thought. . . . In this whole story, man has attained the conscious-
> ness that . . . the human is the immediately present God. . . . It is
> this story [of the appearing of God] which creates the conscious-
> ness, the knowledge, that God is a Trinity.[2]

Trinity and Comprehensibility

One of Hegel's basic motifs puts him at odds with all thoughtless
theology; it is the motif that in the meaning of "God" there is a
content that we can think, or conceptually grasp, and, by grasping
it, take part in its own reality. The doctrine of the Trinity provides
the fundamental test of that motif. Not only has it served over the
centuries as the paradigm of theological mystery, as a way of saying that one cannot say what one ought to say because one does
not know how to do so, and as a way of indicating the limits of
comprehensibility; it was also left untouched in the theology of
the Lutherans and Calvinists, since it was taken over as part
of the theological tradition with which they had no quarrel; and
for the theology of the Enlightenment it represented a keystone in
the arch of ecclesiastical obfuscation and superstition. Yet it was
just this doctrine in which Hegel saw the possibility of the comprehensibility of God and the unity of the divine and the human,
and a theological rescue, as it were, for the subjectivity which the
Reformation had "set free" and which the French Revolution was
to bring, for Hegel in his youth, to its fulfillment. Hence, when
the theologian F. A. Tholuck sent Hegel a copy of his new book
on the Trinity, Hegel replied in indignation that the book pre-

sented the doctrine as though it were an object for antiquarian preservation: "Does not the high insight into God as the triune merit a completely different awe than merely to ascribe it to an externally historical process? In your entire essay I could neither find nor feel a trace of your own sensibility for this doctrine. I am a Lutheran and through philosophy am all the more confirmed in Lutheranism. . . . It is an outrage to me to see these things explained in a way comparable to the lineage and dissemination of silk manufacture, cherry growing, or the pox."[3]

Hegel took seriously, as did the other idealists, the view that, with the Reformation, the possibility of basing philosophy and theology on authority had ended. Henceforth, the only basis for acknowledging traditional doctrines as true must lie in one's own insight into their truth. That the theological doctrines did express the truth, he did not contest or ever seem to doubt; but they were presented in thought images, rather than in concepts, as matters to be believed and not to be doubted or to be comprehended. Whether, like Bultmann in respect to New Testament myth, Hegel saw in the pictorial form itself something that moved the doctrines beyond their pictorial expression to conceptual understanding or whether, on the contrary, this impulse came from the subjectivity that had been set free can here be left as an issue in Hegel interpretation; he did in any case regard the doctrines, and preeminently the trinitarian and christological dogmas—the two most opprobrious ones in the eyes of the leaders of the Enlightenment—as containing the absolute truth, which could be transformed into philosophical concepts and which, in the process, took the particular thinker into its own reality.

There is a difference between this thinkability and that represented in the theology of Aquinas or even Anselm. For, to put the contrast perhaps a bit too simply, while metaphysical theology recognized that in God we have to do with one that can be made an object of knowledge—that basic Anselmian insight was the foundation of medieval scientific theology—it did not regard the thinking or knowing process itself (or the act in which we do the knowing) as a participation in the life of the object being known. The human knower and the divine known remained over against each other, even though, in our knowing of God, God is also knowing us. For Hegel, by contrast, the human activity of knowing is itself a participant in the divine life. When we know God, that act of knowing is an event in the life of the God being known. The human spirit is part of the divine life. So Hegel could say that the elevation of consciousness, which marks the transition from imagistic belief to self-cognizing or self-understanding faith, is one in which we come to know that our knowing of the divine is the divine Spirit knowing itself in our knowing; with that, finite knowledge is elevated to the infinite. This is, as it were, the "mystical" thought that distinguishes Hegel from deistic accounts of the relation of the human and the divine, giving it a "monistic" hue that contrasts with the "dualistic" hue of the supranaturalist tradition.

For his trinitarian understanding, it means that Hegel understood the dogma of the Trinity to express the truth that the human belongs to the divine. But the problem was not one of simply asserting this to be so but rather of putting it into concepts that make it comprehensible. This required, on the one side, a battle against the philosophical concept of an abstract absolute deity and, on the other side, a correction of the tendency in the trinitarian dogma to grasp the identity and difference (the oneness of God and the threeness of the persons) in concepts that imitated the identity and difference in the relation between genus and species—as though the oneness of the divine nature were the oneness of a genus ("tree") and the threeness like the multiplicity of species ("maple," "oak," etc.). Explicitly the dogmatic formulations rejected this kind of understanding of the one and the many in God; but they did so in the form of negations rather than in the form of really different concepts. Hegel's conceptual problem, therefore, which had connections to both the philosophy and the theology of the day, was, first, that of God as living spirit over against God as the abstract absolute of metaphysical philosophy and, second, that of the unity and manifoldness of "spirit" as over against nature or generic being (genus-species-individual). In a global way, those are the tasks carried out in the *Phenomenology of Spirit* and in the *Science of Logic*. I do not mean to suggest that these two works were clearly undertaken as treatises on those two programmatic tasks, for one of the things that make reading Hegel difficult is that in his writing he is seeking his questions as well as his answers. But in retrospect it is possible to see these as the two works in which Hegel came to terms with the tasks and which served as the conceptual foundation for his more readable lectures on the philosophy of religion.

Hegel's basic intention was to work out the concept of spirit in distinction from the concept of objective being. Doing so was also a way of showing the comprehensibility of the imagery of the trinitarian dogma. How do we grasp in thought the life process as compared with objects? In both cases there is a relating of identity and difference. In the case of objects, this is done by referring different species to a genus as their ground: "tree" is the ground of maples and oaks because it represents that with reference to which maples and oaks are both the same and different. This kind of understanding is so common—it is how we understand things in the everyday world as well as in the objective sciences—that the tendency is to make it the measure of all understanding. But the trinitarian dogma is formulated in such a way as to defeat this way of understanding it. For it does not assert that there is a divine nature which, like a genus, is the ground of the differences in the three specifications (persons); it asserts not that Father, Son, and Spirit are alike in being divine but unlike in being different divines, but rather that each of the three, though distinct from the other two, is the one and only God. In doing so it verges on unintelligibility when measured by the standard of objective understanding. Hence, if the dogma does indeed represent the comprehensibility of God, then it does so by some other manner of relating difference and identity to each other. But what other way of understanding multiplicity in unity is there?

One suggestion is contained in a common but not strictly correct interpretation (because it borders on a rejected modalism) that draws on the meaning of "persona" and "hypostasis" as the "masks" or "roles" that an actor puts on or plays. Olivier playing Hamlet and Olivier playing Lear are one and the same Olivier, but they are two persons; and Hamlet when played by Olivier is no less the one and only Olivier than is Lear when played by Olivier; each persona is, at the time of playing, the one and only Olivier, but neither persona is the other persona. Along the lines of such an interpretation, the persons of the Father (Creator) and Son (Redeemer) and Spirit (Life-Giver) can be said each to be the one and only God in the time when it is being played—when creation is going on, the Father is the one and only God; when redemption is occurring, the Son is; when life goes on, the Spirit. From this, one can also work out a theology of history from the standpoint of religion, as Hegel himself did. In its earliest phase, religion shows God as nature; later, as art; and, finally, as self-consciousness or as spirit. Retrospectively, from the last phase, one can see the earliest phase under the person of the Father, the second as the Son, and the third as the Spirit, so that when Hegel wrote in the *Phenomenology* that art is "the night in which the substance was be-

trayed and made itself subject," the allusion to a connection between a religion of art and the crucifixion of Jesus is probably
intentional.[4]

This way of thinking of the relation of the same and the different is, clearly, different from that of objective being. The problems with personae or roles, however, are that one still thinks the
actor as such (Olivier) to be different from the roles played and
that there is no intrinsic reason for the number of roles or personae to be three rather than some other number. Hence, the concept of spirit needs to be formed in another way than through
analogy to an actor and the personae. For this other way, a key
thought is provided by the romantic understanding of the self as
capable not only of expressing itself in something other than itself (as it does in a work of art) but also of recognizing itself in its
opposite, or, more exactly, of being itself in its opposite, through
which it also comes to itself; that the self can recognize and be
itself in what is other than itself is a thought of what constitutes
the identity and difference in spirit as spirit. Even more emphati-
cally, that the self is capable of being both what it is and also what
it is not is the mark of spirit. In other words, when we see sameness and difference in objects, we do so because we can connect
with each other our thought of the object and our sense perception of it; the abstract thought provides the element of identity,
the ground or reason, and the concrete perception provides the
element of difference. In knowing an object as an object, we make
the connection between the two (by a process which Kant called
the transcendental imagination and which Hegel recognized as the
empirical form of reason [Vernunft] itself). If we are dealing only
with thoughts, there is only identity without difference—a dog is
a dog (to use one of Kant's examples); and if we are dealing only
with perceptions, there is only difference without identity. For
something to be constituted as an object it must be a unity of
those two elements. So we can understand how two things can
both be the same, as dogs, and yet be different, as particular dogs.
(This is, admittedly, a simplified reading of the matter, since there
are intermediate concepts and more generalized perceptions than
is indicated in this single example; but the basic pattern is not
changed.)

In knowing spirit, however, something else is involved. All
knowledge, we can say, does involve the elements of identity
and difference; but the way in which those elements appear and
are related is not the same in the knowledge of spirit and in

the knowledge of objectivity. Rather, the knowledge of spirit involves, not sensation and conception, but embodiment and self-awareness (or consciousness and self-consciousness). The self of self-consciousness is the identity in the difference between the many expressions of self. ("Spirit," as Kierkegaard wrote, is the self relating itself to itself.) The relating of the self to itself in its other is, then, what constitutes the life of spirit. This puts objective knowledge as well as art under a single perspective: even in coming to know objects, what is happening is that the self recognizes in the material some of its own self (it recognizes in the material the forms of its own thinking, or it recognizes that the essences of the material objects are the same as the forms of its, the self's, own thinking); similarly, in creating works of art, the self is able to express its selfhood in material that is other than itself. This understanding of spirit provides a different account of identity and difference from that of genus and species. The ultimate that appears in it is also different from an ultimate genus (whether called "being" or "thing"); for, in coming to know the ultimate genus, we abstract the most common ground of all things (anything at all is a thing rather than nothing), whereas, in coming to know the absolute spirit, we elevate the finite self (the self of a particular time or place, of a particular act) to the infinite; every particular self is the place at which self as such, the divine spirit, is acting.

With this understanding of the unity of self and its other, the doctrine of the Trinity assumes a position as the fundamental aspect of life as such. God as spirit is the living God, not the abstract metaphysical God. The three persons of the Trinity, each the one and only God and each different from the other, express, in real images, the fundamental movement of life as such. Creativity, alienation (objectification, separation), and reunion (reconciliation) constitute the moments of life in such a way that each of them is the whole of life in its own moment and each is different from the others. In more Hegelian language, the self in itself, the self for itself, and the self in and for itself are the three moments in which spirit comes to itself as spirit. There is no common "ground" (a selfhood as such) to which these three can be referred as different specific appearances; rather each of them is the one and only self. (One can point up the difference in this way: When we are dealing with different species of a genus, or different examples of a species, we can say: "There is a tree, and there is *another* one." When dealing with the different appearances of spirit, we say, rather, "There is the self, and there is the self *again*.") Christian theology conceives of God, Hegel wrote,

> as necessarily entering into the process of differentiating itself from itself, of positing its other, and as first coming to itself not through relinquishment but through sublating this other. . . . God the Father (this simple universal, being-in-self), putting aside his solitariness, creates nature (that which is external to himself, self-externality), begets a Son (his other I), but by virtue of his infinite love beholds himself in this other, recognizes his image therein, and returns in this image to unity with himself. This unity is no longer abstract or immediate, but concrete, mediated through difference in that it is the Holy Spirit proceeding from the Father and the Son, and attaining perfect actuality and truth in the Christian community.[5]

A consequence of this for the doctrine of the Trinity, however, is that the divine and the human both belong to the eternal life of spirit; otherness is not something added to the life of God but is a moment in it. Understood in this trinitarian way, God includes humanity as the otherness in which divinity is shown. It was this idea from Hegel that seems to have been the spur to Barth's (and not only to Tillich's) doctrine of the Trinity, although Barth's own reading of Hegel's works, rather than of histories of philosophy, seems to have been confined to a couple of hundred pages from the lectures on the philosophy of religion.[6] It provides the basis on which one can, as Barth did, get rid of a distinction between God in himself and God for us, patterned after a common misunderstanding of Kant's distinction between noumenal things in themselves, which are unknowable, and phenomenal objects, which are knowable. The God of revelation—that is, for Barth, the God who is identified with Jesus of Nazareth, or who is manifest in his other, a single human being—is the true God because the true God is the one who is not only in himself but also manifest in his other. It was this same idea of Hegel's which led Karl Rahner to his metaphysics of the "real symbol" (that an entity can express itself in its other, hence, that it can really be itself in its symbol), which is at the heart both of his Christology and of his doctrine of the Trinity.[7]

There are, of course, differences. Rahner uses the Hegelian idea within the bounds of Thomism, which is to say, within the framework of the unchanging and changing aspects of the divine nature. By virtue of its real identification with its other, the divine Word remains the same in itself while changing in its other, its human nature, but this is a real change in the divine nature as well. And Barth's trinitarianism is not only that of the identity and self-differentiation of spirit but also, and more distinctively, that of the movement of subject, predicate, and object in the words and thought of a proposition. Moreover, like Schelling before him and like Jüngel recently, Barth rejected the necessity that was connected with Hegel's God. In his chapter on Hegel in *Protestant Theology* (written before his dogmatics), his criticism was that the God of Hegel "is at least his own prisoner," because in comprehending

> all things, he finally and at the highest level, comprehends himself too, and by virtue of the fact that he does this in the consciousness of man, everything God is and does will be understood from the point of view of man, as God's own necessity. Revelation can no longer be the free act of God; God, rather, *must* function as we see him function in revelation. . . . Hegel, in making the dialectical method of logic the essential nature of God, made impossible the knowledge of the actual dialectic of grace, which has its foundations in the freedom of God.[8]

I do not think Robert Jenson is right in putting the issue of Hegel's and Barth's trinitarianism as he does when he makes it a matter of whether the world or Jesus is the other of God. Jenson writes: "In Hegel, Augustinian trinitarianism fulfills its constant tendency [a tendency visible in Tillich and Macquarrie today] by finally explicitly taking the world as God's Object, rather than Jesus"; he sees in Barth a "christological inversion" of Hegel because Barth puts Jesus in place of Hegel's world.[9] But the alternative of Jesus or the world is itself a false alternative when applied to Hegel's dialectic; for the creation of the world and the crucifixion of Jesus are both moments in the process through which God objectifies and alienates himself from himself, the extreme point of alienation being that of the crucifixion. The issue might rather be—for Barth's as well as Hegel's doctrine—how the connection is made between the historical concreteness of the man Jesus and the idea of the living God. *That* the identification is made by both is clear; not so clear is the kind of thinking which is involved in making it.

Understanding the Modern Age

That Hegel took the extremity of finitude—the absolute finitude of the death of Jesus as the death of God—into his trinitarian theology provided him with a means to understand christologically the modern age. In a critique combining a sharp analysis of contemporaneous philosophy with a shrewd understanding of Protestant piety, he showed how the Protestant principle of justification through faith alone made objective religion impossible and how this, in turn, led in the direction of complete secularization. Tillich made use of this critique in his writings on the philosophy of religion from the 1920s. It has to do with the fact that the Protestant principle (or, as Hegel could put it, the "principle of the North" expressed religiously in Protestantism) rejects the identification between the divine and any finite thing. As Tillich pointed out, this is a fundamental difference between Luther's and Paul's understanding of justification: upon Luther's critique of Catholicism there did not follow, as there did upon Paul's critique of Judaism, a new religious "realization," that is, an incorporation into symbols and cultus of a translegal religion; instead, the Protestant principle of justification denied the possibility of any such realization at all. Protestantism, Hegel noted, "builds its temples and altars in the heart of the individual, and sighs and prayers seek for the God of whom the heart denies any intuition, because of the risk that the intellect will cognize what is beheld as a mere thing."[10] There is an unbridgeable gap between the subjective desire for the eternal and the whole of objectivity. Faith alone is capable of preserving the deity of God; intuition and intellect cannot do so. This is the "poetry of Protestant grief," the source of the "unhappy consciousness," the feeling of the irreconcilability of the deity held in faith with the finite world. If the feeling of grief at the imperceptibility of God should ever pass into an intuition without grief, it would have become superstition.[11]

The piety that cannot find anything in which to behold the object of its faith leads then to a point at which only the finite is recognized as real at all; the infinite cannot be objectified or beheld as a reality. In its extreme form, this leaves over against each other the reality of the finite and the infinite subjectivity of the human I—in other words, nihilism. The religious impossibility of a reconciliation of God with finite reality is converted into a reconciliation with merely empirical existence; that is the spirit of the modern age. But it is a reconciliation that does not do away with the absolute opposition between finite and infinite which was expressed in the Protestant longing or grief; it only repeats it in a different way. Here Hegel's christological reading of the time (which enabled him even to refer to its philosophy as a "speculative Good Friday") focused the issue of nihilism. Either the end result of the Protestant principle was a nihilism unrelieved, ending with the recognition that, because God did not exist, that is, because God was not identifiable with any existing thing, there was nothing to the idea of God; or one could think of this absolute finitude as itself a manifestation of God, in the thought of the death of God. That is to say, the way beyond the nihilism implicit in the modern situation, as an outgrowth of religion in the West, is to elevate the modern feeling that God himself is dead (what Tillich analyzed as the doubt about there being any meaning at all) "to the dignity of a truth which belongs to God and is called forth by him," because, by such an understanding of it, the proposition that God is dead "is saved from being made into an absolute."[12]

With this analysis of the Enlightenment, Hegel set what is still a theological task today, that of understanding theologically the autonomy of the modern spirit (the subjectivity set free) in such a way as to see in it a theological movement. Jüngel takes this as a task of answering the question of "where" God is; indeed, that is how he interprets Hegel's philosophical theology. If the crucifixion of Jesus is seen as the "place" where God is, then the nihilism of the modern age, which results from the impossibility of finding any existing thing that is godly, is transcended by being theologically understood. This is the setting in which I would understand Altizer's theological program.[13] His debt to Hegel is unconcealed. His effort to read the present world against the background of this theological history is probably as ambitious as any current theological program. In *Total Presence* he sets forth the thesis that takes the Hegelian reading to its conclusion: even the absence of a sense of absence (even the loss of a feeling that God is dead) is itself testimony to the total presence of God. This, at least, is the spirit that he finds in contemporary culture—God has become so completely identified with finitude that there is not even any tension between God and the real; God is totally in things just as they are, present also in the absence of a sense of his absence at all. The grieving that the longing of the heart cannot be fixed on any object ("the beauty of subjectivity," as Hegel called it) has given way to a total presence. Altizer's is therewith perhaps the most daring of the Hegelian readings of the present. But it, along with such earlier theologies of culture as that of Tillich and with more recent deconstructive readings of contemporary nihilism, indicates how Hegel is still a partner in the theological discussion.

7

SCHELLING'S IMPACT ON
PROTESTANT THEOLOGY

TRACING THE impact of a thinker by way of direct influences is, at best, an uncertain undertaking. For, in the first place, a similarity of ideas between two thinkers is not necessarily evidence of direct influence, since some ideas seem to present themselves almost as a matter of course at a certain time to those who are thinking through the positions of their predecessors; and, in the second place, the direct influence of one thinker on another may not appear at all in a similarity between the ideas of the two of them. One can think of illustrations of each of these possibilities. In certain points, there are such similarities between Barth's and Schelling's doctrines of God's freedom, or lordship—*deitas est dominatio Dei*—that one might be tempted to regard Schelling, to whom Barth expresses no particular indebtedness, as his secret teacher;[1] yet, apart from documentary evidence, it would be difficult to know whether Barth was actually influenced by Schelling's critique of Hegel or whether he arrived at a similar critique through his own reflections.[2] Again, apart from a scrap of information in the Tillich archives giving such an indication, it would be difficult to see any connection between Husserl's *Logische Untersuchungen* and Tillich's 1919 unpublished essay entitled "Rechtfertigung und Zweifel."

Even apart from those kinds of uncertainty, it is not always clear what is to be gained for theological thinking through the tracing of such influences. In some cases, of course, the gain is clear. For example, it adds to the intelligibility of the role of duty (*Pflicht*) in Kant's practical reason if one is aware of the derivation of that concept not from Kant's systematic thought so much as from his Pietist religious background. It also adds to one's understanding of the inner dynamics of philosophical idealism if one traces the way in which Karl Daub was successively influenced by Kant, Hegel, Schelling, and then Hegel again, in a pattern partly repeated, almost a century later, by Paul Tillich. For to understand how at a certain stage in one's systematic thinking Kant can be persuasive against the whole metaphysical tradition, Hegel against Kant, Schelling against Hegel, and Hegel again against Schelling is to gain a grasp of the living character of problems that are still current.[3] Beyond this, however, it is not clear whether one has gained anything important, except as a biographer or chronicler, by discovering that it was probably Hermann Cohen to whom Barth's understanding of Plato in the *Römerbriefkommentar* and, in turn, Barth's commentary to which Tillich's language in his *Dogmatik* of 1925 are indebted.

In view of these two questions, I shall in the present essay confine attention to two aspects of Schelling's impact or influence: first, to a few important, direct lines of the influence of his writings on theologians and, second, to the nature of the specific influence from Schelling as contrasted with other thinkers of the time. That Schelling did have an impact there can be no doubt. Both his obvious genius and his impressive person would almost have guaranteed it. There is evidence of it not only in the way his name could serve as an accusation—as when Schleiermacher, on coming to Halle, was accused of being a pantheist like Schelling—but also in the deference paid to him by contemporaries and in the interest with which he was read by contemporaneous intellectual leaders. There is evidence of it, too, in the way that Heidegger (and the theologians who studied him) seems to have recovered the ontological question and the meaning of the *Nichts* (in Schelling the "Not-I") through Schelling's studies of the principle of philosophy. That Schelling's activity at the University of Berlin, in which he was expected to undo the damage of the Hegelians, ended in disappointment and that the judgment of his writings during that period—his lectures on the philosophy of mythology and revelation—has oscillated between, on the one side, outright condemnation for being nothing but unrestrained fantasizing (Emanuel Hirsch) and, on the other side, captivation by the richness of their suggestions concerning the meaning of mythology and the history of religions (Dorner, Tillich, Jung and Freud perhaps?) may make it necessary to clarify what the impact was, but it does not alter there being such an impact. Hence, the object of this essay will be to try to contribute toward that clarification.

Direct Lines of Influence

The Protestant theologian of whom one first thinks when the question of Schelling's impact is raised is, of course, Paul Tillich. No other one of either the nineteenth or the twentieth century so explicitly acknowledged his indebtedness to Schelling; and, certainly, no other one has the distinction of having written both his philosophical and his theological dissertation on Schelling. Two of Tillich's main teachers at Halle—Wilhelm Lütgert and Adolf Schlatter—had already come under Schelling's influence and transmitted the basics of his religious thought even before Tillich had read Schelling himself. The impact, when Tillich did read Schelling, was, according to a letter of the time, overwhelming. In the year 1909 he wrote to Alfred Fritz, confiding that he had now gotten to the philosophical presuppositions of Schlatter and Lütgert in Schelling of the second period; he added that there are only two periods, "the usual division of periods is nonsense."[4] But this is reported in connection with Tillich's own response to reading Schelling, whose works he had recently purchased. So strongly was he affected by them that he was unable to produce anything of his own—he spoke of "die Unfähigkeit, aus der Fülle des zu Rezipierenden auch nur das Geringste zu produzieren" as the reason for his silence. Schelling "kept me completely down" so that "I was listening but could not speak because I was hearing too much."[5]

The effect on Tillich was permanent; Schelling remained his mentor in a way that no other predecessor did. In his autobiographical sketch of 1936, "On the Boundary," which was first published as an introduction to his essays on the interpretation of history and then was issued as a separate volume in 1966, he wrote that he still found in Schelling more theonomous philosophy than in any of the other German idealists[6] and that it was only Schelling among the idealists who saw that systematic thought, too, is conditioned by the situation of the thinker, although, unlike Kierkegaard, he did not manage to incorporate this recognition into his philosophy.[7] In short, it was the thought especially of the later Schelling which enabled him to relate the theological ideas he had learned from such teachers as Martin Kaehler with philosophy and which opened the way to a unification of the two.[8]

But the influence of Schelling was not so unambiguously welcomed as Tillich's references in later years indicated. There was a negative, oppressive side to it, which, alluded to in his letter to Fritz, is made explicit in an exchange of letters with Emanuel Hirsch almost a decade later. Replying on 20 February 1918 to a letter he had received from Hirsch, he called the letter "the profoundest" thing since Schelling's positive philosophy that any theologian had written, and he was reminded of the way in which the *düstere Kraft* of that positive philosophy had originally affected him, "deeply shaking [him] religiously" with the idea of the lordship of God, so that he first interpreted Schelling II (the apparently heteronomous Schelling) by Schelling I (the Schelling of freedom) and then left Schelling for Hegel and, later, for Nietzsche. "A whiff of those days came to me," he added, "from your letter," containing the summons: "Don't forget Schelling II."[9]

Although Tillich went on to say that he had not really forgotten that part of Schelling, these remarks are an indication that his relation to Schelling was more dialectical than his other, later comments suggested. He was initially both overpowered and repelled by the conception of God which Schelling had set against Hegel's and which finds so audible an echo in Karl Barth's; for the conception seemed to be in radical opposition to the principle of autonomy for which Tillich stood and in which he undertook to live. It may be historical irony, or it may be a reflection of the personal bitterness left by the later controversy between Hirsch and Tillich during the Nazi period, that, in his history of Protestant thought, Hirsch found precisely this later Schelling so worthless and that Tillich ascribed to just this Schelling the decisive influence. In 1918, Hirsch had replied in turn to Tillich's letter, "I blessed Schelling II when I received your letter, even though I still do not like him. You do owe him *very* much."[10]

What, then, did Tillich owe to Schelling? Three basic ideas, probably. The first idea, which is contained in Tillich's interpretation of the symbol of the cross as a self-relativizing symbol, combines thoughts from Kaehler and Schelling. From Martin Kaehler—or, perhaps, it would be more accurate to say "through Kaehler," since the idea is not expressly his—Tillich had received the notion that the Protestant principle of justification is applicable not only to the moral but also to the intellectual realm; justification is not only of the sinner but also of the doubter. From Schelling's philosophy of revelation, he received a notion that made this principle itself not something merely reflective or philosophical but rather a philosophical appropriation of a religious and theological expression. Schelling had identified the *Grundidee* of Christianity in this way: "The Son *could* exist independently of the Father in his *own* glory [lordliness]; he could not, of course, be *true* God outside the Father, but he could indeed be *God*, that is, Lord of being, outside and without the Father, not, indeed, in *essence* but, even so, in *act*. *This* glory [lordliness], however, which he could have had independent of the Father, the Son rejected, and *therein* he is Christ"; that he rejected this possibility and instead "chose the cross"—"herein lies the basic idea of Christianity."[11]

In other words, the connection between the principle of justification (that the mind can seek truth in the midst of its error because truth itself has already been given it) and Christology is that the act through which one appropriates the divine is one of giving up any claim to possess the divine. The systematic significance of this is seen already in Tillich's earliest systems (from 1913 on) in what he called the paradox of the theological standpoint.[12] It asserts that the theological system, through which the absoluteness of any truth is denied (its anti-idolatrous role), must have the same criterion applied to itself—it is not the absolute truth. By being thus subjected to the same principle to which it subjects everything else, it remains continually open to reformulating and revision even while being systematic. What Tillich owed to Schelling, then, is the recognition of how the systematic idea, which was one of the major contributions of idealism to Western thought, can be prevented from becoming absolutist and of how this self-application of a criterion is a reflection of the self-denial of the Christ.[13] When Tillich, in volume 2 of the *Systematic Theology*, formulated the paradox of Christianity by remarking that a defeated Messiah is no Messiah and that Christianity acknowledges and accepts this paradox,[14] this formulation focuses what Schelling had called the basic idea of Christianity—that the fulfillment of the Messianic vocation on the part of Jesus lay in his not being the Messiah. The only thing that distinguishes between him and any other human being—no one else, after all, is the Messiah either—is that, by a combination of freedom and destiny (as Tillich put it), he *could have* been but freely chose not to be the one. Schelling's kenotic Christology, similarly, had rested on showing that the Son *could* really have been God without and outside the Father—that is how he is different from humanity as such and also from divinity as such—but that he freely chose not to exercise that power. (Schelling, in another context, also defined "nobility" as the not exercising of power or privilege that one could exercise if one chose to do so.)

Besides these christological readings of justification and paradox, a third debt of Tillich to Schelling—although this is one that he does not explicitly acknowledge—lies in his concept of the "demonic" as the other side of the "divine," both of which are included in the "holy" as such.[15] The idea of the power of the deity loosened from its unity in the deity, which is the leitmotif of Schelling's philosophy of mythology and revelation, has such close affinities to Tillich's concept of the demonic, and may be what Tillich meant with his reference to the "dark power" of Schelling's philosophical theology, that one cannot but think there is a link. It is significant that, in *On the Boundary*, Tillich includes the demonic in a triad: human-divine-demonic, in which the divine is the synthesis of the human and the demonic (just as the prophetic is called the synthesis of the sacramental and the secular, and theonomy the synthesis of autonomy and heteronomy). This is somewhat different from his account of the demonic in his works on the philosophy of religion; for in them, the "demonic" and the "divine" are two powers in the "holy": both are creative and destructive, as is the holy itself, but they are distinguished because the demonic is creative in the service of destruction (it creates forms in order to destroy forms, even the forms it creates), whereas the divine is destructive in the service of creation (it destroys forms in order to create new forms that take the old into themselves). In these formulations there is as much of Rudolf Otto as there is of Schelling. Still, that Tillich can also use the human and the demonic as the opposites which are synthesized in the divine is at least enough of an echo of Schelling's mythology to make one think that this idea does have its roots in Schelling's doctrine of God, a doctrine according to which there is a dual principle in deity itself, which cannot be reduced to a metaphysical or dialectical monism.

Although the line connecting Schelling with Tillich's concept of the demonic may be at least smudged, it is clearly traceable from Schelling to Barth's unique interpretation of divine election.[16] The line—a thin one, to be sure—runs from Schelling by way of Daub's *Judas Ischariot*, a book Daub wrote during his

Schelling period and a book that Barth cites (though only briefly and not favorably),[17] to Barth's understanding of a double predestination that establishes rather than undercuts the universality of the divine grace. Daub had taken Schelling's point seriously, that the origin of both the negative and the positive, which cannot be derived from each other, must lie in the divine being. (The meanings of "negative" and "positive" here are not simply their logical sense, since the negative principle, the sheer givenness or freedom of the divine existence in contrast to the divine essence, is, like all data, something positive when viewed in empirical terms. But that qualification need not be taken into account here.) This must mean, with respect to theological history, that Judas is an incarnation of the one principle in the same way that Jesus is the incarnation of the other; aboriginal evil is embodied in the person of Judas, as aboriginal grace is in Jesus. Daub never finished the book, not only because it proved to be almost unreadable but also because, by his own testimony, the effort to think through that line of thought was debilitating in the extreme. Barth's doctrine of predestination can rightly be regarded as a completion of Daub's attempt to apply Schelling's idea of the original duality in deity to Christology and history—in that sense Lambinet may be right (see n. 1). Barth found a key, which Daub lacked, in the thought that the object of the divine decree of rejection, the negative side of election, is none other than Jesus—so that the answer to the Calvinist question of who is elected to damnation is Jesus—and that Judas, by being the incarnation of that self-rejecting side of the divine will, was a manifestation of the saving will of God. God's choosing of rejection for himself and acceptance for creation is the one divine will that is doubly incarnate in the figures of Judas and Jesus. In retrospect, Daub's effort foundered, not only psychologically but even logically and speculatively, on the sheer contradiction of trying to think or imagine (and portray) an incarnation of radical evil, since the very thought or portrayal either reduces the radicalness of the evil or defeats itself—"damns itself," one might say—in the attempt; it was this that led him from Schelling back to Hegel, a path along which Tillich briefly followed in the period during and after World War I, but a path which Barth did not have to follow because he struck a new one. Had Barth written nothing else than his treatise on divine election, he would have done enough to earn himself a place among the creative interpreters of nineteenth-century idealism, if not specifically of Schelling's doctrine of God.

There are other aspects of Barth's theology that seem to have their origin in Schelling. His doctrine of God's freedom has echoes of Schelling's proposition that God is not identical with being but is the Lord of being (a conception in which he found himself allied with Newton). Again, what Bonhoeffer named Barth's "positivism of revelation" has echoes of Schelling's logical empiricism and philosophy of revelation. Schelling had maintained that, while it might be possible in a system of concepts to derive the concept (for example) of a plant, without making reference to the empirical world, it is never possible to know on the basis of the concept whether there actually is such a thing. Thus, while it might be possible to say *what* God is on the basis of concepts alone, Schelling had maintained, it is not possible to say *that* he is or what his will is, without reference to a revelation of that being and will; these do not have their ground in any anterior thought, they are just given, *unvordenklich*. Finally, Schelling's and Barth's constructions of a suprahistorical history, a prehistory (in which, according to Schelling, there occurred the original Fall, an "intelligible" fall, that determines the historical condition of the race) which is the background or origin of actual history, are similar enough to make it probable that there was some influence, at least indirect, of Schelling on Barth. All such connections between Schelling and Barth, however, are more difficult to trace clearly than the one from Schelling to Barth's doctrine of predestination.

A third theologian (apart from contemporaries like Daub and Marheineke) in whom there is evidence of a direct impact of Schelling is I. A. Dorner. He was one of the few theologians to have seen the point Schelling made against Hegel's concept of being. (Eberhard Jüngel has recently resumed the same discussion in *God as the Mystery of the World*.)[18] Schelling had argued that the concept of being does not have any content by virtue of which it can "move" at all toward the concept of nothing and thence toward *Werden* (the "shall" or "will," the futurity, of being); the movement is, rather, imposed upon the concept by a reflective recognition that pure or abstract being is nothing in particular. For that reason, Schelling took as the original concept not being (*Sein*) but the potentiality-to-be (*Seinkönnen* or *Seinwerden*). What is beyond being is, in Aristotle's terminology, τὸ τί ἦν εἶναι, which Schelling read literally as "that which was to be." This is to say that, from the standpoint of actual being, the origin is to be thought not as pure being (because pure being makes no transition to actuality) but rather as the was-to-be or the can-be (the futurity, the potentiality) of actual being. Unlike the idea of pure being, the idea of able-to-be (or free-to-be-if-one-chooses-to-be) does contain movement in itself; for the idea of possibility already leaps forward to that of actuality. Furthermore, this movement, unlike the necessity that Hegel saw in the dialectical movement of being to nothing to becoming and, finally, to spirit, is not necessary but free. There is no indication in the can-be whether that which can be something actually will be that thing.

In *A System of Christian Doctrine* Dorner made use especially of Schelling's philosophy of mythology and revelation in order to show how this philosophy, even more than Hegel's, contained the elements for a reconstruction of the doctrine of the trinitarian God.[19] Although Dorner's own reconstruction may, by its biblicism, fall short of the promise, it was clearly influenced by Schelling on those points in which there was a difference with Hegel. Thus, after noting Schelling's criticism of Hegel's concept of being ("It is not evident by what power Hegel can make pure Being veer round to Nothing, as to an idea different from Being"), he called "more promising" Schelling's beginning his ontology with the possibility of being (the potentiality to be) instead; for the very indeterminateness and ambiguity of this concept contains the recognition that "we must seek to advance by the agency of separations of the defects still remaining in our first, and still insufficiently determinate, idea, or apparent possibilities," instead of, with Hegel, introducing something as "wanting in the original idea, the annihilation of which would form the process of advance."[20] Similarly, the basis of the trinitarian conception is then seen to be in the relation of the can-be (being in itself), the must-be (pure being), and the shall-be (self-possessed being).[21] In short, whatever may have been his reservations about the early writings of Schelling, Dorner saw in the later Schelling an advance beyond the idealism of Hegel just in the matter of its providing an ontology of freedom.

The Nature of Schelling's Impact

In his *Gott: Nochmals Martin Heidegger* Alfred Jäger points out, among other things, that the structure of Heidegger's question of being is made more accessible and intelligible by reference to its background in Schelling and the problem of pantheism or, what is the same, the problem of the "identity" of being (of the copula or "is" in such a proposition as A = A or I = I or "God is All").[22]

This provides one way of describing the nature of Schelling's impact. He raised the question of the "ground" of being, or of what is beyond being and thinking, beyond being and nothing, in a form that still appears to be more radical than the way it is raised in Hegel. Theologically, this is expressed in the distinction that Schelling made between free spirit and necessary spirit. He did not regard it as sufficient to conceive of God as spirit; rather, the task is to form the concept of God as free spirit, for it is in that freedom that the distinction between God and man and between God and the whole of being is to be located. Dorner may be right in suggesting that this places Schelling's later philosophy closer to biblical theology than was Hegel of the *Logic* and *Phenomenology;* that might then account for the attraction that this later Schelling exercised on Protestant theologians. Whether or not that is the case, however, Schelling's raising the question of the ground of being and thinking at all does seem to add a dimension to the concept of spirit that is not obvious in Hegel. Schelling himself may not have followed through—Tillich, who in his dissertations on Schelling argued that Schelling used that principle of identity to break the idealist system of identity, and Georg Picht, who sees in Schelling the first appearance of that break with the Western metaphysics of being that Heidegger came to represent, agree that Schelling saw the matter rightly but was unable to incorporate the break into a constructive philosophy.[23]

The question of the ground of being, as Schelling formulated it in his *Philosophie der Offenbarung,* shows its connection both to the Neoplatonic tradition and to Heidegger's ontological question. "At some point of its development," Schelling wrote,

> the human spirit will feel the need to get, as it were, to the bottom of being—to "get to the bottom of it" [*hinter eine Sache kommen:* lit., get behind a matter] is a colloquial expression that I am deliberately using because such expressions help to make things clear— one would like, as we say, to "get to the bottom of a thing." But what is the "bottom of a thing" here? Not being; because this is the surface (*das Vordere*) of a matter, that which immediately catches attention. . . . The bottom of a matter is thus not its being but the essence (*Wesen*), the potency, the prime matter (*Ursache*)—these are all synonymous here. Thus at the point of its highest development the deeply implanted and ineradicable human inclination to comprehend will also demand to get to the bottom not only of this or that matter but of being at all—to see, not what is *above* being,

for this is a quite different concept, but what is *beyond* being. It reaches a point where one has to become free not only of revelation but of every reality in order to flee into the complete desert of being, where one meets nothing real any more but only the infinite potentiality of all being, which is the only immediate content of thinking, in which thought moves only in itself, in its own ether.[24]

Or, again, in the first lecture: "Far from its being so that man and his activities make the world comprehensible, man is himself the most incomprehensible and drives me irresistibly to the view of the unhappiness of all being. . . . If I cannot answer that question, everything else sinks into the abyss of a bottomless Nothing."[25]

Put simply, the impact of Schelling, and particularly the later Schelling, in theology is at least that of continually raising the question whether the Hegelian system, or even the Hegelian concept of spirit, is theologically adequate—whether it has, so to speak, reached the bottom of things. This is the question of whether God who is verily God can be identified with being or spirit or whether, instead, such a God is beyond the whole of being.

The contribution that post-Kantian idealism made to theology—most directly to Christian systematic theology but potentially to any theology—lay in its conception of God as spirit (which was accompanied by breaking the equation of God with the infinite and the equation of the creature with the finite—spirit is both infinite and finite). In the being of spirit, identity and difference are related to each other not as they are in objective entities, where to be of one kind means not to be of an opposite kind (if a thing is generically a plant, it is not an animal), but in such a way that the self is itself in its other. The capacity to be itself in its other, indeed, to come to itself by showing itself in its other, is the capacity that defines the can-be of spirit in contrast to nonspiritual entities. Idealist thought—and this is as true of Hegel as of Schelling—drew the theological consequence of this by recognizing that the nature of God as spirit, which was dogmatically expressed in both the trinitarian and the christological formulations, is that there is an other in the divine being itself. In Schelling's philosophy of mythology and revelation, Christ is really the other God in God, who can actually be God apart from the unity of the divine being, who is driven from that unity in the prehistorical human Fall and who returns to the unity through the mythological process (a necessary process taking place within the human consciousness) and through revelation (a free deed of the historical person Jesus). Apart from the unity of God, the other God could actually be God but could not be the true God. That the Christ in the person of Jesus freely chose to forgo actually being God was the deed through which the disrupted unity of God was restored. That is one reading of the meaning of spirit, a reading which laid the foundation for a whole theology of religion and of history. Hegel's reading of it in the *Phenomenology* appears less fanciful and more descriptive, and in the *Philosophy of Religion* it appears to have more basis in historical research than Schelling's. Even so, Hegel too depends on the concept of spirit as that power of being in which the identity and difference mean that the one can be itself in its other and that it actually is itself in becoming its other for itself.

What then is the difference between the two? On what basis can one say that Schelling puts the metaphysical foundations of theology more radically into question than Hegel? The answer can be given, I think, by saying that Schelling raises (1) the question whether even being and thinking have a ground or reason and (2) the question how the connection is made between thinking and being, which may be, in effect, Schelling's question of the difference between necessary spirit and free spirit. The intention of these two questions will be briefly elaborated to conclude this essay.

It seems to me that Schelling was on the right track in thinking that the concept of being does not get to the very origin, because being does not of itself move toward nothing and thence toward futurity (or becoming). This is to say that one can ask not just for the origin of all things in being as such but that one can ask, intelligibly, about the origin of being—not just the origin of the physical cosmos or even of the lawfully ordered whole of the physical and spiritual universe but the origin of being as such. If the question is formulated in terms of the "ground" of being, then its sense can be indicated in the following way. The "ground" of something is that with reference to which the thing is both the same as and different from another thing. For example, the concept of "flower" represents the ground of the concepts of "rose" and "tulip" because it is that concept with respect to which roses and tulips are the same and different—they are both flowers but they are different flowers. A ground is the origin both of the sameness and of the difference; and, for there to be a ground, two things need to be over against each other in such a way that they are both comparable and contrastable. When one asks about the ground of *being,* however, the conceptual problem lies in there not being anything over against being with which it can be compared and contrasted. What is over against being is, literally, nothing (and by "nothing" we are to understand a referent that is already contradicted by our naming it). The concept of the ground of being cannot, therefore, refer to any thing or to being as such but to whatever it "is" that is between and beyond being and nothing. (In the Schelling of "Vom Ich als Prinzip der Philosophie" this is God as the identity of I and Not-I). So the concept raises the question: How can one think what is totally other, that is, what is neither being nor nothing, what neither is nor is not anything? In more Kierkegaardian language—or in the sense of the legend of the medieval monk who had agreed, before his death, that he would send back a message from the beyond to answer whether that world was like or unlike the present world, and whose message, when it came, said *Nec taliter nec aliter sed totaliter aliter*—how does one think *totaliter aliter,* the totally other?

The question of God as free spirit does raise, it seems to me, the issue of how the spheres of thinking and being (of Schelling's negative and positive philosophies) are related to each other. This can be focused in the interpretation of the ontological proof of God's being. Granted that this proof, rightly understood, shows that we cannot both understand the meaning of "God" and also deny that God is real as well as ideal. (The only case in which the proof would fail to have such a result is the case in which the meaning of "God" would itself be a negative, so that to be only in the mind and not also in reality would be better or greater than to be both ideal and real. That is why an ontological proof of Satan is different from a proof of God.) Both Hegel and Schelling acknowledged such a proof, not as a logical demonstration, which moves from premises to consequent, but as what Schelling called a "necessary deed" in which understanding the meaning of the word simultaneously involves seeing it as realized in the world; the deed of thinking, through which one becomes conscious of God, is, in this way, comparable to the deed of understanding the meaning of "I," through which consciousness is elevated to self-consciousness.

But how is the link then made between the God understood as being, in any case, someone or something (that is, not nothing), on one side, and, on the other side, the empirically given world? If God is necessary spirit, then it seems to follow that from the idea of God alone a connection is made with the whole of reality. This is to say that, at a certain point, the idea converts itself, as it were, into reality: the idea of God becomes identical with the appearance of the whole of reality. If, on the other hand, God is free spirit, then God *can* in principle be identified with any reality, with no reality, or with the whole of reality. With what God is to be actually identified we cannot know just on the basis of the idea or on the basis of speculative thinking but only on the basis of whether, *in fact* (and freely), God appears as this or that or some other thing. To put the difference more pointedly: for Hegel, God *is* real in everything (and reason's task is to see into that truth); for Schelling, God *can be* real as anything (but experience, rather than reason, will tell us where the reality actually is). Schelling seems to me to point more clearly toward the role played by symbols and real signs; they are the realities through whose mediation free, that is, rationally underivable, connections are made between one's consciousness of God and the self-presentation of the real world. If this is so, then the nature of the impact of Schelling on Protestant theology is not only that it opened the door to a "positivism of revelation" (with its danger of becoming a repristination of supranaturalism) but also that it prepared the way for a new understanding of symbols as those actual things (persons, events, objects) which are not God but as which God exists.

PART TWO
Science and Culture

8

THE NO TO NOTHING AND
THE NOTHING TO KNOW
Barth and Tillich and
the Possibility of
Theological Science

IF IT is true, as John of Damascus said, that we cannot say *what* God is; if, in other words, all we can say of God is that God is *God*, then how is a knowledge of God, a theological science, possible at all? If one cannot know what something is, how can one know anything else about it? Aquinas answered the question by likening theology to those sciences in which the effects of the undefinable subject take the place of the definition of its nature. The world, with everything in it, can be read as the effect of its cause. And the link between, on the one side, the cause of the world, and, on the other side, the God of whom what is known is only that God is God is forged by the negative jointly contained in the name of God and the name of first cause: the first cause is, in any case, not the world or anything in it, and God is, in any case, not the world or anything in it, so that, by the link of this negative, everyone can call the first cause God. First cause is not, then, a definition of God—it does not tell us what God is—but a name linking the cosmos, in the category of causality, to deity that is not the cosmos. This kind of theological science is possible—to put the matter non-Thomistically—to the extent that the world and everything in it can be read as the sign of another than itself and to the extent that that other is understood as the meaning of the name "God."

But what of theology in the stronger, or the authentic, sense as the knowledge of God that is God's knowledge, the knowledge of that other which is another knowledge—the theology intended in *sacra doctrina*, in other words? Can there be a theology in this authentic sense when the possibility of sacred doctrine at all has become a matter of question? This is an issue with which, in the early 1920s, the new "dialectical" or "crisis" theology came upon the scene. It is a fundamental issue on which Tillich and Barth were united in opposition to what Tillich called the "self-sufficient finitude" of existence in the late nineteenth century. It is also the issue on which the first breach in the ranks became publicly visible in the *Auseinandersetzung* of Tillich and Barth. Not incidentally the matter on which they divided was formulated in a question of Barth that recalls the principle stated by John of Damascus: "Why not call God—God?"

The question was formulated with a little more Barthian flourish. But it did call attention to a fundamental problem in the notion of theological science. In addition, it pointed out, or at least pointed to, a basic difference between Barth and Tillich. The theological difference between the two may in the end be less great than the similarity, especially if one thinks of both of them as a theological voice against the historicism of the late-nineteenth-century liberal theology with which they broke. The difference is, in any case, less great than would be indicated by the widespread understanding of Barth's theology as a neoorthodoxy. Even so, there is a difference, which for purposes of this essay I have formulated as the "no to nothing" that is the name of God in Barth's theology and the "nothing to know" that is the symbol of God in Tillich's. What is of interest here, however, is not so much the question of what their theologies were as it is the question of what those theologies still offer as food for one's own theological thought.

Tillich and Barth were, if they were anything at all, theological thinkers of the first rank. That there were differences between them can hardly be denied. Their styles of thinking were different; their methods were different; their relations to political, social, and cultural matters were different; their persons and manner of life were different. Barth called his theology a church dogmatics, Tillich's was a theology of culture and an apologetics. Tillich acknowledged his debt to Barth, saying that it was Barth who awakened him from the slumber of almost equating life-processes with divine revelation.[1] Barth acknowledged no similar debt to Tillich, whose theology he called, even in his later years, "abominable" and with whom he maintained cordiality only despite the theology.[2] Tillich wrote a highly compact language, in which everything of nonessential detail had already been eliminated; Barth wrote an effusive language, varying in mood from self-mockery to utmost aggressiveness and not sparing, or hiding from, readers his journey through detailed debates with the theological tradition. Barth's theological development is on the surface marked by a turn from the anthropological to the theological as sharp as, and in nature similar to, the turn in Heidegger's philosophy from the analytics of *Dasein* to the poetry of *Sein*; Tillich's is on the surface a successive unfolding of the original principle that the paradox of thinking and the paradox of believing are the same paradox.[3] Barth's was a maverick ego that never lost the sense of continuity with itself. Looking back in later years on the theology of his Romans commentary (specifically on his interpretation of Romans 8 : 24) from which he had meanwhile distanced himself, he could mockingly commend himself with the English words inserted into his German text: "Well roared, lion!"[4] Tillich's was a punctiliar ego—if one may put it so—that seemed uninterested in its own continuity but always recovered itself in new matters. Tillich commented that in looking back at his early writings he often seemed to be reading the works of someone else. Tillich's aesthetic sense was for the visual arts, and he could find in expressionistic painting a contemporary revelation of God; Barth's was for music, and he not only began his days by listening to Mozart—as well as reading the newspaper—but also ventured the judgments that there is no theological visual art but that in Mozart's music one can hear the original goodness of creation.

Yet, despite these differences, they were alike in being singularly occupied with thinking through the content and meaning of theology: What does it mean that the word *God* has appeared in the language, and how, in a nihilistic age, is one to answer for that word and the tales and judgments connected with it? To *think*, not just to repeat and rearrange or paraphrase what has been said and written, and to think *theologically*, so that the thinking and the thought-about are fitted to each other—this, we might say, is the task they undertook to accomplish and also bequeathed to be done, still and again. So the question for our consideration is this:

Do they, and how do they, still enable one, by their example, to think and to think theologically? Barth's theology is founded on the name of God as the existing name whose meaning is the eternal no to the meaning of the word *nothing*; Tillich's is founded on the symbol of God as the symbol whose reality contains the nothing that we know in knowing the negation of nothing that is God. What shall we make of that in a theological science today? I shall proceed by asking two things: What was Barth's question to Tillich and Tillich's to Barth? What is to be made of their answers?

What Were the Questions?

With some reluctance, Tillich had in 1923 opened the exchange between them with an essay entitled "Critical and Positive Paradox," an essay which, together with Barth's response, shows how far off the mark it is to compare Tillich and Barth by saying that the one starts from below and the other from above. Tillich's reluctance to write was not due to doubts about the criticism he wanted to make; it was due, rather, to his fear that such a public exchange would deflect attention from what dialectical, or crisis, theology had to say to its time. Nonetheless, he obliged the editor of the *Theologische Blätter* and presented his argument that the theology of crisis was in danger of being either a self-defeating positionlessness or a covert supranaturalism. In Tillich's vocabulary, supranaturalism is a species of idolatry. Barth replied: If it is true that the fear of an idolatrous use of the word *God* is justified and if it is also true that one can see through that fear as amounting to nothing, then "why not with all good and bad Christians call God God?" Why play hide-and-seek with an "icy monster" called "the unconditioned"? The unconditioned—"a big word . . . ! God is perchance the one meant? . . . Would not the familiar, plain 'God' in the mouth of a theologian . . . finally be more secure against dialectic, over against which I do not exactly consider '*das Unbedingte*' to be weather-tight either?"[5]

With that, the issue between them was joined, though hardly yet with the clarity it attained over the years. Can the word *God* be used idolatrously? Yes, they both agreed. Should theology then take precautions against its idolatrous use? Yes, said Tillich, because the fight against idolatry is as necessary as religion is universal. No, said Barth, because one can see through the fear of idolatrous use of the name, as a fear which, though well founded, does not amount to anything. But what did Barth mean by saying that the fear does not amount to anything even though there is a good basis for it?

He does not elaborate the point in this rejoinder. But possibly he meant this: of course, there is a danger that human beings will absolutize or make idols out of things that are neither absolute nor God. In that sense, the fear is well founded. Yet it is exactly that idolatry which is met and taken into the divine grace by virtue of the name. It is precisely as idolater that one comes to know what is the redeeming grace of God. In that sense the fear of idolatry amounts to nothing. Idolaters is what we are in any case; the question is only whether our being idolaters, our denying the deity of God even in the efforts to affirm it, is of any importance to the relation to God. Once one has seen through the fact that we are all idolaters—there is nothing else that we can be—one can also recognize that it is the idolatrousness of idolatry that is made negligible by the manifestation of God. The appearance of God is, in other words, the denial of our denial. In that sense the fear of idolatry can be seen through as amounting to nothing. So one might read Barth.

Tillich's analysis—which, along with Barth's reply, I am as much reconstructing as reviewing in these paragraphs—hinged on the distinction between a positive paradox and a critical paradox. The question he put to dialectical or crisis theology was whether it was in effect different from nihilism and, if so, whether it was still working with an absoluteness that it itself prohibited or was willing to acknowledge the positive conception of paradox that is presupposed in the critical concept of it. Barth, with perhaps some justice, confessed that he might not entirely have understood the point but, to the extent that he did, what surprised him was not the point itself but that Tillich seemed to think he was saying something to them that they did not already know. "I think I understand what Tillich means," Barth wrote in his reply; "but then I am baffled by the fact that Tillich is obviously of the opinion that he is calling our attention to something of which we are presumed to have heard no more than the disciples of John had heard concerning whether there was a Holy Spirit." What, then, was the question connected with critical and positive conceptions of paradox? What was the content of Tillich's argument that dialectical or critical theology presupposes something nondialectical and positive if it is not to be either nihilism or absolutism in disguise?[6]

Dialectical theology had as its fundamental contention that

every theological position had to be denied because it was not, and could not be, authentically theological. "Only God himself can speak of God," Barth said in 1922. "That means the defeat of all theology and all theologians."[7] To every word claiming to be the word of God, dialectical theology said: "No, that is not the word of God." To every equation of the worldly with the godly or of the human with the divine, it had only the message of no. But dialectical theology said this no to every word claiming to be the word of God *as* a human word claiming to be the word of God and then said no to this claim in turn. But could it say this no *as* the word of God against all words of God and then against its own saying without defeating itself before it attacked any idols? Could this no be the unity of the worldly and the godly, of the human and the divine, which it itself denied? Is the only unity of the divine and human to be found in the negative: the one is *not* the other? This is the question that goes to the foundation of dialectical theology. If its basic theological position is that no position is theological—because it is a position of human beings, not the position of God—then is it not self-consuming or self-defeating?

Tillich's assessment of the dialectical theologians—he had in view Friedrich Gogarten and Karl Barth in particular—was twofold: they were consistent in being willing to apply to their own position the same no that they applied to all others; but they did not draw from this consistency the right inference, namely, that the critical paradox presupposes a positive paradox. A critical paradox is the human no to every word that claims to be a word of God, a no which, as that human no, is also the no, the judgment or *krisis*, of God. It is paradoxical in that it is what it denies anything can be—a divine word in the form of a human word. It is critical because its content is the negative judgment that the worldly is not the godly and the human not the divine. Formally Tillich's argument against a merely critical paradox is a variation of the refutation of skepticism. If skepticism is the view that nothing can be shown beyond doubt to be true, then it faces the question whether this view itself can be shown beyond doubt to be true. If the view can be shown to be true beyond doubt, then it contradicts itself; if it cannot be shown to be true beyond doubt, then it is incapable of refuting a given other claim to an indubitable truth. Skepticism can be consistent as an attitude, parasitic upon positions, but it cannot be converted into a position; it presupposes the givenness of something to doubt. Skepticism can be a position only paradoxically—as the assertion that the one indubitable truth is that there is no indubitable truth. But then it faces the question of how that position can be a position at all. How will one show that this one indubitable truth is indubitable?

Dialectical theology had to face a similar dilemma. In its form as what Tillich called "critical paradox," it applied to itself the same no that it applied to everything else. But, in doing so, it created for itself a fundamental problem. For, if even the theology that there cannot be a theology cannot be a theology, then what is to prevent one from saying, theologically, that there can be a theology after all—since the denial that there can be a theology cannot be a theology or it consumes itself before it denies anything? The no to all theology turns out to incapacitate itself by falling into an infinity of negations, unless it has a hidden basis from which the no is being issued. The positive paradox, by contrast, is the human word which asserts *as* the word of God that every word is both a human word and the word of God. The critical paradox is the human word which says that no human word, including this human word, is the word of God; the positive paradox is the human word which says that the human word which says that no human word, this human word included, is the word of God shows the word of God. In personal form, the critical paradox is the human being whose existence shows that no human being, including this human being, is divine; the positive paradox is the human being whose existence shows that the human being whose existence shows that no human being, including this human being, is divine shows the divine. Phrased differently: the human being who shows that human beings who show that human being is only human and not divine are human, not divine, shows the human being that is divine. A three-tiered relation is involved here. There is the human word itself. Then there is a word about that human word. Finally, there is a word about the word about the human word. The critical paradox can appear at the second tier, when the assertion is made that no word, not even a word about the word, is a word of God; the positive paradox is at the third tier, when the assertion is made that the word that no word is a word of God shows the word of God.

The force of Tillich's critique can best be illustrated by making reference to Barth's dialectical position in his essay of 1922 entitled "The Word of God as the Task of Theology." For that is the essay in which he raises the question of how theology can say anything that is the word of God if the only words there are are human words; and that is the essay in which his reply to the ques-

tion is most purely dialectical. There Barth outlines the dilemma
of theology—when theology is understood, authentically, as a
speaking of God by God—as consisting in its being both necessary and impossible. This is to take up theology in the strongest
sense of the concept—not as a human reflection on the divine, or
a human speaking of God, but as a speaking of God that is God's
own speaking. That such a speaking is impossible seems obvious.
Everything said or thought is said or thought by human beings
about things or persons which, whatever else they are, are in any
case not God. That is true even if one tries to reserve a book as
sacred scripture or its words as the word of God. For, at the least,
the judgment or the thought that scripture is sacred is itself a human judgment and thinking. Hence, the impossibility of a theology in this authentic sense seems plain. That such a theology is,
however, necessary may seem less obvious. Does its necessity ex-
tend beyond the Protestant pulpit, which, in Barth's case, was the
occasion of the predicament? The Protestant sermon did not purport to be a human discourse about things in heaven and earth but
a *sermo de Deo* in the double sense of a talk of God—an address
in which the addresser was not the human preacher but the God
about whom he was preaching. Worshipers, Barth said, do not
come in order to hear the views of a parson, however learned or
wise, on this or that subject matter. They come in order to hear
addressed to them a word that can be heard as the word of God.
Without that presupposition, Protestant preaching is an anach-
ronism or it is, in kind, no different from any other public address.
It is always possible to say, of course, that that is only a contingent necessity. The idea of a sermon that was genuinely the address of God to the assembled worshipers, and the more so the
less they believed it to be that, may be an idea of a form of speech
that belongs to a specific epoch of religious history. Once its time
has passed, it cannot be recovered and need not be retained.

One can read Barth's essay simply in this context—as the way
in which he had to come to terms with his obligation, as a Protestant parson, to preach a sermon—and that is indeed the factual
framework of the writing. Yet Barth develops the problem in such
a way as to show the necessity of there being a speaking that is
both of and by one who is other than we in our humanity are, a
necessity connected with the question of the beginning and the
end, of what was before birth and will be after death; for this is a
question that is both humanly inevitable and humanly unanswer-
able. That we are not God and our speaking is not God's speaking

is the obvious fact; in that sense authentic theology is impossible. But that, as human beings, we can ask, do ask, and must ask what is the beginning before our particular beginnings and the end after our particular ends, and that we ask as ones who cannot answer our own questions, not even by saying that the questions cannot be answered or that they are illegitimate, is equally obvious; in that sense theology, as a word not our own, is necessary. This is Barth's purely dialectical reading of the human situation in respect to theology—theology is both its impossibility and its necessity. His answer is equally dialectical. To carry out theology in such a situation is to think theologically by recognizing both the impossibility and the necessity and thereby to let God appear as God, or, as Barth put it, to give glory to God. The recognition of that dialectical state is itself the way in which God is acknowledged as God, and the very freedom to ask the question to which there is no answer shows the answer to that question. It is not that one gets the answer but that the question is liberated and one is freed for the question despite its unanswerability. This is Barth's dialectical theology—thinking in the contradiction between the necessity and the impossibility, without resolution, is the thinking that lets God be God by redeeming the question of finite infinity.

But now comes Tillich's question. For, having said that theology is both the necessity and the impossibility of a speaking of God, one has to ask: Is this speaking about theology as both necessary and impossible in its own turn a theological speaking? Or is it but a human speaking of the limitations of human being? On what is it based? Either the dialectical position reiterates itself ad infinitum, and is indistinguishable from nihilism, or there is something nondialectical presupposed by it—and that nondialectical base is either, as Tillich called it, a positive paradox or a hidden absolutism, a supranaturalism. Increasingly Tillich became convinced that, in Barth's case, it was a supranaturalism and not a positive paradox. In 1923 he still posed it as a question or a challenge to Barth's theology. That Barth could not see anything in the charge of supranaturalism seems clear. He could rightly point out, in reply to it, that he did not equate the biblical words with the word of God. The biblical words were human words as much as were any other words. They were not sacred, they were not a special religious language, they were common human language; the biblical books were to be read as critically as any other books. In all of this Barth was right—he was not a supranaturalist.

He was, however, a supranaturalist with respect to that part of Tillich's criticism which he appears genuinely never to have grasped at all. Though he did not exempt the scriptures from the critique, historical and other, to which all other writings are subjected, he did continue to say that it was *this* language, the language of the Bible, on which theological critique was based. It was to this language, not to any other language, that one was to look for the dogma which is the content of theology and which says a no to even this language. What Barth reserved from critique was not the biblical or traditional ways of speaking of God—he was not supranaturalist about them; what he did reserve from critique was the decision that *these* are the ways of humanly speaking of God to which exclusively theology is to turn. True, he may have explained the reservation, as he did in the introduction to his Romans commentary, by reference to his vocation as a Protestant minister: that vocation called upon him to interpret the Bible. Were he in other circumstances, he would read, say, Lao Tzu or Goethe with exactly the same presuppositions with which, in his given circumstances, he read Paul, namely, that the book being read is a good book and that it is worth one's while to take its thoughts as seriously as one takes one's own.[8] But his affirmation of that vocation as such remained uncriticized, not subjected to the no to which everything was to be subjected. That, at least, is a supranaturalist reservation. To it Tillich's critique pertained.

That Barth might, in turn, have scented something like a supranaturalism in Tillich is indicated by a certain indignation of his over the way in which Tillich pronounced judgments "*vom Unbedingten her*"—from the point of view of the unconditioned. How, Barth wondered, does one find one's way to the position of the unconditioned from which to see these things? But the more important question of Barth to Tillich is connected with that "icy monster" itself. Does the name "unconditioned" say anything more than the name "nothing"? Can such a concept provide a key to understanding what the name of God means? Or is it not the case that one can understand the unconditioned to mean anything at all only if one silently imports into the term the meaning of the name "God"? Can one distinguish between nothing and God by means of the concept of unconditioned?

There is a word in our language, the word *nothing*, which makes it possible for us to think beyond everything there is. Nothing does not mean some mysterious thing, and talking about it—*pace* the positivists—does not come about by a confusion between words or things or by the reification of a meaning. Rather, it is that, when we understand the word *nothing*, we also understand that what the word means is contradicted by there even being a word for it. In that understanding we can, as it were, leap for an instant beyond everything there is at all, beyond the whole of entities and beyond the understanding of being as such. But that is all we can do. Any positive content we give to it contradicts, as does the existence of the word *nothing* itself, the meaning we understand it to have. Nothing is just nothing, not anything, not even *a* nothing. The noun "nothing" only fixes the meaning of what we readily understand in passing when we use the word *not* in our ordinary language, and fixes it by abstracting just the "not" as "not," or the not-ness of the "not," from the flow of discourse. We readily understand the difference between "I am coming" and "I am not coming," "It is good" and "It is not good." To formulate the concept of nothing as nothing is to try to understand what it is we understand when we unreflectively understand the negative in such negative judgments.

But what of the unconditioned, *das Unbedingte*, of Tillich? Is what is un-thinged, or not-thinged at all, distinguishable from nothing? Is it, in other words, even less than an icy monster? A *frostiges Ungeheuer* is at least something. But is the unconditioned, the un-thinged at all, anything at all? In short, is *das Unbedingte*, which Tillich takes as a key to understanding the meaning of the word *God*—a key to be thrown away after it has unlocked the meaning—either just an ersatz-name for God or just another name for the concept of nothing?

With this we have the double question to the theology beyond theistic or sacred theology announcing itself in Barth's and Tillich's writings of the 1920s. To Barth, it is the question: Can a dialectical theology avoid being either the nihilism of an infinitely reduplicating no or the idolatry, the supranaturalist reservation, of the biblical writings? To Tillich, it is the question: Can the unconditioned be anything? Barth's answer is contained in his understanding of the name of God; Tillich's, in his conception of the religious symbol.

What to Make of the Answers

Though Barth had no answer to Tillich's question at the time of the exchange between them, the answer at which he arrived was crystallized in 1931 in his study of Anselm's proof of God, in which he seems to have been following the guideline once given by Kant in *Der einzig mögliche Beweisgrund zu einer Demonstration des Daseins Gottes* (1763): the only possible basis for proof of the existence of God is that the denial of it amounts to nothing.[9] What emerged was not exactly the positive paradox of which Tillich spoke but an understanding of the name of God that makes the impossible of theology possible and the necessary free. How so? Basically thus: When God is understood as, in Anselm's formulation, "that than which a greater cannot be thought," then the very name "God" instantiates the one who is known when it is known that we are not God and that God is not we but not nothing either. It is, in other words, just in thinking the meaning of the name that one becomes a creature of the creator and that the creator is revealed as the eternal no to nothing out of which creaturehood comes. In that sense the name of God *is* the revelation of God, *when* it is thought through; for the thinking through of the meaning in the name is not the basis for an inference to the existence of a metaphysical entity, but it is the way in which God exists and the way in which God is shown; our understanding the meaning of the word is the way in which the one meant by the word is revealed as being there.

Attention is often called to Barth's statement that the presupposition of this proof is faith. But usually the wrong thing is made of this statement, as though it meant that if one already believes in God then the proof will show that the belief is rationally tenable, or as though this were a peculiarly theological proof. That is not the sense of the statement. All it means is that the demonstration starts not just with any understanding of God but with a specific one, namely, with that understanding which accords with biblical faith and is formulated in Anselm's words as *id quo maius cogitari nequit*. If one understands "God" to mean a supreme being, there is nothing in the name "God" to prove that such a being is a reality as well as a concept. But *if* one understands "God" to mean that than which a greater cannot even be thought, then that very understanding makes perceptible the relation to the one meant when one thinks through the meaning. One does not have to so understand the word; in that sense, the meaning of the name is the presupposition, not the content, of the proof. But one can so understand it, and because it has been so understood in the tradition, Barth from that moment on considered the question of the reality of God as one already settled before theology even begins its work. The plain ordinary words that convey the meaning are the manifestness, the being there, of the one of whose name they provide an understanding. The word *God* itself *is* the manifestness of God when the word is thought through as the name with this meaning. This is not, then, an idolatry of the name "God" but a recognition of the instantiating power of the name when understood in this way, that is, when understood as containing a rule of thinking that shows to thinking the one it is thinking about. Just as Descartes's method of doubt uncovers the instantiating capacity of the word *I*, so the rule of thinking contained in Anselm's formulation of the meaning of the name of God uncovers, in Barth's interpretation of it, the instantiating capacity of the word *God*. One could almost take as a superscription of Barth's later dogmatic theology the words with which Maimonides opens his *Mishneh Torah:* "The foundation of foundations and the pillar of all wisdom consists in knowing that the name exists."

The development of Barth's dogmatic work can be viewed as a transference of the instantiating capacity of "God" as a name to the whole of the biblical books. This is, as far as I can see, the only way of reading Barth's biblicism nonbiblicistically or nonsupranaturalistically: the tale of God's election becomes a real history in the telling, if the tale can be so told as to exclude the possibility of thinking of it as not real. Though it may sound far-fetched to call a work which at thirteen volumes and over nine thousand pages was still not complete an experiment, it does seem to me that Barth's *Dogmatics* is just that—an experiment with the possibility that, or a wager that, one can use the concepts of the dogmatic tradition in order to tell the tale of divine election so that when one thinks through what is being told the narrative shows its story as a history which one cannot but think of as real. It is an experiment or a wager because Barth never found a link between the book and real history comparable to the rule of thinking that links the name "God" with reality.

If the question to Barth was how to avoid the infinity of negations on one side and absolutism on the other, the question to Tillich was whether the concept of the unconditioned was anything more than a poor substitute for the concept of God or, if not, whether it had any more content to it than the concept of nothing. Tillich's answer is given in his notion of symbol. If, for Barth, the name of God is, in the thinking of it, the no to nothing that steers a path between nihilism and supranaturalism, then Tillich's symbol of the unconditioned contains in itself the nothing that we know when we know God as not nothing—the symbol "God" is self-negating as a symbol, or it is demonic, and the God who appears in and with the symbol is known only through knowing that negative of the symbol, which has the capacity to become demonic. In a sense one can say Barth's theology is free to ignore the negative as already belonging to the past; Tillich's is not.

Behind this difference is also a difference in Barth's and Tillich's own experience of nihilism. Barth concluded—rightly, as it seems to me—that the not, *das Nichts*, of which Heidegger spoke in "What Is Metaphysics?" as the nothing into which human existence is extended and which is experienced in the mood of anxiety, is less radical than is the negative, *das Nichtige*, that is God's nonwilling.[10] To think the thought "There is nothing that God does not will" (if this correctly paraphrases the meaning of the nothing that is the "object" of God's nonwilling) is to face a negative more radical than the thought of nothing beyond all being. (Doubtless it is also the source of more theological mischief than the thought that there is nothing beyond being.) But there is no indication that Barth himself ever experienced, or understood the experience of, either form of the not; for he provided no phenomenology of the terror before *das Nichtige* comparable to Heidegger's or Tillich's phenomenology of anxiety before *das Nichts*. If this is true, it is not unambiguously a drawback. It may be one of the reasons why it took Barth longer than it took Tillich to recognize the demonic potential of national socialism. That is a drawback. But it may also be one of the reasons why, unlike his speculative forerunner Karl Daub (*Judas Ischarioth*, 1816–18), Barth was able to think through *das Nichtige* so as to turn the doctrine of double predestination, the doctrine based in what Calvin admitted was a *decretum horribile*, into a doctrine of salvation that excludes no one.

In Tillich, by contrast, the nihilistic experience was constitutive. His analysis of contemporary meaninglessness as arising out of the development of religion in the West since the sixteenth century reflects not only his understanding of the dynamics of religious symbols, with their nihilistic as well as their demonic potential, but also his own experience of the possibility that religious substance can be lost. Tillich lived more really than Barth with the question: "What if all of this is not true?" Even so late a work as his Bampton lectures, *Christianity and the Encounter of the World Religions*, attests the force of that question.[11] Hence, unlike the name of God in Barth's theology, the symbol of God in

Tillich's is not the eternal no to nothing but the incorporation of the negative in a reality which provisionally overcomes it but in which the negative still has the possibility of emptying or demonizing the symbol. That is the nothing that needs always to be known in religious symbols as their risk.

The concept of the unconditioned is the concept of what is not anything or anyone but not God and not nothing either. It is a concept exactly midway between the concept of nothing as nothing and the concept of God as God; it is the concept of God in something. If the experience corresponding to the abstract concept of nothing is to be found in the mood of anxiety, the experiential content for the concept of the unconditioned is given by the mood of ultimate concern, the concern about what matters ultimately—being or not being at all. Tillich's answer to Barth's question of why one should not call God God is connected with the symbolic character of the word *God* and its history of in part having lost its meaning and of in part having been used for suppression and terror. Calling God the unconditioned is an attempt both to rescue the meaning of the word *God* as a symbol and also to counteract its idolatrous use. The unconditioned is not God, but it is the actual question of God, in correlation with which the symbol of God is the answer. To know the word *God* as a symbol is to know the nothing that is in it, for the symbol of God refers neither to anything nor to nothing, but, as symbol, it continually negates everything and nothing. If one does not recognize the nothing in it, it becomes an idol.

In the theology of both Barth and Tillich, the starting question is not whether there is something that is God or whether one can know God; it is, rather, whether what presents itself as God *is* God at all. Theology in this mode does not start with the idea of God in order to ascertain whether there is a corresponding reality; it starts with a reality *as* which God is God—as the reality in the name or the symbol. But the first thing to be said of the name or symbol is that, though it is that as which God appears, it is not God. What is one to make of this fact? Something different, it seems to me, from what either Tillich or Barth made of it. For it implies that the starting point for theological knowledge is not, as Tillich formulated it, the assertion that God is being-itself, the continual no to nothing that is embodied in anything at all and expressed in the symbol, nor is it, with Barth, that God is the one manifest in the name of God; it is, rather, that God is God as what is not God. It is such an "is as not" that makes a connection of the pure identity of God as God with the whole of being that is not God and that God is not—God *is* God *as* what is *not* God. Perhaps this is a path along which one can travel further if, both as metaphysical science and as sacred doctrine, theology has reached its end in the declaration, *as* the word of God, that no word is the word of God. That, as it seems to me, is what the theology configured in the works of Barth and Tillich gives us to think about.

9

CONSTRUCTING
THEOLOGICAL MODELS

THE IDEA that the mind deals with reality by constructing and testing models is, of itself, not strikingly new. But attention has been drawn to this subject in recent years because of some developments in physical science, where models have come to play an increasingly important role since the breakdown of the conception that the formulated laws of physics were literal descriptions of the laws or inner structure of nature itself. For their use in science has raised parallel questions in other disciplines. In theology, too, it has been proposed—for example, by Ian Ramsey and Frederick Ferré—that models, either in the looser sense of some handy construct or in the stricter sense of a distinct cognitive device and method, are a useful tool. The present essay, taking up the conception of model in the stricter sense, is directed toward showing what theological models are by analyzing how they are constructed and how they are related to nontheological disciplines. This latter task is important because of what seems to be a great danger in this undertaking, that of doing nothing more than giving a theological title to something quite nontheological. The analysis I am making differs from those of Ferré and Ramsey on points where, as I judge the matter, their description of the character and operation of models seems to be either incorrect or inadequate.

Ferré and Ramsey have provided contrasting ways of employing models in theology. In 1963 Ferré published his "Mapping the Logic of Models in Science and Theology," in which he drew a comparison between the operations of models in natural science and in theology.[1] What is common to both is that theories and models are different and that one of the functions of models is to make the "abstract calculus" of the theories immediately perceptible; a model is "that which provides epistemological vividness or immediacy to a theory by offering as an interpretation of the abstract or unfamiliar theory-structure something that both fits the logical from of the theory and is well known" (p. 75). Thus, the concept of God in theology is a theoretical term that is "constantly interpreted in terms of epistemologically vivid personal models" (p. 77). An example of this is the way the "epistemologically vivid stories and anthropologically immediate images" of the Judeo-Christian Scriptures represent "the nature of ultimate reality" (p. 77). And Christians believe Jesus of Nazareth to be "the one and supremely reliable model for God" (p. 78). However, there is a difference between scientific and theological models because the latter are metaphysical in scope; "there is nothing in principle beyond the scope of the biblical model of nature, man, and God" (p. 81).

Because of their "epistemological immediacy," models provide one way of defining the terms of a theoretical system. It is true in theology as well as in science that "implicit definitions" of systematic terms are always possible. The terms "God," "Christ," and "world," which Ferré regards as theoretical terms in the statement "God was in Christ reconciling the world to himself," can be defined by being related to other terms in the same theoretical system. But such implicit definitions are never more than formal, never more than the "manipulation of empty tokens," and, when applied to this particular illustration, would not yield anything more than the paraphrase "A was in B relating C asymmetrically to A" (p. 83). Models get beyond that emptiness and mere formality.

Yet Ferré sees an important difference between science and theology, because science has, besides the purely formal method, two other ways of defining its theories and theology has only one. Theoretical terms in science can be given an indirect definition through prediction of consequences that can be put in the form of "observation-statements" which can be verified or falsified. That indirect method is not usable for theoretical terms in theology because here theories are metaphysical in scope and cannot entail any particular observation-statements—or they may entail all observation-statements, which comes to the same thing as far as testing them is concerned. Models are the sole explicit means, direct or indirect, for defining the theoretical terms; they provide "the particularity of concept that would otherwise be missing from theology" (p. 83). For this reason, theological models are held more tenaciously than scientific ones. Scientific models can be changed and in fact are changed rather frequently; but the change does not bring about a scientific revolution, because the theories remain standing. Scientific revolutions occur only when the scientific theories are themselves changed. Theological models—at least those "highest-level" models which occupy a "key position" in an "overarching model of reality"—are different (p. 92). Changes in them are resisted because they "signal a religous revolution."

To this picture, as Ferré has sketched it, we can add an additional stroke by noting that changes in theological theories are possible as well. If a change in high-level models, when the theory they define is retained, is attended by a religious revolution, a change in theological theory must mean either a shift from a theological to a nontheological metaphysical theory (e.g., from the basic concept "God" to that of "ultimate reality") or a theological revolution (say, when the change is from "Elohim" to "Jahweh" or from "Jahweh" to "Allah," each of these being meant as a theoretical concept and not a model). Ferré's exposition is admittedly incomplete here. But if this additional stroke can be added, the parallel between models and theories in science and theology can be maintained even on the question of revolutionary changes.[2]

Ian Ramsey, in his *Religious Language, Christian Discourse,* and *Models and Mystery,* has analyzed the logic of theological or religious (the two terms mean the same here) statements as operating according to models and qualifiers.[3] In this view, theology characteristically takes a situation, or event, or idea as a model to which it attaches a qualifier, and the function of the qualifier is then to direct the use of the basic model so as to lead to a "cosmic disclosure." Thus, the idea of omnipotence is a model ("power") with qualifier ("omni-"), and what the qualifier does is to tell us to keep magnifying the conception of power ("still more . . .") until "the penny drops" and "power" becomes more than an ordinary idea—it becomes a cosmic disclosure.

A problem with Ferré's analysis is that it treats models and theories as distinct in kind. What seems to me, however, to differentiate the contemporary notion of model from the familiar theological notion of analogy is just the fact that a theory is nothing more than a model that has undergone sufficient testing to be generally accredited. Ferré thinks of a theory as providing a high-level abstract formulation of that for which a model provides immediacy or perceptibility. Such a definition of model is, as such, certainly legitimate. But it seems to me less fruitful than a definition that does not make a distinction in kind between models and theories. It does not allow for the possibility of high-level theological models which are as discardable as scientific models or for the possibility that some theological models (even if not all of them) might be empirically testable; for, if their scope and use are metaphysical, they can be tested only as are metaphysical theories and models. For that reason, it seems to me advisable, first, not to distinguish in kind between theories and models and, second, to account for the difference between tenacious and discardable models, not as a difference between highest- and lower-level models, but as a difference in kind between models and religous symbols.

The problem with Ramsey's proposal, on the other hand, is that it does not analyze the structure of the "models" that are theologically "qualified"; it describes model after model and shows how they are "qualified," but it does not probe the materials of a model for anything like a structure in them.

Unlike Ferré, then, I shall treat models and theories as the same in kind, the difference being only that theories are well-established models. And unlike Ramsey, I shall not be operating with models and qualifiers but with the *basic structure of domains* as providing part of the material for a theological model and with *conjunctives* as providing the other part. In Ramsey's analysis, some nontheological material provides the model, and this model is qualified so that it becomes a theological model; when it then serves for "cosmic disclosure," it is an actual model. In the analysis I shall be giving, the nontheological material is provided by some domain of thought, and this material is incorporated into a theological model when a conjunctive is introduced in the manner to be described. With this different analysis, I hope, in the first place, to avoid two objections that Ramsey's analysis has met: namely, that it seems to turn theological insight into merely a psychological event (the "penny drops," and I see things in a new way) and that it seems to imply that theological models are no more than tools for mediating insight, or cosmic disclosures. The first objection is, I think, only partly warranted;[4] the second seems more justified. Then, in the second place, I hope with a different

analysis also to make use of the turn given to theological thinking, first, in dialectical speculation of the early nineteenth century and, subsequently, by dialectical theology of the 1920s.

As I shall be using the concept, a model is distinguished, on the
one hand, from an observational or analytical description and, on
the other hand, from a symbol. It differs from a description because the content of a model is not intended to be a replica of how
an object appears or really is. Yet, at the same time, it does intend
to provide a way of cognitively dealing with that object. Even if
the model contains no description of the object it refers to, it does
allow one to come to terms with the object. That it can do so is
due to its two attributes of being constructed and being testable.

Models are constructed, not naturally given. They may be constructed in the imagination or in physical fact, but in either case
they are constructed, put together, made up. Thus, a computer
can serve as a model of the brain, although it happens to be a very
limited model. A diagram on paper might serve as a model of a
system of thought. A mental image may serve as a model of a person we deal with. The concept of a supreme being has served as a
model of God. The fact that these models have been constructed
gives them one of their main advantages as a cognitive tool: we
know them from the inside because we have put them together;
hence, we somehow get an inside way of dealing with the objects
for which they are models.

Models are also testable; we must have means for determining
the reliability with which a given model allows us to understand
the object of which it is a model. Indeed, if a construct cannot be
tested, it is not a model. To be a model, it must permit of testing,
a process that distinguishes between true and false models, in
whatever gradation of truth and falsehood. The testing of a theological model differs from that of scientific or other models, but
what is common to all models is that some means of testing must
be available if what is claimed to be a model is indeed to function
as a model.

Second, a model differs from a symbol. The two are alike in that
they provide means of dealing with a reality without providing a
description of it. But they differ in that a symbol results from the
impress of reality upon the mind; it is constructed as a response
to a real impression. Hence, a symbol does not possess the apparent casualness and discardability of models. It arises as a subject's response to an imposition of reality, whereas a model arises
out of the free play of a subject's imagination. Both of them are

replaceable, for, if a model no longer enables a subject really to deal with the object in question, there is nothing to prevent its being replaced by a different and more adequate one; and, if a symbol no longer expresses the reality it originally expressed, it can be replaced.

In sum, what we mean by a model is a construct that provides us with a methodological way of dealing with an object being investigated. Can theology develop such models? Can a theologian develop models of God, or God's view of things, comparable to a physicist's models of the world of nature or a historian's models of the course of history? I think it is possible to do so, but one is dependent on nontheological domains for the material. The recognition that theology does not have a material domain of its own, not even the domain of religion, is one of the consequences— enduring, I think—of dialectical theology's critique of religion in the 1920s. Theology may use materials from religion, but it cannot claim religion as its proper domain; for it has no closer kinship with religion than with science, art, and other domains. If Schleiermacher divorced theology from speculative metaphysics, associating it instead with religious feeling and construing it as a reflection upon that feeling—so that what defined distinctively theological assertions about God was their traceability to immediate self-consciousness—dialectical theology, with its "totally other" God, who was free from and for anything finite, freed theology in principle from religion. Material for theological models may consequently be taken not only from religion but from any definable domain of human activity and knowledge. The definition and analysis of such domains is not properly theological but metacritical work.

The technique for constructing theological models involves, then, two tasks: (1) that we identify the basic structure of a domain, and (2) that we introduce a conjunctive into that structure. An example from Tillich's theology can serve as a guide here. Tillich's analysis of the meaning of theological statements like "God is freedom and destiny" illustrates this technique. I shall take this statement as such a model and analyze the way in which it has been constructed.[5] It will become clear then what is involved in the two tasks of identifying a domain by its basic structure and providing a conjunctive for it. The whole model here is "God is freedom and destiny," taken as a model of transcendence in the domain of the study of being. The structure of that domain is the polarity of freedom and destiny, as further specifications of

the polarity of self and world. The connective in the model is
"God is." Thus, the difference between "Every being is both free
and destined" and "God is freedom and destiny" is that the former describes a characteristic of the structure implied by anything, insofar as it is at all, and the latter presents a model of transcendence, or depth, in any being as a being.

The *domain* used in this model is ontology, as distinguished
from a generalizing metaphysics.[6] Such a metaphysics generalizes
from particulars until it reaches those generalities which apply to
all things. It may do so in a more abstract way, in which case it
results in a logistic kind of metaphysics; or it may do so by taking
a typical instance of reality as representative of all reality, in
which case it is a more concrete and vivid kind of metaphysics.
Ontology, by contrast, analyzes and describes the elements implied in being and thinking at all, not as generalized patterns but
as fundamental constituents of being. For example, the statement
"All things are ultimately atomic in nature" is a metaphysical
generalization, but the statement that the subject-object relation
is the basic structure of being is ontological. The one is a generalization, the other an analysis. A metaphysical generalization
can normally be tested only as part of a whole system in which
everything finds its explanation at one place or another. An ontological statement can be tested directly by asking whether it
does describe elements implicit just in the fact that something is
at all: if the negation of an ontological statement does not ex-
hibit the structure the statement describes, the statement is not
true. Metaphysics in this sense is thus a universalized description
of what things are or what reality ultimately is. Ontology is an
analysis of the structure implied in the fact that anything is at all.

The *basic structure* of this ontological domain is that of subject
and object, or self and world. These terms designate the extreme
opposite elements which constitute the domain and which are
equally essential to it; they do not designate ultimate metaphysical entities. Tillich derives them from the ontological question
"Why is there anything at all?" as the most fundamental question
about being that it is possible to ask; a more radical question is
not even thinkable. Whatever else the question implies, it implies at least a subject (the agent who asks the question) and an
object (that about which the question is being asked). The test of
whether subject and object are ontological elements is to see
whether one can deny the statement without presupposing the
structure it claims as basic. Since, structurally, a denial too im-

plies a subject ("I" deny) and an object (I deny "it"), the elements of subject and object are ontological.

The terms "freedom" and "destiny" as used in the model "God is freedom and destiny" are further specifications or characterizations of the ontological poles "subject" and "object." Freedom expresses the spontaneity of subjectivity, its activity; destiny expresses the objective conditions of freedom. Freedom is always freedom over against destiny and destiny is destiny over against freedom, just as objectivity is such for subjectivity and subjectivity is such for objectivity. As taken from the domain of ontology, these two terms do not mean observed or hypothetical characteristics of the world or of human beings; they mean characteristics of the basic ontological elements, derived by an analysis of the structure implied in the fact that anything is.[7] In other words, freedom means "subjectivity as freedom" and destiny means "objectivity as conditioning power."

I think it is necessary to be aware of that distinction between metaphysics (in the sense given it) and ontology in order to avoid confusion about this particular model. However, my concern here is not with the ontological structure itself; instead, the concern is to show how ontological material is incorporated into a theological model. In their own domain, "freedom" and "destiny" are interrelated opposites, united only by the context of being. In a theological model, they are united by a "conjunctive." Using the ontological materials for constructing a theological model requires a construction in which the ontological poles are connected by something other than being. Any act of being is a unity of subjectivity and objectivity, freedom and destiny; but an act of being is not a theological model. A theological conjunctive provides a different sort of unity, one established by transcendence or depth in the domain. The unity of polar opposites in any being, as such, is formally a balance, and organically it is an interaction. In such a unity each pole conditions and supports the other; freedom is freedom toward destiny, and destiny is destiny for freedom. The unity provided by the theological conjunctive is not a balance of the poles but a deepening of each pole made possible by reference to a "third," which is the depth of each. When the depth is fully manifest, the greatest freedom is also the most definite destiny. The material making up that "third" in the present case is "God is," a religious or systematic-theological term.

It should be noted that calling this a model does not amount to saying that freedom and destiny are models of God's being, or that human freedom and destiny are models of God's freedom and destiny. Rather, it is saying that "God is freedom and destiny" models a transcendence present in the ontological domain, a unity-in-depth of being, different from the unity provided by being as such. Since this difference between the unity of a domain itself and the unity of transcendence in that domain is important for understanding how a theological model can have its content even when it does not have a proprietary domain, this point should be made as clear as possible. Within any domain (science, art, history, religion), there is a unity of some sort provided by the context itself. Thus, the scientific character of works of science gives all of them some unity; the fact of being in all beings gives them some unity. That unity can be analyzed into its basic structure by discovering the elements which constitute it. So the basic structure of being, for example, is the ontological polarity of subject and object. But there is another unity, which is related not to the general character of the domain itself and its structure but to the factor of transcendence in it. It is this latter unity that the theological connective expresses. (One may regard "conjunctive" as a neutral and somewhat colorless word for the cognitive aspect of Spirit.)[8] Hence, it is the introduction of the conjunctive into the model that identifies it as a theological model.

"God is freedom and destiny" is a theological model using material from the domain of being. To illustrate the pattern further, three additional models can be adduced at this point. If the primary domain is religion, instead of being, and if its basic structure is the polarity of God and man, three different models for its unity in depth are provided by Whitehead's *Process and Reality*, Karl Barth's *Kirchliche Dogmatik*, and F. W. J. Schelling's *Philosophie der Mythologie und Offenbarung*.

Whitehead develops a model in which "creativity" is the connective for the polarity of God and the world (of which man is part). This is clearest in the last part (part 5) of *Process and Reality*, where God and the world are described as conditioning each other and as both expressing creativity. Creativity is divine and human. To view the God-world relation in cosmology and the God-man relation in religion from the standpoint of creativity is thus to view them from the standpoint of the depth, the transcendence, the ultimate in the cosmological and religious domains.

Barth's theological model for the religious domain employs neither the concept of being itself nor that of creativity nor a philosophical system but the God-man Jesus of Nazareth as a connective for the polarity of God and man. As the unity of God and man, Jesus is not a religious unity, resulting from direct interaction between God and man, but a unity in the depth of the God-man interaction. "Jesus is the unity of God and man" formulates this basic theological model. If Whitehead's system is an elaboration of the basic model "Creativity is the ultimate unity of God and the world," Barth's system is an elaboration of the model "Jesus is the unity of God and man."

Schelling's model uses "God himself" as the third-term connective for the religious God-man polarity. "God himself is man and God" would formulate his model. Schelling develops the concept of the monotheistic God, God who as God is the one, although he does not, of course, think of it as a model but as a speculative concept, a reflecting mirror, of the divine life.

These examples, besides further clarifying what theological models are, also illustrate the point that theology is free both from religion and for religion as well as from and for other domains. For it is possible to construct a theological model by using religion as the primary domain and some other material as the connective. In "God is freedom and destiny," a religious symbol serves as the connective. But we may take religion as our primary domain instead, as is done in "Jesus is the unity of God and man" (Barth) or in "God himself is God and man" (Schelling). We may define the basic structure of religion as constituted by the God-man relation. In this polarity, "God" means that to which one responds unconditionally, and "man" means the responder. In the religious domain itself, the two are united by "religion," that is, the interaction between the two in which God is the initiator and man is the responder. This relation is used as primary material in a theological model when a third term is introduced, a conjunctive to express the unity of the two poles that results not from their interaction but from the relation of both of them to that third as their depth. Besides Barth's Jesus or Schelling's one God, we might also have used for this purpose "Being itself," which is the ontological concept for the depth that is always beyond the ontological polarities, always sought and expressed but never grasped in the ontological question and the ontological structure. This would result in the model "Being itself is God and man" (a parallel to "God is freedom and destiny"). As a theological model, it should permit us to understand being itself (the depth of the religious relation) and also to view religion from the standpoint of its own depth. Such a model might be exemplified by Martin Heidegger in his "What Is Metaphysics?" (1929).

Perhaps a caution is in order here. The foregoing description makes theological construction sound like a very mechanical procedure. Yet of itself it is not mechanical, first, because defining the basic structure of a domain correctly and selecting a third-term conjunctive for it requires familiarity both with the domain in which one is working and also with ways of expressing depth or transcendence; and, second, because not all domains or connectives are equally useful at any given time. Both of these points are evident enough that they do not require great elaboration, but two further observations might be made about them.

First, one cannot normally analyze a domain for its basic elements if one is not familiar with it. Like all real analyses (in contrast to mechanically formal ones), the analysis of a domain for its basic structure requires insight and penetration as well as analytical clarity. Insight and penetration are possible only when one has a feel for the material and its own character and movement. It is not even clear in advance that the basic structure must be constituted by only two polar terms. Although it is true that the domain of being is so constituted in existentialist ontology generally, it is possible that the basic structure of being is, in fact, tripolar instead (self, world, other-self). In such a case, the conjunctive would obviously be a "fourth" instead of a "third." A correct analysis is important, for without it a theological model sacrifices its actual import, and that kind of correctness cannot be ensured by mechanical rules.

Furthermore, not all domains are or need be equally available for theological models. Although it is true in the abstract that one might use any domain, it is also true that at given times in history some are more useful than others because of developments within that domain itself. Contemporary physics is a case in point. Since the rise of quantum mechanics, something like a "transphysical" question has appeared, and is being modeled, in physical science itself. In addition, the theoretical discussion of the nature of statistical probability, which in quantum mechanics has replaced the strict cause-effect relation of Newtonian mechanics, has brought to the fore one aspect of a basic structure in the domain of microphysics, namely, the polarity of potentiality and actuality. How one gets from a whole set of possibilities on one side to those out of that set which become actualized on the other side has become a question about the connection between two basic poles in microphysical reality; possibilities and actualities have replaced causes and effects as the two terminals. In other words, developments within physics have both crystallized a basic structure of the domain of "nature" and exposed a factor of transcendence in it. How a physicist answers the question of the connection between the two poles—whether one says there is, for example, a deeper level of reality at which the apparent randomness of elementary particles can again be fully determined—is not decided by his scientific competence. It has to do, rather, with the construction of models that are, strictly speaking, theological instead of physical. Thus, physics at this point in history is particularly open to the introduction of something to deepen the domain, a conjunctive for the poles of potentiality and actuality; and the debate between those physicists who maintain a hidden determinism and those who hold something else is in kind a debate about two different theological models: the norms for deciding between them are the same as those for deciding among any proposed theological models.

One such model in physics uses the basic polarity to say, "God chooses which of the possibilities becomes actual."[9] In this case, "God chooses" is not to be interpreted as a physical explanation competing with the statistical description of probability. Statistical probability defines the unity as given in the physical domain itself; it is the physical unity of potentiality and actuality. "God chooses" expresses a unity that relates potentialities and actualities to each other indirectly. It competes, not with statistical explanations, but with other models such as the claim that there is a "hidden determinism" in microphysics. In such a model, one sees the connection between possibilities and actualities indirectly, relating each of them to God's choosing as a third term. Statistical formulations are a description of the direct relation between the potentialities and actualities; "God chooses" expresses an indirect relation, for the "choice of God" in the model lies in the depth of potentialities and actualities.

In this model, as one may note, use has been made of a device different from the predication which the model "God is freedom and destiny" employed. Physical potentiality and actuality are connected, not by being predicated of "God" ("God is possibility and actuality"), but by being made the object of God's choosing. The conjunctive here is not "God is" but "God chooses"; the model does not say what God is but what he does. The effect of the connection is to deepen the physical domain by expressing a transcendence in it and to make possible a view of physical reality as the concrete expression of God's choosing.

This theological model, using primary material from the domain of physics thus illustrates how particular domains may be more available at certain times than at other times or than other domains are. Even in Newtonian physics, one could, in the abstract, construct a theological model with its materials. One could connect the cause-effect poles of the physical structure by the notion that God created the whole mechanism to start with; but, in such a case, the theological model remains more extrinsic and has less real weight than in cases where there is an opening, a transphysical factor, that is the object of attention in physics itself. The present model illustrates a second point as well: that theological models can use primary material from domains without first giving a metaphysical interpretaton of it. Physics is no farther from and no closer to theology than are metaphysics and ontology. Any domain, even if it is but part of the whole, has a basic structure in which the depth can be manifest. Hence, a theological model does not require ontological or metaphysical material—although it may use them also. In principle, it can use material from any domain directly without filtering it through a metaphysical interpretation.

To this last assertion it might be objected that any analysis of the basic structure of a domain is itself a metaphysical or ontological interpretation. I do not think this is the case. Such an analysis does bear a "meta"-relation to the domain, but it is not metaphysical. It is meta-religious for religion, meta-ontological for ontology, meta-physical for physics, meta-artistic for art, and meta-ethical for ethics. As a single term to apply to all of these "meta"-possibilities, the term "meta-critical" seems best. A meta-critical reflection always occurs with reference to some primary domain, such as physics or religion. The "meta"-factor is provided, not by a whole of which the domain is a part, but by a self-transcendence of that domain. A metareligious stance is not a metaphysical stance toward religion; it is a stance in which religion transcends itself. The language that is used for articulating such a standpoint need not be a metaphysical scheme; it might be any domain different from the first one. Thus, religion might provide a metaphysical opening in physics, and physics might provide a metareligious opening in religion. But the metareligious dimension of religion is not, as such, physics, and the metaphysical dimension in physics is not, as such, religion; it is, rather, the self-transcendence of the domain in question.

Our whole picture, then, has two parts to it. In the first part, we have, on the one side, a set of domains, the exact number and character of which I have not sought to ascertain here at all but each of which has a basic structure;[10] and, on the other side, the material that is used to constitute the conjunctive for the poles of the structure and to provide a unity in depth for the domain. The second part of the picture is provided by the fact that the material for the conjunctive can be either a coinage taken from a different domain (as when "God is," which in the first instance means a religious event, is used as a conjunctive for the ontological elements of freedom and destiny) or a coinage that arises within a given domain (as when "being itself" conjoins the ontological elements). This fact can cause a certain amount of confusion, for one needs to know that "God" in "God is freedom and destiny" performs another function than it does as the direct object of religious experience. As the direct object of religious experience, "God" is one polar element of the basic man-God structure of the religious domain; in "God is freedom and destiny," it is the conjunctive providing a unity in depth for the domain of being as defined by the basic self-world (or subject-object) structure.

Similarly, the idea of a "hidden parameter" in microphysical reality arises within the domain of physics, defined as the context of statistical lawfulness whose basic structure is that of possibility and actuality; but its function is to express a unity in depth for that domain—in which statistical probability already provides one sort of unity. To speak of a "hidden parameter" that conjoins possibility and actuality is to reach the same level as when one speaks of "God's choosing" which possibilities become actual. The difference between the two lies in the fact that, in the one case, the term for the conjunctive comes from a domain (religion) other than physics. Parameters, as such, belong to physical calculations; gods do not. But a "hidden parameter" in physics today gets beyond the structure of physics by expressing a unity in depth. It differs from normal parameters just as much as Schelling's monotheistic God (God who, as God, is one) differs from a God who is the direct object of religious experience and just as much as Tillich's being itself (the depth of the ontological structure) differs from being as the ontological structure.

Thus, if we refer to a transphysical element appearing in physics today, we mean that there is at least one physical term or idea performing the dual function of designating a physical entity (parameter) and expressing a unity in depth for the structure of the whole domain ("hidden" parameter). To the extent that it performs the latter function, it is directly competitive, not with the

ideas that define the general unity of the domain (statistically cal-
culable process), but with other conjunctives that may be drawn
from other domains ("God chooses").

"Theology," then, refers either to the whole set of conjunctives,
in whatever domain, or to a theologics that, like mathematics, is
an a priori symbol system needing some incorporation into models before it can provide knowledge of actual reality. In the present essay, I have not gone into the question of whether such a
symbol system as theologics exists at all, for it does not affect the
description of theological models given here. But I think a plau-
sible case can be made for saying that the Christology of the Protestant Reformers was in fact a mythics, a dereligionized mythology,
just as modern mathematics, which began about the same time,
was a dereligionization of the Pythagorean number system and,
further, that the speculative dialectic of Hegel, Daub, and Marheineke (and perhaps Schelling) was in effect an a priori theologics in which the mathematical and mythical are combined. If that
is so, then mathematics, mythics, and theologics comprise three a
priori symbol systems contributing materials that can be incorporated into models. We should then have further support for draw-
ing clues about models from contemporary physics; for, in its own
models, physics has discovered how to relate the a priori symbol
systems of mathematics to physical reality. But whether there is a
theologics is a question that need not be pursued further here.

We may ask, finally, what the construction of theological models accomplishes. "Cosmic disclosures," Ramsey might answer.
A better answer could be given if one divides it into two parts.
First, what the model does for the primary domain is "deepen" it;
it exposes the transcendence in that domain. Then, from the theological side, what the model does is to provide us with a way of cognitively dealing with transcendence and, at the same time, with a
way of understanding the primary domain by means of its own
depth. The theological model—to put it in theological terms—
gives us simultaneously a concrete knowledge of God and a theological knowledge of the other domain. "God chooses which possibilities become actual" gives me, in the form of a model, a
knowledge of physical reality from the standpoint of God. "God is
freedom and destiny" does the same for being, and "Being itself is
divine and human" or "God himself is God and man" do so for the
sphere of religion.

Moreover, the construction of models is a means for discovery.
What is God doing now, say, in the domain of history? One way of

answering that question is to construct and test theological models of current history.[11] Beyond what Ramsey ascribes to them, these models would not merely mediate cosmic disclosures, they would say, specifically, what is going on in the depth of a given domain.

Constructing theological models is an alternative, or at least a supplement, to several other kinds of theological research and thought. It is an alternative to confessional theology—theology as witness, which always ends in exempting theological statements from the control that any cognitive statement must have. It is also an alternative to metaphysical theology, which always seems to avoid the serious question of how metaphysics is even possible for historically conscious thought. It is, thirdly, an alternative to biblicistic theology (Christian or otherwise), which always seems to end either in an authoritarian theology or in a tolerant nontheology. It is, finally, an alternative to theology as religious thought, which runs the risk of ignoring secular consciousness in the same way that uncritical metaphysics might try to ignore historical consciousness. It is a free theology in the sense that it can make use of those materials—confessional, metaphysical, biblical, religious, and secular—without being bound to them. Perhaps it is the kind of theology Tillich was pointing to in the phrase he used in his last public address, "the religion of the concrete Spirit."[12] But, in any case, it holds prospects for a direct interaction between theology and other spheres of culture.

10

BIBLICAL TRADITION
AND LIBERAL LEARNING

DESPITE THEIR difference, what seems to be common to liberal learning and the biblical tradition today is their impotence against the spirit or demands of technological thinking. The decline of liberal arts, which many in those arts feel, may in part be only a delusion; for it is difficult to estimate whether it is really a loss of standing in preprofessional and postelementary education or only a result of the expansion into mass education at the higher levels. Even if the decline is partly a delusion, however, there is clearly a difference between what vocational and technical training demand and what a liberal arts education and the biblical tradition can provide; and it is also clear that the technical and economic demands predominate. Liberal learning has always presupposed a condition of freedom from economic demands; it requires a certain kind of leisure, whether this be afforded by financial independence or by an educational system that grants such leisure to youth during a period of life. The strict answer to the question whether liberal arts are useful is always no. Almost by definition, and at least by Aristotle's definition, liberal pursuits are just those that are not necessary or useful. They are the province of the free.

But as such they are also a matter of concern both to the humanities and to the biblical message. Neither the biblical tradition nor classical or modern humanism ever produced an adequate theory of the relation between liberality and economic necessity (there is no way around the circumstance that some of the basic necessities of life itself depend upon having and using money); if they had, they might be in a somewhat better position to incorporate such necessities without subverting themselves into products to be sold through advertising. Disregarding this matter, however, the present essay undertakes to show some basic ways in which the liberal arts and the biblical tradition are both concerned with values that cannot be replaced by anything else in the contemporary world.

The Hermeneutical Experience

The liberal arts are marked by their regard—at least in the ideal—for the study of languages. A Bachelor of Arts normally has studied more languages than has a Bachelor of Science. This was not a feature of what Aristotle called the liberal arts nor even of the liberal arts which Philo of Larissa numbered at seven (grammar, rhetoric, and logic; arithmetic, geometry, music, and astronomy) and which Boethius entitled the trivium and quadrivium. But it has some rooting in the way in which the subjects were taught since the fifth century—by way of mastering commentaries on the subjects—and has become a mark of the humanities since the time of the Renaissance. Sometimes this interest is justified by utilitarian or political considerations—commerce with foreign countries is better if one can speak the natives' language, and one should not be so provincial as to think that everyone else must learn one's own language. There is, no doubt, some validity to those illiberal justifications; for it stands to reason that we can get along better in the world if we show enough interest in other people to learn their language than if we go our way assuming they must learn ours. But the role that the study of language plays in the free or freeing arts is different from this justification. It has to do with the principal feature of language—that it is a unity of sign and sense. Human freedom is involved with the same process that marks the formation of language, the distinction and merging of sense and sign which makes possible our act of understanding anything. The liberal arts are specifically concerned to cultivate an understanding of meanings, just as the sciences are directed toward cognition of corresponding realities. Learning involves the capacity both to detect sense in a sign and to refer the sense to a reality: the former is the province of the liberal arts, the latter that of the sciences. If we designate the basic concern of all learning as truth, or the correspondence between understanding and reality, then the study of language is preeminent for the skill of understanding as the study of science is for the perception of reality. These are two different sides of the experience of truth, which is that of seeing the correspondence between understanding and reality.

At the beginning of the modern period in Western intellectual history, the revived interest in classical Greece and Rome brought with it a renewed study of the ancient languages. It came to be recognized that we cannot rightly understand what the literature of the classical period meant if we cannot read it in the original language. Especially was this the case with respect to the Scriptures. They communicated the divine message in the signs of an ancient language. To understand exactly what was being communicated required learning the system of signs in which it was "entongued." The distinguishing between signs and senses and the recognition of different senses in different signs, together with the new fusion of sign and sense that results from translation or from learning a foreign language, constitute, in essence, the heart of what now is known as the hermeneutical experience, or the experience of language, of how signs mechanically learned become the bearers of meanings and thus come to life.

Language is a unity of sense and sign. What makes an acoustic or visual figure (a series of letters or sounds) into a word is the capacity to bear a sense. To one who understands English, "tas" is as much a sequence of letters as is "has"; yet the latter is a word, the former is not. In the latter figure and sound we can detect a sense. Indeed, when we understand the word *has,* we go immediately through the sound or sight in order to pick out the sense that it bears; we do not dwell on how that combination of letters looks or sounds. A sign is a pointer that, as much as possible, calls attention not to itself but to what it is pointing to; it becomes transparent. The capacity to be a sign is an indispensable characteristic of language.

Hermeneutical experience is the conscious recognition that the sense of words can be liberated from the particular signs with which they are usually connected and can be associated with other signs. This liberation is similar to the one which disengages names from the things named, or words from realities, and which required the sustained effort of Greek philosophy; in ancient Greek, that "most eloquent of all languages [*die sprechendste aller Sprachen*]," as Heidegger called it, the confusion between words and things was pervasive and probably cost Socrates his life. But the additional effort of distinguishing senses from signs in words themselves has become the concern of modern hermeneutics. That such distinctions can be made is due to human freedom; the degree to which they are made is the degree to which that freedom is actualized in the use of language. A beginning language student soon learns that what is said with the words *Good day* is the same as what is said with "Bon jour." This ability is the basis for being able to make comparisons between a sense that appears in one sign and the same sense in another, between different signs that carry the same sense, between the sign as such and the sense it carries, and even between sense and significance.

When the sense borne by signs does not refer to physically perceptible objects but to other objects—such as beauty, truth, and goodness—which, though they are more than logical objects, appear only to the mind in concepts and images but not to sensation, the hermeneutical capacity is especially important. It may not take great discernment to see that a Frenchman speaking of an *arbre* and an Englishman speaking of a *tree* are using different linguistic signs for the same thing, because the thing can be pointed out as a physical object. But it does take discernment to see, for example, that when Aquinas writes of justification he is not speaking of the same thing as is Luther when he uses the same word. Since here there is no physical object to which reference can be made, it is easy to imagine that people using the same word are speaking about the same matter. Some realities are given only in the words themselves, unlike physical objects which are also given to our sense perception; and in those cases the temptation is to think that the word and the thing are inextricable. This need not occur in a crude fashion, as when one assumes a word always means the same. It can occur, and frequently does, when with respect to nonphysical realities we cannot distinguish between the sense of the words and that which the sense signifies. Hence we are tempted to think that since the theoretical sense of a word like *truth* (correspondence between understanding and reality) is different from the practical sense (faithfulness) of the same word, the two different senses must be referring to two different things or have two different significances. Or, to take another example, we think that it is impossible to retain the significance of the biblical message if we do not retain the signs and sense of the biblical words; and we land in biblicism. What frees one from that temptation is the capacity to distinguish and associate signs and senses and senses and significances. Both liberal arts and biblical tradition have this kind of freedom in view as one of their aims.

In the stricter conception of liberal arts, the hermeneutical experience is shaped through the classical languages of Greek and Latin. But, while these may, because of their elaborate grammar and extensive inflection, be particularly suitable for that purpose, still the same could be accomplished with other languages or even—as Mortimer Adler once suggested—by using basic English, in contrast to standard English, as the second language in the case of those who for whatever reason find it impossible to learn the signs of a foreign language. Sign-learning is largely mechanical and tedious work, and if it can be dispensed with in certain conditions, without destroying the hermeneutical interest, one need not object to doing so. To be able to translate meanings from everyday English into basic English engages the same kind of skill as does translating English into Greek or Latin or some other foreign language. Other aspects of the experience of language are, of course, not conveyed or learned in this manner. One does not learn, for example, the way in which some languages seem to have a greater signifying power than others—they can almost present the realities they mean.

Liberal learning is to free one from the power of words, not in the reduced sense that it teaches one to be suspicious of words which have rhetorical or emotional power and to confine oneself to words that are exactly denominative of what is meant, but in the amplified sense that the ability to distinguish between sign and sense is the condition for being able to give full range to language as such—it frees one from the bondage that comes from having to use a language in which signs, meanings, and significance are so intimately fused that a given sense or significance can be conveyed only by a given sign and the sign cannot be regarded as such because its sense or significance always intrudes. One cannot then enjoy just the flow of sound, say, in a line of poetry because what one hears or sees is always forthwith the sense, or lack of it, in the words. Language is the medium of being human, as water is the medium for swimming; and it is worth learning for that reason.

Furthermore, the aspect of the biblical tradition which has to do with understanding the world as creation cannot be appropriated except through something on the order of the hermeneutical experience. For to be able to understand a thing or a person as the creature of one who created it by speaking it is to see its whole being as a sign carrying a meaning. In book 10 of his *Confessions* Augustine narrates how he interrogated "the mass of the world" and how "it responded." What could it tell him of his God? All things exclaimed in reply, "We are not, he made us." "My questioning," Augustine continues, "was my intention"—that he was looking at the mass of the world with a view to seeing a sense in it. Their reply was their very appearance (*species*). Everything appeared as pointing away from itself ("not we") and as pointing out what it was pointing to by the words *He made us*. In that manner everything was a sign carrying a meaning, everything was a word whose significance was creation. Things can be read as words when they can be understood as signs bearing a sense; but to read them so requires the ability of interpretation. The more one is able to recognize what it is to be a sign with a sense, the more one is able to read the world of physical reality as the book in which the meaning "creation" is inscribed. For to be a creature is to be a sign carrying a sense; and to understand creaturehood is to understand the sense that the sign carries. The same is true in particular of human being. Though intellectually we are still under the dominance of the concept of person—to be human is to be a person—the more original conception of human being is that of a "word," a sign with a sense seeking to be understood, perhaps a sign without an interpretation (*Zeichen ohne Deutung*), as Heidegger put it, but for all that a sign. The ethical relation, which consists in unconditionally acknowledging the person as free and worthy of respect, depends on that more basic relation, in which the existence of another is a sign through which we can understand the meaning of creaturehood. But we cannot articulate this relation without being able, first of all, to disengage the sign as such from the sense it carries and from the significance that the sign and the sense together constitute. To learn to do that is part of the task of the liberal arts.

Freedom

The matter in which liberal learning and the biblical tradition have a common interest is that of freedom. Liberal learning can mean, as it did for Aristotle, the kind of learning suitable for free men and also the kind of learning which brings freedom by disciplining the mind and making the practice of virtue possible. In the *Politics* (book 8) Aristotle contrasts the liberal arts or pursuits or sciences with the useful or necessary ones and warns that even the liberal pursuits can become illiberal if they are followed too assiduously or if the object is not moral but subservient; and any pursuit which deteriorates the body or which earns wages is vulgar, not liberal, because it preoccupies and degrades the mind. But despite their common interest in freedom, liberal learning and biblical tradition are often opponents, because they conceive of it differently. Bultmann and Heidegger were almost personifications of that opposition. For in the one case freedom is thought of as a gift that comes by proclamation; in the other case it is an acquisition. One should not too hastily blunt that opposition in the interest of a religious or Christian humanism by contending that it is a different freedom that is involved in the two cases—the freedom to be human, on the one side, and the freedom to face God, on the other. Instead, one should recognize that in their self-understanding humanism and the biblical message do have opposing notions of how human freedom comes to be. Freedom as such is a matter of being the self that one is on one's very own. The question is whether that mode of being can be achieved through arts or whether it is bestowed through a proclamation of the gift of God.

A key to understanding the relation between the opponents lies doubtless in an aspect of Christology which has to do with the identity between the "I am" of Jesus in the Gospels and the "I am" that is thought and said by any other self-conscious being. That freedom can be bestowed through proclamation at all implies that there is such an identity between the "I" of the one who was Jesus and the "I" of any human being. It may be an identity within a difference, as indicated by Paul's adversative phrasing "not I but Christ in me"; yet even so, the difference does not disrupt the identity between the two, and the Pauline conception of baptism as a participation in the death of Christ is not merely a metaphor but a real account of what takes place. To understand that identity is a major task of Christology.

The christological relation is one in which the human self encounters the "I" outside itself embodied in another. This relation is distinguished from the ethical; it involves not the relation of a person to another person as such but that of the self with itself outside of itself in another. The power that was Jesus' authority over his disciples, his *ex-ousia*, was not that of an ethical demand for respect but that of one whose command was of itself the same as the free decision of the disciples who heard and could obey it; and to the extent that his saying was identical with their will, he was, for each of them, their "I" in another person. Luther's formulation that faith *ponit nos extra nos*—posits, or shows, us outside ourselves—contains a recognition of this relation. In an ethical person-to-person relation, the self recognizes the other as

being on its own what "I" am on my own, but the other so recognized is one that I can never be, analogous with what I am but
never identical with me. The christological relation, however, is
one in which the "I" of the other, the one who is the Christ, is the
same as the one I am on my own; it is "I" outside of myself.

This is a relation which Christian theology has had difficulty
explicating adequately. But it is strongly suggested by the way in
which Bultmann, and kerygmatic theology generally, speaks of
the authenticity of the self in relation to the proclamation of
Jesus. In the announcing person, the herald who proclaims the "I
am" of Jesus, the possibility of being one's self on one's very own
is actualized for the hearer. When Bultmann objected to Heidegger's analysis of human existence in *Being and Time*, he did so on
the grounds that such an analysis can show the inauthenticity of
existence—that "I" am not the self in fact that I should be on my
very own—but can do nothing to remedy it; the analysis can pro-
ject the possibility of such being on one's own, but it cannot accomplish it. By contrast, the proclamation of the resurrected
Jesus presents the actuality of being on one's own that is otherwise only projected as a possibility. The kerygma of Jesus as resurrected is the language in which the power to be one's self on one's
own is actually mediated. Contrary to much popular preaching,
then, the kerygma of Jesus is not the message: "You cannot be
yourself authentically, therefore Christ must be it for you"; instead, it says essentially, "You *can* be yourself on your own," but
by saying this through the kerygma of Jesus it makes the authentic existence possible. How it can be that the Jesus of the gospel is
the same as the "I" that I am to be on my very own may be explained in one way by Paul's image of the head of the race; but
Christology today would require other theories for its explanation
of that identity, and they are by and large lacking. The theory,
however, does not undercut what is taken to be the actuality—
namely, that the self as "I" is enabled to be a self on its very own
by being presented with itself in the "I am" told of Jesus. Kerygma
does not intend to remove freedom but to bestow it. And in that
concern it is at one with the aim of liberal arts learning.

The deep chasm between the two on the question of whether
this freedom is a gift or an acquisition can be bridged, as it was in
the Christian humanism of the Renaissance and Enlightenment,
to say nothing of nineteenth-century idealism. For the identity
between the "I" of "I am this one here" (Dasein) and the "I" of

Jesus' ἐγώ εἰμι also implies an identity between accomplishment and gift; and the actual failure to achieve the liberality aimed at in the arts is matched by the actual failure of kerygma to bestow what it announces. The obvious fact that, like everything else, a liberal arts education falls short of its aim is of itself no more a proof against its conception than the failure of proclamation is an evidence that it is an untrue illusion. Bultmann's strictures on the accomplishment of existentialist analysis must be tempered by similar observations about the results of actual preaching. In the end Christology implies an identity between what one can do on one's own and what one is given to do.

Showing Other Worlds

The literary side of the liberal arts shares with the biblical tradition the task of showing worlds that are not otherwise visible. In this they differ from a science of the physical world. Their objects have first to be shown; they do not exist for the senses otherwise. Language does also interpret the objects of the everyday world. That we call a tree a "tree" (a word whose etymological root is the same as "true") instead of something else shows it in a certain way, by interpreting it while naming it. But the characteristic of literary objects and of the object which is the concern of the biblical tradition, the kingdom of God, is that while they can be shown upon objects of the world they are nonetheless of a different order. They must be shown first as creations of the imagination before they can appear upon literal objects. Good literature shows worlds which are other than the world of everyday relations, worlds in which the truth of the everyday may indeed be better understood but which are not the everyday. Once seen, they can become the meaning to which the world of physical objects points; they can turn the everyday world into a meaning-bearing sign. Thus, the reading of a fictional work like Updike's *Rabbit Run* or Camus's *The Stranger* may open up a world which is other than the one with which we are already familiar, by presenting the characters with their relations and inner states to our imagination. That world remains fictional so long as we do not refer it also to the already known world. But such fictions are always capable of enriching the everyday when we can see the everyday as a signifier of the different world which is portrayed in the literary work. The liberating effect of such literature is not that it permits us to es-

cape from the "real world" of the everyday but that it turns the
objects and persons of the everyday into symbols of the worlds
portrayed. Literature thus opens up—at least it has the potentiality for doing so—a world of freedom beyond the world of con-
straints and experienced limitations that is the everyday world.
Even ethical failures and physical debility can, in the light of
what is thus shown, be understood through the creations of art.

In this function the literary side of the liberal arts is similar to
the biblical tradition. For the depiction of the kingdom of God too
is a way of opening up a world not given to everyday intuitions. It
is often forgotten that that phrase "the kingdom of God" is at first
only the name of what human being is open or exposed to; it does
not name or further describe any actual realm. It is a name designating that to which human existence as such is open, another
name indeed for that openness itself. What has been newly recognized and analyzed as a consequence of the existentialist movement is that the nature of human being is just the absence of
a fixed nature; the essence of being human is perpetual self-
transcendence, a matter of being always opened to . . . ; and what
it is open to remains to be filled in ever and again. To designate
the other end of that openness, to say what it is that this human
being, a "sign without interpretation," is pointing to, the biblical
tradition speaks of "the kingdom of God." This kingdom is that
which must first be shown through what is said of it before it can
be seen or known. This is what makes the language of the parables of the kingdom of God unusual when compared to ordinary
talk of objects. For the subject about which it speaks is not something already known and then further characterized by what is
being said of it. If one says, "The tree in my yard is an evergreen,"
as one may in normal talk, the subject-term "tree" has the function of pointing out what one is speaking about. That is always
the normal function of the subject-term in predications or judgments about things of the everyday world. Predications add further characterizations of the thing that the subject-term shows or
designates. But when one says something about the kingdom of
God, the subject-term does not show what is being spoken of. Instead, the parable as a whole is to show what is named, but not
yet shown, by the subject-term. A parable comparing the kingdom of heaven to a grain of mustard seed (which, though the small-
est seed, grows into the greatest shrub) is told so as to show that
to which human existence is always open and which is named
"kingdom of heaven."

In mundane language the subject-term of speech is a name which designates and shows an object in the world, or even the whole world; and the aim of the speech is to interpret further the object so designated, by saying what it is. In parabolic language the subject-term does not show anything but only names an openness for what is to come, so that the function of the parable is not to interpret what is already shown by the name but to show the object by telling what in the world it is "like." To the extent that we can imagine a mustard seed as it grows into a vast tree we can also form a picture of what is designated the kingdom of God. To that same extent we can see the world that is named as "the kingdom of God" and that is the terminus of our openness. It is a picture of that to which human being is as such always open or exposed. This does not make the mustard seed, or anything else in a parable, the basis for inferring the existence of another world, but it makes the image of the mustard seed a potential meaning which we can understand as borne by the openness of human existence. What does the form of existence mean? It means the kingdom of God. What is the kingdom of God? It is what can appear as the image of a mustard seed growing. That very picture can be superimposed upon the relations of the everyday world, so that this world becomes a signifier of the one portrayed in the parable, just as what is portrayed in the parable is a likeness of what is named as the ultimate direction of human openness.

Liberal learning and the biblical tradition share the task of showing worlds beyond the world of physical things and personal relations—of providing the tools and skills to free the mind for such creations; the difference between the two lies in the world which each is showing. The kingdom of God, with which the biblical tradition is concerned, is a certain inversion not only of the everyday world but also of the world of literature. Our images of beauty are inverted by the kingdom of heaven just as much as is our everyday perception of objects and persons. Parables like that of the laborers in the vineyard show the kingdom of heaven by way of an inversion of justice. Within this difference between the biblical and liberal learning, the arts and the biblical tradition are similar in their tasks and aims and different from those of the sciences; for they do not start with familiar objects and worlds in order to find out more about them; they start with the unknown worlds in order to display them by bringing them into being, first in our imagination, then as the meaning to which the everyday points.

Understanding and Technology

The split between the humanities and the liberal arts, on one side, and the sciences and technology, on the other, is a product of the modern world; it appears with the Italian humanists during the Renaissance but was not characteristic of earlier periods. Since then it has been deepened by the advances in technology which have created instruments of power that do not readily fit into either the world of nature or that of the humanities. Francis Bacon's motto "Knowledge is power" designates a way of thinking that is different from the premodern arts and sciences and, as it were, inaugurates the modern technicized world. It does not wonder at the world as it is but seeks to conquer it and change it. And human being is accordingly understood as the subject of its own history more than as the product of destiny.

Science and technology have created an artificial world which, unlike art otherwise, does not answer to the needs of the life processes. Moreover, these instruments evolve at an ever increasing rate, producing a permanent revolution that is independent of political or social powers. It endangers the known world and seems indifferent to the values represented by the liberal arts, which too seem incapable of bringing technical rationality under control. One cannot assume that the answer is to make certain that the people whose hands are at the controls of technology are liberally educated and humanely disposed; for the autonomy of the technicizing process prevents it from being subject to such control. There is an intrinsic lawfulness about the technological that draws those who are associated with it into its own dynamics. Those who in recent years have fled to the countryside or to communes in order to escape technology's power have at least recognized that truth about it. Hence the current question is not so much that of the relation between the liberal and illiberal pursuits but that of the relation of the liberal to the power of technique.

What liberal learning and a religious tradition can do in these circumstances is perhaps no more than to provide the possibility for understanding what is going on. To understand why and how the technical works as it does is to begin to come to terms with it; for there is no reason to believe that the technological world is utterly incapable of becoming a meaning-bearing sign, just as is the world of nature or that of ethics. Here, once more, is a point at which the biblical tradition and liberal arts have converging interests. They not only are concerned with the skill of understanding,

of detecting sense in things as signs around us, but have the re-
sources to do so. The power that technology exercises is not always heteronomous. Technology saves labor (and prevents one
from becoming victim to the illiberal pursuits that, according to
Aristotle, deteriorate the condition of the body), and it overcomes
limits of time and space and makes communication possible.
Moreover, as Friedrich Gogarten sought to show, the biblical tradition has a certain affinity to the unbridled freedom represented
by technology—at least as much to it as to the acceptance of a
cosmic order that was characteristic of Greek science. It has often
been remarked that the injunction given to Adam by the Lord
God was to subdue the earth, not to admire and wonder at it; and
the spirit of subduing is more closely akin to that of technique
than to that of wondering cognition. In this respect there is a mutual reinforcement of Protestant biblical religion and the new
technology; for each of them the earth is a field over which man is
to be the lord, and the techniques of modern thinking are but one
means for expanding and improving that dominion.

The first application of this new way of thinking, based upon
unbridled technical freedom, was made to the earth and not to
human being; and it was made on the assumption that what was
done to the earth did not directly affect the human beings who
were using the instruments. With the exponentially increasing
technology of the present century, however, it has become clear
that action upon the earth cannot be separated from action upon
the human being that inhabits the earth. The will to universal
dominance, which in the first place could be interpreted as the
will to subdue the earth but not the *species homo*, now comes
into question as it recoils upon the human beings through whom
it was first invented.

This whole process is one that calls out for understanding, for
the showing of a meaning that the process might, as a sign, bear.
For biblical tradition this amounts to asking how the kingdom of
God can be like what appears in the technicizing process. The
specific freedom offered by the liberal arts and biblical tradition is
that which comes from being able to read the meanings in the
signs; and that applies to the technological world as well.

11

THEOLOGY AND MUSIC

THEOLOGY AND music have often, if not always, been closely related to each other. This is particularly true in Protestant theology, since it developed, in its early stages at least, hand in hand with music. Indeed, Karl Barth, certainly one of this century's leading Protestant theologians, assigned to music a place that he denied to the visual arts. There is, he said, no theological visual art; but there is theological music. He made this observation in connection with a special praise for the music of Wolfgang Amadeus Mozart, who, of course, was not Protestant—unless being an irregular Catholic is the same as being Protestant. No doubt Barth was unjust in allowing theological import to music while denying it to the other arts. But his statement does call attention to the fact that, while theology and art always have a close affinity— the Muses, so Homer tells us, sang to Apollo's accompaniment for the entertainment of the gods—there is a particularly intimate connection between music and the kind of theology that came with the Protestant reformation. The reasons for this are as much historical and cultural as they are religious. For the theology of the Reformers was formulated just at that point in Western cultural history when people's attention was turning away from the sense of sight to the sense of sound—when rhetoric was gaining dominance over formal logic or dialectic and music over painting. One notices this shift, for example, in Luther's conception of the act of faith. It was an act of receiving one's true being from God, made possible only through a *hearing* of the divine promise.

This connection between the sense of hearing and the central religious act in Protestant theology accounts in large measure for its special interest in musical art. The objective reality of a God who can be heard is different from the objective reality of a God who can be seen or contemplated in vision, in exactly the same way that the objectivity of sound and music differs from that of sight and painting; it is objectively real in time rather than in space, known through the ear rather than through the eye. Perhaps that is why the Muses in ancient Greece were divinities without a cult. Thus it is no great surprise if Barth could hear theology in music but could not see it in painting. To make the story complete, however, we should add that a second, equally significant Protestant theologian of this century, Paul Tillich, showed as much interest in theological interpretation of painting as Barth did in theological interpretation of music—which is enough to indicate that the interest even of Protestant theology is not necessarily restricted to the art of music.

In the present essay, the question is limited to the theme of theology and music or the theologian and the musician, leaving aside the other arts and other forms of theology. Three matters in particular will claim attention: the similarity of music and theology; the difference between them; and finally the interaction of theologians and musicians.

Some working definitions are needed for this purpose. Both music, as art, and theology, as thought, deal with reality and bring aspects of reality to expression. So I shall define music as the work which makes reality *audible in sensuous forms*, and theology as the work which makes reality *audible in verbal forms* or *thought forms*. Neither music nor theology adds any new objects to the world of physical things that already exists. Of course, the notes which indicate what music is to be played or the books in which theology gets written down are objects like all other objects. But everyone knows that the score is not the music, and everyone should know that the written words are not the theology. Both music and theology, in this sense, must be actually heard to be what they essentially are. This is to say that I shall be using "theology" in a restricted sense. Theology here means the activity in which reality becomes audible through words. This essay itself is neither art nor theology but a systematic reflection upon art and theology. With good fortune, a systematic reflection can be artistic and theological as well as systematic. But properly speaking, all one can promise is systematics, not art or theology.

One more observation and our preliminary definitions will be finished. I have pointed out what is common to music and theology—namely, that they are the means through which reality can be heard, through sensuous forms or thought forms. But another aspect of the matter is introduced by the distinction between secular and sacred music. What is the difference between them? Certainly not the fact that the one is played in church and the other in the concert hall. After all, everything seems to get played everywhere these days, and one is not safe in using the location of performance as a guide for distinguishing kinds of music. Rather, the difference between secular and sacred music is like the difference between poetry and theology. Poetic words are those which bring *aspects* of reality or the whole of reality to audition; theological words are those which make audible the *depth* of reality—the quality of reality in everything that is real—the power and grace of being in everything that is anything at all. The forms in both cases are in the sounds of words; what distinguishes the two is that in the case of poetry aspects of reality are heard, but in the case of theology the depth of reality is heard. One can make a parallel distinction in a musician's use of sensuous forms. There are musical pieces through which aspects of the real can be heard; there are others in which the depth of reality can be heard. The former are the secular, the latter the sacred, compositions. In the case of music as well as theology the line between the two is never permanently fixed. Poetic words can become theological, and theological words can become poetic, just as the secular in music can become sacred and the sacred secular.

Having fixed these definitions we can move on to a consideration of the *act of creation* which is involved in the production of music and of theology. For it is in this that they are most similar. The act of production or creation is the opposite of the act of abstraction which characterizes reflective knowledge. The faculty involved in art and theology is not conceptualization but symbolization. The power of conceptualization is the capacity to abstract forms from what is physically perceived; the power of symbolization is the capacity to produce a physical perception for something that otherwise cannot be physically perceived. Thus, concepts abstract from physically perceived objects in order to reach the logical or mathematical forms in them. Symbols bring something which at the start is imperceptible into physical perception. So symbolization is just the reverse of conceptualization. A concept of tree, for example, abstracts from what is physically perceived; a symbol of tree uses what is physically perceived to make perceptible something that is essentially invisible. A word used as a concept abstracts from its own sound; a word used as a symbol takes the physically perceived sound in order to make audible what is essentially inaudible.

Music and theology are both activities of symbolizing rather than of conceptualizing. They do not begin with physically perceived objects but with a theophany—the appearance of something undefined and inaudible, which urges the one to whom it appears to give it embodiment; and the embodiment given it is a response to this god who appeared. The response is the way of saying what it was that appeared and elicited the creation. Neither the artist nor the theologian starts by having a perfect picture of something in mind, which is then copied into a pattern of tones or words. Artists or theologians have nothing clear to start with, only that undefined energy or presence that elicits the response. They do not know what it is that is addressing them and urging them on, apart from the actual embodiment that they give it. It is this impulse to create, this impelling presence that surrounds them and will not let them rest—this it is which constitutes the theophany, without which, if one may indulge a bit of romanticism to say it, no one ever was or is a musician or theologian but only a musical or theological technician.

Like all responses to theophanies, the actual piece of music or the actual theological work is simultaneously an achievement and a failure. It is never an adequate embodiment of the presence that elicited it. Even though we are unable to say how or where it falls short, we are acutely aware that it is an inadequate response to the impulse from which it sprang and the power to which it responded. This is another way of saying that every response to a theophany, which lets the god be heard, is at once judgment and grace.

The similarity between the work of the theologian and that of the musician extends further than their origination in a theophany, for it includes as well the acts of repeating, in performance, the original creations. For musicians and theologians are not only creators but also performers, and they live not only in the present but as inheritors of the past. The task of a performing musician with respect to pieces of music from the past is like that of a theologian with respect to the documents of theology from the past. To perform Bach's *St. Matthew Passion* is to be able—or at least to try—to redo the original act by which it came into being and to hear, by means of it, the indefinable God to whose appearance it owes its origin. Each musical piece is both a pathway to, and a definition of, that reality to which it responds. When theologians interpret material from the past, they too are endeavoring to redo the original act, so as to be able to hear what was heard by the one who first gave it expression. If there is any difference between the two sorts of performance—and I am not sure there is—it must lie in the fact that history seems to corrode theological words more than musical sounds. One can today listen to the *St. Matthew Passion* and experience its impact immediately, without an effort first to transpose it into something contemporary. But one cannot listen to a sermon or theological treatise from the same period and really hear it as theological, without first transposing it into something more modern. This seems to suggest that words lose their symbolic power before musical sounds do—perhaps because they are not pure forms but signs carrying a sense, and the sign and sense can split apart. But I am not certain how much this is the case; for it is possible that I am mistaken in thinking that a person in the twentieth century *can* hear the *St. Matthew Passion* of Bach any more readily than theological words from the same period can be heard. It is possible that both of them require preparation and induction. Perhaps the performing musician has the same difficulty in bridging the historical gap between the then and the now as does a practicing theologian; and the musician's task only *looks* different to a theologian because the latter is not a musician. Or perhaps the theologian labors under an artificial burden. If, like a musician who assumes that music from the eighteenth century was and is genuine music, the theologian were to assume—contrary to a widespread practice today—that theological words from the same century were and are genuine theology, the gap might not be so great as theologians think. That is to say, perhaps the trouble is not that history has made theological words impotent, but that theologians have only forgotten what theology is, whereas musicians have not forgotten what music is.

I have spoken about the similarity between the work of a theologian and that of a musician. Now I come to the chief difference between them, one which is, of course, quite obvious but needs to be stated: a musician works with tones; a theologian works with words and thoughts. Or, to put the distinction somewhat more precisely, a musician deals with sensuous forms, a theologian with thought forms. The one is aesthetic, the other cognitive. The one is impersonal, the other personal. The one is addressed to appreciation, the other to the personal center. Through musical forms reality becomes audible, though impersonal; through verbal forms it becomes audible and also personal. Here we have the difference between cognitive and aesthetic hearing. This difference is reflected in our usual ways of speaking about music and language. Music is performed through an instrument, even when the instrument happens to be the vocal chords of a singer. But words are spoken by people, and they are addressed not to a person's sensuous appreciation of sound but to the personal center. Thus, through sacred music, the depth of reality does become audible, but it remains impersonal; through theological words it becomes not only audible but personal. (It is no accident or arbitrary connection, then, when the "word of God"—that is, the word through which the reality of God becomes audible—is equated with a person rather than a set of words or a book.)

We need an illustration of this difference, and there happens to be a three-word phrase that serves this purpose well. In the Gospel of St. Matthew we are told that Peter, after his denial of Jesus, went out and wept bitterly. The three words of importance here are "and wept bitterly." Let us make several different assumptions. Let us suppose, first, that we hear the sound of someone weeping. This sound itself is neither artistic nor theological, but a natural sound. Let us suppose, in the second place, that we hear, not the sound of someone weeping, but the words in which we are told that someone wept—someone says to us, "He wept bitterly." These words, again, are neither artistic nor theological, but informational. They tell us something about someone; they tell us what Peter did at a certain time and certain place. Now let us make the third supposition and combine the words "and wept bitterly," which of themselves are not aesthetic, with the tonal line to which Bach puts them in his *St. Matthew Passion*. Immediately the same words, in that combination, become aesthetic. This is all the more so when the music is sung not with the English word *wept* but with the German word *weinete:* the diphthong *ei* can carry the tonal line as it descends, then suddenly rises and descends again, thus approximating the natural sound of a wail even while transfiguring it into a sensuous form. For, artistic now, those words do not simply give us information about Peter, but they let us hear the sorrow of reality which becomes audible in the musical phrase connected with the words. Finally, we make a fourth supposition. Let us assume we are conscious of the whole context surrounding these words in Matthew's Gospel, so that the statement "Peter wept bitterly" becomes more than a statement about Peter; it becomes a word which makes Peter's weeping an expression of the sorrow and regret of humanity itself. So understood, these words, in combination with the music, become a powerful expression—aesthetic and cognitive, musical and theological at once—of the infinitely deep sorrow that moves through all being. What started as a natural sound, a symptom of a particular interior state, has now become a sign of something other, the sadness of finitude itself.

This illustration not only shows the difference between aesthetic and theological sounds; it also brings us to our third major consideration: the interaction between theologians and musicians. The ultimate task of theology and sacred music is to make audible the grace of being that is deeper than all sorrow or regret. When ideally joined, theology and music unite in giving an expression, simultaneously aesthetic and cognitive, sensuous and personal, to the inexhaustible grace that pervades all being. The "Kyrie eleison, Erbarme dich, Gott, um meiner Zähren willen"— an alto solo that follows the Evangelist's recitative of the weeping of Peter—expresses just that: a plea for compassion, yet uttered in a melody through which can be heard a grace which already understands all. But in actual life this ideal unity is prevented by the corrosion of all forms, sometimes of theology, sometimes of music; and so it happens that at some times, or for some people, there is no way of making the grace of being audible in words, but only in music. In such circumstances music can do what theology cannot. Sacred music can let grace be heard, even when words have become too corroded or distorted to do so. This is parallel to a phenomenon widely recognized today, namely, that many people learn more of the substance of theology indirectly by way of novels than directly by way of theological treatises. Aesthetically or mythopoetically they can be opened to something that cognitively remains closed to them. Insofar as music and theology both minister to the infinite divine grace, they have complementary ways of performing the same task. But because their forms of expression differ, the one can sometimes do what the other cannot and thus maintain a living contact with the reality of grace until the other has recovered its voice.

This brings us back to a point with which I began: Barth's praise of the music of Mozart. It is interesting to notice why he is so generous in that praise, and why, during his life, he liked to begin the day by listening to Mozart's music. It is because, in Barth's words, Mozart in his music "knew something about creation in its total goodness that neither the real fathers of the Church nor the Protestant Reformers, neither the orthodox nor the Liberals, neither the exponents of natural theology nor those heavily armed with the 'Word of God,' and certainly not the Existentialists, nor indeed any other great musicians before and after him, either know or can express and maintain as he did." This is quite a claim. But Barth says even more. Mozart in his music was "pure in heart," far transcending both optimists and pessimists. "1756–1791! This was the time when God was under attack for the Lisbon earthquake, and theologians and other well-meaning folk were hard put to defend Him. In face of the problem of theodicy, Mozart had the peace of God which far transcends all the critical or speculative reason that praises and reproves. . . . He had heard, and causes those who have ears to hear, even today, what we shall not see until the end of time—the whole context of providence. . . . *Lux perpetua lucet eis*—eternal light *does* shine upon them—even the dead of Lisbon."

Here, in these quotations from the *Church Dogmatics* 3:297–99, Barth has said it all in a splendid summary. The goodness of creation, simultaneously our most ancient past and our most novel future, which has never yet been theologically heard anywhere by anyone, has been and can be heard in the music of Mozart, a composer who, though "he died in misery like an 'unknown soldier'" and, "in company with Calvin, and Moses in the Bible . . . has no known grave," had heard creation "unresentfully and impartially." What the musician has accomplished has not yet been accomplished by a theologian anywhere. Those who have ears for music and for theology, can, therefore, find something audible in music which is still nowhere audible in theology. So it is not the case that a theologian has nothing to hear or learn from a musician.

This passage from Barth is a specific illustration of what is meant by saying that musicians can sometimes do what theologians cannot. The earthquake of Lisbon, which shattered naive beliefs in the goodness of God, received no answer from the theologians who tried to prove God's justice in view of innocent suffering; but it did receive an answer through the music of Mozart, for he was able to hear deeper than all tragedy and suffering to the goodness that is infinite and to give it audible expression.

12

GOETHE'S AND
BERLIOZ'S FAUST

THERE ARE portions of Goethe's *Faust* which call out for musical settings, and Goethe himself awaited some composer who could meet the requirement. Berlioz wrote the first pieces for his *Damnation of Faust* under the direct inspiration of Gerard de Nerval's French translation of Goethe's drama.[1] He sent the music to Goethe as a tribute to the master, but unfortunately he never received a reply. Goethe, who was by that time an old man and unable to judge the music, asked his composer-friend Zelter for an opinion about it. Zelter ridiculed it—probably in part out of jealousy since he, Zelter, was to have written music for the *Faust* but was unable to do so. Goethe therefore decided against his initial impulse to reply to Berlioz.

Despite this first inspiration from Goethe's drama, Berlioz's *Damnation of Faust* is an independent work. The libretto, most of which he wrote himself, is on a much smaller scale than Goethe's drama. This is evident already in the omission of a host of characters that appear in Goethe: Margaret's brother Valentin and Faust's assistant Wagner, for example, to say nothing of the array of figures from Goethe's part 2. Goethe's *Faust* is set on the same cosmic scale as the Book of Job and the *Divine Comedy* of Dante. It is a drama of universal salvation, even if it is called a tragedy; in it the apparently destructive power of secular love is in the end unmasked as the creating grace of divine love, and the Eros that drives Faust is disclosed as a service of Faust to the Lord. The action follows Faust through the stages of his quest for sense and identity, or for true life. Having sought true life in science and learning, he has discovered that the sum of what he knows is that he does not know anything. Neither sensual love, in part 1, nor art, in the first portion of part 2 of the tragedy, comes out any better—the ideal is impotent against the real. So Faust becomes a man of action and deed, and in so doing he meets the irreconcilable conflict that lies at the basis of all the others, the conflict in the conscience itself—a sensitive conscience can never be a clear conscience, and a clear conscience can never be sensitive. There is no resolution to this in the conscience itself until the conflict is disclosed as the working of the Eternal, which in the form of the Eternal Feminine spans the opposing members in the conflict and which Goethe embodies in the figure of Gretchen or Margaret and the other female figures such as the Virgin Mary and Helen. They bring to light the otherwise invisible salvation of the guilty conscience; and they bring it to light by turning all of nature and history into a likeness of this saving—making them warranties that it is true though not yet literally manifest. Goethe's concluding words, which Nerval did not include in his translation, are:

> Alles Vergängliche ist nur ein Gleichnis;
> Das Unzulängliche, hier wird's Ereignis;
> Das Unbeschreibliche, hier ist es getan;
> Das Ewig-Weibliche zieht uns hinan.

The Eternal Feminine, which is both the occasion of the fall into guilt for Faust and also the source of redemption, is Goethe's representation of the New Testament evangel on a cosmic scale.

Berlioz's libretto is, by contrast, a small-scale drama, reminiscent of a medieval morality play, in which the question of the duplicity of the free conscience has not yet arisen. Not only does Berlioz restrict himself to part 1 of Goethe's drama—which has Faust sent off to hell and Margaret saved (although in the first draft Margaret was not saved either)—but he has cut down the size of that part in itself to give greater prominence to the three figures of Faust, Mephistopheles, and Margarita. Faust is the proud soul, *l'âme fière*; Margarita, the innocent soul, *l'âme naïve*. Mephistopheles knows he has no chance against the naive soul directly, but he traps the proud soul with charms and trickery. The action begins on the Hungarian plains. (Why Faust should be on the Hungarian plains is explained by the circumstance that Berlioz had a Hungarian march that he wanted to use for something.) Faust here begins to fall victim to ennui, his utter boredom with everything. His solitude is interrupted by the chorus of peasants and soldiers. He envies the simplicity of the peasants as well as the soldiers' unquestioning exultation in military glory. "All hearts throb to their victory song," he sings, "mine alone remains cold, indifferent to glory."

In part 2 we are abruptly transported to North Germany, to Leipzig, and the Elbe river, as Faust, contemplating suicide, is saved by the Easter hymn of the chorus, "Christ has risen." The ennui has pursued Faust even to this country solitude ("without pleasure I see again our proud mountains"), and he has resolved to risk the poisonous drink that will either illuminate his reason or destroy it. The Easter chorus changes his resolve and he declares, "Heaven has won me back." In Goethe's text he is won back, not for heaven, but for earth. In this and the next part of Berlioz's work the sequence is roughly that of Goethe's drama, though with many omissions and some dislocations. Mephistopheles suddenly appears, mocking Faust for letting himself be swayed by the sentimentality of the Easter hymn and promising Faust to show him what real life is. "The pious feeling of those silver bells has marvelously charmed your troubled ears"—"Instead of shutting yourself up . . . Come, follow me—a change of air." He then takes him on a bawdy tour through Auerbach's tavern, bewitches him and Margarita with dreams of each other, has them meet and make love. It is in the tavern scene, Auerbach's cellar in Leipzig, that a characteristic feature of Berlioz's *Faust* becomes clear. Brander sings his tale of the rat which lived in luxury in a kitchen until one day it ate poison and rushed around frantically as if in heat; it took refuge in an oven, which unfortunately was turned on, so that the dead rat was in the end literally in heat. The tale of the rat is taken from Goethe's text. But Berlioz immediately has it followed by a *Requiescat in pace* with *Amen* sung by the chorus of drinkers as a solemn fugue that sounds like something from Handel. The fugue sounds "learned, truly religious," Mephistopheles comments, and it demands to be followed by something equally worthy. Mephistopheles then sings of the flea that lodged with a prince, who fell in love with the flea, had a tailor clothe it, and so cared for it that the flea invited all of its relatives to come along. In the end they turned the court into an assemblage that scratched all the day long. This mocking juxtaposition of the ridiculous and the stately betrays Berlioz's hand.

Part 3 is set in Margarita's bedroom, where Faust and she meet and make love. Abruptly in part 4 we find Margarita alone, already forsaken by Faust, and singing her lyrical Romance, the song of longing and resignation which was Berlioz's first composition in this work. With some minor changes in the first two lines, the text of the Romance is that of Goethe. This is the climactic scene for Margarita, as she faces the fact that Faust will never return—"He comes not. He comes not. Alas!" Disquiet at his absence has turned into tranquil resignation. With a few mediating notes, the scene shifts to Faust and his invocation of nature. He comes to life again ("je crois vivre enfin") through an invocation that has the character of a question to nature, to which the answer is the nonanswer of nature's turbulent vastness: "To you . . . a soul insatiable cries out for the happiness it cannot seize." Once again Mephistopheles appears, diverting Faust a second time from his newfound life, this time by informing him that Margarita has been imprisoned for parricide—the sedative which she has been giving to her mother while Faust was there or she was expecting Faust has, over the weeks, killed the mother. Faust rides with Mephistopheles, purportedly to rescue Margarita. Too late he learns that he has ridden, not to the rescue, but to the abyss of pandemonium. "Il est à nous," "He is ours," Mephistopheles cries out, as he did after the chorus of sylphs and gnomes had bewitched Faust with the first vision of Margarita. And now he adds, "Je suis vainqueur," "I have won." Pandemonium follows. The princes of darkness ask Mephistopheles whether Faust signed the document of his servitude freely. Mephistopheles replies that he did, "il signa librement." The chorus then strikes up a song, whose language is a parody of the *Laus, Hosanna* that the angels sing in Latin for Margarita later and whose music is reminiscent of the choruses of the soldiers, students, and drinkers. The *Hosanna* or *Laus* to Mephistopheles comes out as "*Has Mephisto*"—a Hosanna and *Laus* twisted into *Hélas;* and the earlier *gaudeamus igitur* of the students is distorted into "irimiru karabrao." The chorus is followed by an epilogue on earth and the apotheosis of Margarita, who is taken into heaven accompanied by spirits and a chorus of children. For her, who was led astray by love, the nightmare is over; she is to "hope on" ("conserve l'espérance") and come with the heavenly messengers. At this point Berlioz eliminated a passage that more explicitly mentioned Faust's redemption and kept only this brief allusion.

If one compares the libretto of Berlioz with the text of Goethe's drama, one is likely to think that Berlioz's text is something of a throwback to an earlier conception of Faust. Goethe set forth on stage the salvation of the free and active man who, daunted by nothing, can break all taboos. Berlioz leaves unsaid what the eventual destiny of that man is; his possible salvation is left as a hope, nothing more. Goethe's drama reworked the whole of classical and contemporary culture into a drama of the age that was also a portrait of the whole of history. Berlioz's libretto is on the order of a morality play—with the implicit exhortation to be on guard lest one be subverted by the evil one, who need not come as a roaring lion but may appear as a trickster and charmer. According to this impression of the libretto, there is a conflict between the repristinating character of the story and the innovative character of the musical score to which it is set. It is then difficult to see how the same man could have been the author of both.

One might, of course, conclude that Berlioz the composer was ahead of Berlioz the literary artist. This is not an unheard-of phenomenon, since different talents can be developed in different degrees in any one person. But a second interpretation is possible, and I offer it here as a conjecture, which comes from one who, as an amateur in this material, does not need to be deterred by soundness of judgment that comes from knowing what one is talking about.

My conjecture is this: What fuses the music and the text of Berlioz is irony in the form of self-mockery. The tavern scene is a prime illustration. The song of the rat is itself a kind of mockery on natural love. One cannot tell the difference between a rat that is in heat and a rat that is poisoned. This is followed by a high, solemn *Requiescat in pace, Amen,* which gently mocks the mockery. It is concluded by a moral tale to the effect that it is best to squash the first flea right off before it has invited all of its relatives to join it. The mockery in this moral story is that Mephistopheles calls it a subject no less touching than the rat and the Amen.

A second illustration of this self-mockery, or self-limitation, is provided by the scene in the abyss. Faust has signed the document of servitude to Mephistopheles because that is the price exacted to rescue Margarita. When asked whether the signature was given freely, Mephistopheles says yes. But to call a signature given under duress a free one is to make mockery of the sense of freely signing anything. Mephistopheles declares himself the winner, but his victory is only as durable as the freedom of Faust's signing is real—which is to say, it is a victory that is negated as soon as it must find a reason for its claim. The epitome of the mockery is no doubt contained in the near gibberish that Berlioz, apparently in imitation of Swedenborg, calls the infernal language. The only parts of this language that are undistorted are the names of the abysmal characters—Mephisto, Beelzebub, and the rest. The other parts have only enough sense to show that they are non-sense or distorted sense. If this language is intelligible, then Faust is damned.

This element of self-mockery may be a clue for suggesting that Berlioz's scaling down of Goethe's drama of human history is intentional, as though to say that the "damnation of Faust" can be taken only as a threat that has always already been exposed as a delusion. A portrait of the damnation of Faust then has the character of a self-mocking likeness of what has really happened. The terror that is awakened by the ride to the abyss and the plunge into it, which leaves the abyss bubbling and finally silent, is more like the fright caused by monster movies than the anxiety of conscience that runs through Goethe's *Faust*. But this fright, in its self-mockery, becomes a likeness of that ontological anxiety.

In the end, then, Berlioz may not have been able to depict in his libretto what has really happened, as Goethe thought he had depicted it in the attraction of the Eternal Feminine. But he has been able to make it audible: the self-mockery of the text makes one listen to the music accompanying it, and self-limitation or self-relativization of the music, which is expressed by the juxtaposition of the tranquil and the tender, the harmonious and the dissonant, together with the wide range of musical moods that the score creates suggests that Berlioz's *Damnation of Faust* may, after all, be on a scale that, contrary to first impressions, is equal to the vision in Goethe's *Faust*.

13

DEMONS, IDOLS, AND
THE SYMBOL OF SYMBOLS
IN TILLICH'S THEOLOGY
OF POLITICS

IN THE whole of Tillich's theology of culture, politics and architecture seem to have a special place because each of them involves a juncture between symbol and literal fact that appears to
be different from other cultural works. Architecture is different
because a building not only is a symbol but also has a real or technical purpose; even a church is, as Tillich put it, a symbol and
Zweckbau in one.[1] Hence there is a certain constraint of factual
need placed upon an architectural work that is not imposed on a
painting or a musical composition; and, perhaps as a result of
this, Tillich was able to pronounce a remarkably positive judgment upon church architecture in the twentieth century. The
double character of architecture was, he thought, one of the reasons why, among all the visual arts, architecture made the most
rapid and most impressive advances in this century,[2] and he concluded that, despite some failed experiments, the astonishing
thing is the triumph over the dishonest, the unquestioned, and
the anxiously conservative: the "new church building is a victory
of . . . the creative human spirit and of the Spirit of God that
breaks into our weakness."[3]

Politics, too, differs from the other cultural spheres in a theology of culture. This is so for two reasons: one is that the political
is the basis of all culture; the other is that a theology of politics,
as theology, demands active engagement with real political forces
and the techniques of political power. Even in the last volume of

the *Systematic Theology*, Tillich called attention to how the political sphere is "always predominant" because political unities "remain the conditions of all cultural life"; for that reason he thought it significant that the "symbol in which the Bible expresses the meaning of history is political: 'kingdom of God,' and not 'Life of the Spirit' or 'economic abundance.'"[4] This is, moreover, the one sphere of culture in which Tillich himself, between the years 1914 and 1933 (or, at least, 1917 and 1926), sought to be culturally creative. However successful or unsuccessful his participation might be judged to have been, there is no doubt that he intended to help shape the political events in Germany in those years. One would not expect this on the basis of what Tillich wrote in his essay on theology of culture. In that essay, he concluded that a theologian of culture does not seek to be culturally creative but adopts, instead, "a critical, negative, and affirmative attitude toward autonomous productions on the basis of his concrete theological standpoint."[5] Not only does this observation appear to contradict his own political activity in the years after the First World War; it is also at odds with remarks made about the relation between theology and politics in other essays, in which his theology of politics specifically required active political participation. Religious Socialism served as the example here. From the mid-1940s Tillich could look back and describe the "basic impulse" in Religious Socialism as the "feeling of living in the center" of a fight between the divine and demonic.[6]

This requirement of political engagement carried over into Tillich's interpretation of how *Gehalt* and form are united in the symbol of the kingdom of God. For the effectiveness of this religious symbol depends upon its having a connection to real political technique; otherwise it is only a version of utopianism. Religious symbols do not otherwise depend for their truth upon their attachment to realities other than what is already in the symbol itself. The symbol of the kingdom of God does seem to do so. It *seems* to do so. One needs to make this observation somewhat cautiously because there is no clear warrant in Tillich's texts for attributing such a distinction to this religious symbol; there are only indirect indications that this is so when we compare it with other basic symbols. Consider, as examples, two other symbols, the symbol of creation and the symbol of the Christ. The symbol of creation expresses the meaning of being finite; its truth is that it bestows the courage to face anxiety. The symbol can have such meaning and power even though there is no occurrence that we can recognize as the occurrence of creation and even if we do not ourselves create anything. Its power does not depend upon its being attachable in fact to a real event or to an actual production. So too the symbol of Jesus as the Christ: in one sense this symbol does indeed have a necessary connection to historical reality; yet, even so, its truth does not depend upon its being attached to the facts of history as does the symbol of the kingdom of God. Tillich did maintain that the symbol of Jesus as the Christ, precisely as a religious symbol and independently of the results of historical research, does guarantee that the Christ was a real human being, even if that human being did not in fact bear the name of Jesus and did not in fact say and do the things reported of him in the New Testament accounts. There is, in this way, a necessary historical reference contained in the religious symbol; the symbol of Jesus as the Christ would not be true if the Christ had never appeared as some actual human being. Even this symbol, however, does not have the attachment to facts or to human technique that the kingdom of God has. It does not require that one become engaged in historical research in the way that the kingdom of God as a symbol requires political engagement. No metaphysical disappointment would be the result if historical research made it clear that there never was a person named Jesus who lived at the time and said or did the things reported by the authors of the Gospels. In such a case, the conclusion would be drawn that Jesus the Christ had some other name and other factual features; the conclusion would not be drawn that Jesus was not and is not the Christ. This is to say, in other words, that, although it may have a necessary connection to history, the symbol of Jesus as the Christ has no necessary connection to any particular facts. No changes in our knowledge of historical fact alter the effectiveness of the religious symbol. Nothing about the christological symbol urged Tillich to engage in historical research, as the eschatological symbol pushed him toward political activity. And this is the difference: the symbol of creation did not lead Tillich to become culturally creative for its sake; the symbol of Jesus as the Christ did not lead him to take part in historical critical research (although he was willing to make use of it); but the symbol of the kingdom of God did demand of him that he engage in politics and did raise against him the accusation of not having been active enough.

The kingdom of God, then, is unlike other symbols in having a necessary connection to the historically factual. It is a credible symbol only when some actual political order is its bearer; it can have real power only when its coming is identifiable with techniques of political activity. Hence, this symbol, unlike the symbols of creation and the Christ, can be shown to be untrue by historical events themselves, and anyone affirming it runs the risk not just of historical defeat but of metaphysical disappointment. Preliminary defeats are not the final test, of course; yet in the end the truth of the symbol does depend upon the coming of a new theonomy.[7] The kingdom of God is real as something that is "at hand"; its mode of being can be said to be a being-near-at-hand. The term "at hand," when used in this context should not be confused with the Heideggerian *zuhanden* or *vorhanden;* for Tillich takes the term from the New Testament. According to the Gospel of Matthew, John the Baptist called on his hearers to repent because the kingdom of the heavens was "at hand," and Jesus, similarly, sent out his disciples with instructions to preach that the kingdom of the heavens was "at hand" (Mt 3:2, 10:7). The Greek word is ἤγγικεν, "has come near," and Tillich's German was *nahe herbeigekommen.* This, rather than the now familiar Heideggerian sense of "at hand," is what is meant in saying that the mode of being of the kingdom of God is that of being-near-at-hand. Unlike other religious symbols, the mode of being of the kingdom of God is that of being near "at hand." In other religious symbols, the literal points away from itself; in this symbol, it points to itself. Tillich, admittedly, applied this notion of being-near-at-hand not just to the kingdom of God but to the mode of presence of the Holy as such—presumably, therefore, to all religious symbols. Yet the context in which he spoke of it was the political context, when he contraposed the holy as near-at-hand to the holy as the consecration of something given in time and space;[8] and he did not in the same way speak of the Christ or the creation as being "at hand."

The concept poses the question of idolatry and demonry more acutely than do other aspects of Tillich's thought concerning symbols. For it makes one ask how we can identify the coming of the kingdom of God with a real political order and our own activity without falling victim to idolatry. What is the difference between making such an identification and elevating the conditional to the status of the unconditional—which is Tillich's formulation of the nature both of idolatry and of demonry?[9] Can one apply the symbolic criterion of all symbols—that is, the symbol of the cross which, as a second-degree symbol, is the self-relativizing element in all other symbols—to the symbol of the kingdom of God without depriving it of its effectiveness? What is the mode of being that is a being-near-at-hand? How is the kingdom of God near-at-hand in an actual political reality?

The Being-Near-at-Hand of the Kingdom of God

The clearest indication that Tillich gives of the mode of being characteristic of the political religious symbol is to be found in an essay of 1930 entitled "Der Staat als Erwartung und Forderung." For it is in the opening paragraphs of that essay that we find his description both of this mode of being and of the stance or *Haltung*, the mode of thinking, corresponding to it. "Expectation" and "demand," the two terms used in the title of the essay, designate the polar opposites with reference to which Tillich defines his stance as that of "responsible, cooperative review or intuition [*verantwortliche, mitschaffende Schau*]," in which expectation and demand are united.[10] One calculates what is coming not by detached observation but by seeing matters in a view which is responsible for the present and which actually works along with the forces of the present. (The term "Schau" is probably carried over from the Husserlian *Wesensschau*—intuition of essence—that was important for Tillich's early studies in method; but here the emphasis is on the answering for, and the working along, that are contained in the review.) The unity of the expectation and demand, moreover, is paradoxical. It is not as though some points were a matter of expectation and others a matter of demand but that in all points one is aware of both the demand concerning what things ideally should be and the expectation concerning what they realistically can be. The ideal is not an abstract construction but a surging beyond the present that is born out of the present. If being-near-at-hand is the mode of being meant by the ἤγγικεν of John the Baptist's preaching, then "responsible, co-working review" is the mode of thinking contained in his μετα-νοεῖν, or repentance.

What expectation and demand have in common is that they represent two ways in which one can think of the state in terms that are not merely historical or systematic. To think or speak with real effectiveness in the present requires something other than a historical or systematic presentation, neither of which gives direction and encouragement for what needs now to be done. Both demand and expectation are categories of effective thinking and speaking; but they represent opposite extremes. To think in the category of demand is to demand a state in which the ideal of the state has been fulfilled, regardless of what contemporary possibilities might seem to be. The other way—"expectation"—is to calculate what kind of state can realistically be expected on the basis of what it now is. These two polar possibilities Tillich calls the "utopian" and the "dialectical." Utopianism is the demand for the ideal state, irrespective of contemporary circumstances; dialecticism is the calculation of realistic possibilities on the basis of present actuality. "Utopianism looks at the ideal and sets it in opposition to actual reality as a demand upon this reality and as the goal of working in it. Dialectics [as exemplified by the Marxist fight against older socialism] looks at reality and the tendencies that are immanent in it and places itself in the service of these tendencies."[11]

This mode of thinking, one in which demand and expectation, observation and action are paradoxically united, is warranted or justified by the fact that the opposition between utopianism and dialectics is not a clean one—utopianism has a dialectical element in it (because it cannot form an ideal without being conditioned by the actual situation) and dialectics has a utopian element in it (because one cannot observe tendencies in reality without some notion of the ideal as well). Thus Marxism may have been a fight of dialectics against utopianism, but it took the utopian element into itself as well; Marxism was a political party, but at the same time it transcended the partisan. That is also the basis of what Tillich regards as the methodical ideal of a theology of politics, a "responsible, coworking review."

How this stance, or this mode of thinking, which Tillich characterizes as being "born of the present [gegenwartsgeboren]," as involving a tension-laden unity of demand and responsibility, and as related to the depth rather than to the surface of the "present," differs from the calculation characteristic of realpolitik depends on the distinction between the depth and the surface of the present reality. Realpolitik is opportunistic, it is *augenblicks-* but not *gegenwartsgeboren*, it reads the present superficially, and its unity of responsibility and demand is an intellectual accomplishment without being a responsibility in the ultimate dimension of the self.[12] For that reason it lacks inner tension and has no real power. *Verantwortliche Schau* is a responsibility based upon the "depth" *(die Tiefe)* of the present, that is, that point in the present at which something unconditional breaks into it, giving it meaning, and driving it beyond itself and its own accidental features.[13] Only such a viewing of the present combines expectation and demand in a way that has tension and power.[14]

Critical Questions

A series of questions arises from this way of identifying the kingdom of God and temporal realities. The questions are summarized by asking whether the concept of being-near-at-hand can be so defined as to avoid an idolatrous or demonic view of the state. This concept does make possible some identification between theology and politics and between the unconditional and something conditional so that a theology *of* politics can replace a juxtaposition of theology *and* politics.[15] Can this be done without lapsing into idolatry or demonry? The kingdom of God, as the depth of the present manifest politically in it, is what makes action toward the ideal possible in such a way as to maintain the daring and courage that enthusiasm brings even while protecting against the disappointment that inevitably comes when the efforts to establish the ideal state do not succeed.[16] This seems to be the only case in which a symbol is so intimately bound to a concrete reality that even a *theologian* of culture must become culturally creative and the only case in which a theology of culture is asked to contribute to culture by working in it. So I shall direct our further considerations just to the matter of whether being-near-at-hand can be differentiated from the mode of being of the idolatrous or demonic.

Tillich not only was willing to assert, but did assert, that at a particular time a decision for Religious Socialism was also a decision for the kingdom of God. This is, at first blush, a remarkable claim, if one considers Tillich's thoroughgoing critique of all efforts to equate the unconditional and the conditional and the pervasive role played by the self-relativizing symbol of the cross— the symbol of symbols—in his theology. There can be no doubt that any political movement or program, even that of Religious Socialism, is something conditional, devised by human beings and dependent upon political techniques. Indeed, Tillich asserted that very thing not only of other political parties or programs but of Religious Socialism too. Even so, he could say that a decision for Religious Socialism, at the right time, was a decision for the coming of the kingdom of God. Did his theory thereby, despite himself, fall into the idolatry against which he was otherwise so vigilant?

Possible Answers

One way of dealing with these questions is simply to say that Tillich was inconsistent, that, indeed, he did violate his own theological criterion in the claim he made for Religious Socialism. Tillich would not be the first nor the last thinker to have entangled himself in such an internal contradiction. Such a way of dealing with the questions was, in effect, suggested by the charge that Emanuel Hirsch made in his response to Tillich's open letter. As Reimer concluded in his study of this correspondence, it was, according to Hirsch, Tillich who, ironically, "tend[ed] to confuse the divine and the human realms by speaking about the kingdom of God . . . as if man were involved in bringing about the kingdom of God."[17] For his part, Hirsch wanted to hold consistently to the position that the kingdom of God is purely a matter of divine promise without the involvement of human activity. He objected to Tillich's notion that the coming kingdom of God is somehow simultaneously promised to us and demanded of us. He saw the connection to earthly reality not by way of a demand to do something, laid on us by the coming kingdom of God, but by way of law and duty, the performance of which has no bearing on God's activity but through which God leads the believer into an "undisclosed eternity."[18] The difference with Tillich carried over into the conception of the demonic as well. What troubled Hirsch was Tillich's notion, expressed in his essay on the demonic in 1926, that the demonic, like the divine, is an aspect of the holiness of God, instead of being human rebellion against the divine.[19] In effect, Hirsch's reply was, then, really to charge Tillich with a kind of idolatry, although those are not the terms in which Hirsch put it.

Now, Tillich was himself perfectly well aware of this kind of criticism of his position, and he addressed himself to the objections. Hence, we need to consider how he undertook to answer it. Part of his answer lies in the concept of *kairos*; the other part lies in the mode of affirming something as the coming of the kingdom. With respect to the first part: the qualification that Tillich placed on the identification of the kingdom of God with a political concreteness was that *only at the right time* is it true that a decision for a political movement, such as Religious Socialism, can be a decision for the kingdom of God. It is never a matter of elevating the conditional as such to the status of the unconditional; it is a matter of seeing how when the time is ripe, in the *kairos*, the two converge so that dealing with the conditional is at the same time dealing with the unconditional. Neither Religious Socialism nor any other political order is the kingdom of God; rather, it is that in the power of the *kairos* the conditional can really be so near to the unconditional that a decision for the one is a decision for the other as well. When the time is ripe, the two come close; but even then the conditional is not unconditional. The most illuminating passage in this connection, and perhaps Tillich's most precise formulation, is one that appears in *On the Boundary.* There Tillich wrote: "The concept of the fullness of time [*kairos*] indicates that the struggle for a new social order cannot lead to the kind of fulfillment expressed by the idea of the kingdom of God, but that at a particular time particular tasks are demanded, as one particular aspect of the kingdom of God becomes a demand and an expectation for us. The kingdom of God will always remain transcendent, but it appears as a judgment on a given form of society and as a norm for a coming one. Thus, the decision to be a Religious Socialist may be a decision for the kingdom of God even though the socialist society is infinitely distant from the kingdom of God."[20]

Tillich had conceded to Hirsch that the Religious Socialists may not have protected themselves adequately against the abuse to which, in Tillich's judgment, Hirsch was putting the idea of *kairos* by using it to sanction the National Socialist government. (That Tillich's appraisal of Hirsch's political work may not be just to Hirsch is something one would have to concede, I think. But that aspect of the issue need not detain us here; I can simply refer for further discussion of it to the article by Reimer.) He had accordingly made a clearer distinction between revelation and *kairos*, revelation understood as the breaking of the eternal into the temporal and *kairos* understood as a time ripe for a new response to that revelation. "The *kairos*, the historical time, can . . . never of itself be a revelation. . . . It designates the moment when the meaning of revelation discloses itself anew for knowledge and action."[21] Later, in the introduction to *The Protestant Era,* Tillich fixed the terminology, which is also used in the *Systematic Theology,* by distinguishing the "unique" *kairos* from the "dependent" *kairoi.* The unique *kairos* is the moment when the eternal breaks into time—what Tillich otherwise called revelation. For the Christian view, that is the appearance of Jesus as the Christ. The dependent *kairoi* are those moments when a new creative response is made to the original *kairos,* and these dependent *kairoi* determine the periodization of history.[22] A dependent *kairos* is, in this sense, the time for which the present is ripe. If the depth of the present is rightly grasped, the result is a new epoch in human history.

The changing terminology does indicate, at the least, a certain unclarity, if not a real problem, in Tillich's use of the idea of *kairos* and, especially, in his contention that, in a fulfilled time, a decision for a particular political cause can itself be a decision for the kingdom of God. The fight for a new social order cannot bring in the kingdom of God itself; he conceded that. But, in a *kairos*, a particular aspect of the kingdom of God "becomes a demand and an expectation," and at such a time it can be said that a decision for a political program may be a decision for the kingdom of God. An aspect of the kingdom becomes a "demand and an expectation," appearing as a "judgment" on a given form of society and as a "norm" for a coming one. Religious Socialism represented such a judgment upon capitalist society, the bourgeois liberal nation-state; and it contained a norm of a coming form of society in the ideal envisaged in its programs, surviving its destruction in Germany and spreading "through all countries" afterward.[23] In expressing this judgment and presenting this norm, it was the appearance of the kingdom of God.

The important distinction is the one between an aspect of the kingdom of God and the kingdom itself. But it is not clear that this would solve the problem of idolatry; for to say that something conditional is identical with an aspect of the unconditional must be as idolatrous as to say that it is identical with the unconditional. Equating something with an aspect of the kingdom of God is surely elevating the conditional to the unconditional as much as is equating it with the whole of the kingdom of God. Nothing worldly can literally be an aspect of God any more than it can be God. That seems at least to be an obvious feature of any anti-idolatrous stance. In this instance, however, Tillich seems to be saying that whatever, or whoever, expresses a judgment upon the given form of society and provides a norm for a coming form is one who represents the appearance of the kingdom of God so that acceptance of the judgment and norm is a decision for the kingdom of God and rejection a decision against it. This will be so not because the person or group which expresses the judgment is God, and also not because the form of society espoused by it is the kingdom of God, but because the unconditional judgment and norm are expressed in the particular judgment and particular form of society.

This is, as I said, Tillich's most direct formulation of his answer to the question why the equation of deciding for Religious Socialism with deciding for the kingdom of God should not be considered idolatrous: it can occur only in a *kairos*, and it is only an aspect of the kingdom of God that becomes manifest as demand and expectation. Normally, the situation is such that any decision is ambiguous, and no particular decision can ever be either for or against the unconditional as such. The decision about the unconditional is a transcendent decision, as Tillich put it in "Kairos and Logos"; it is not the object of a specific decision, but it is expressed in the attitude, or *Haltung*, that is in the decisions.[24] The kingdom of God seems to be different. In this case, on Tillich's account, it is possible to say that, at certain times, a particular decision for a particular political program is a decision for the kingdom of God. That this is so is the reason why, as it seems to me, the being-near-at-hand of the kingdom of God is a mode of being different from that not only of other worldly things but also of other religious symbols. But the fundamental issue is one of distinguishing between this mode of being and the mode of being of demons and idols. How can the kingdom be near-at-hand, even in this sense, without being idolatrous or demonic? So the question of idolatry reappears.

Indeed, to all those who are not theocrats, Hirsch's position might seem to be, at least when abstracted from its association with National Socialism and from its technical theological vocabulary, both the more consistent and the more appealing. Suppose the position to be formulated in the following way: we cannot look for a way of making political decisions that depends upon deciding where the kingdom of God is at a given time. All we can do is make our human decisions, recognize them as such, and do so in the frame of the destiny that is ours, without knowing how they are connected with the eschatological fulfillment that is a matter of divine grace and promise. What we are to decide is determined by where we are in this world. It is a fundamental mistake to think that we can discern where the kingdom of God is and join our actions to God's, for it is just the revelation of the gospel that severs the connection between all our doing and the fulfillment promised by God. There is surely something appealing about the modesty of this position, which, when so described, flirts not in the least with any form of idoltary. Why did Tillich not adopt it? The answer does not seem to me to lie, as Hirsch thought, in Tillich's failure to understand Luther's distinction between the workings of the law and the gospel. I think Tillich understood it very well, but rejected it. But did he reject it at the cost of unintentionally espousing an idolatry or demonry himself? Might it be possible to destrue, or deconstruct, the occasional hints of his own disillusionment as symptoms of an inner contradiction in Tillich's theology of politics?

An important clue to the way out of the problem lies in Tillich's elaboration of the nature of affirmation which is involved. This constitutes the second part of his answer to the question of avoiding idolatry. "That each of us must bear the risk of having decided for this finite possibility," so he wrote to Hirsch, "and must answer for it before eternity and that, in so doing, we are dependent on grace, as we are in all our doing, are certain for a Christian," but one cannot derive from such a conviction the right to say "an unrefracted religious and theological yes to this finitude"; indeed, such a view "stands in complete contradiction to our human situation." In contrast to Hirsch's unqualified yes, Tillich "could say yes only in connection with many a no" because he believed "that, from the point of view of the eternal, this is the only thing that can be said about something finite and to someone finite."[25]

The corrective to the threat of idolatry appears, then, in the way in which the decision for the symbol is expressed. If a decision for Religious Socialism—or for any other political reality that is in the making, one in which, at the right time, the kingdom of God is felt to be near—had the nature of an unqualified yes, then it would be idolatrous. But if it is a yes qualified by "many a no," then just this qualification is what breaks or refracts the appearance, preventing a complete identification between the conditional thing and the unconditional that is near-at-hand in it. This gives us a clearer indication of the difference between being near-at-hand and being idolatrous or demonic. Like idols and demons, the appearing of the kingdom of God elevates something conditional to unconditional status—it declares, as it were, that, at this moment, *this* political unity, in contrast to others, is a working of the kingdom of God. But unlike idols and demons, whose being does not brook critiques of them, the being-near-at-hand of the kingdom of God elicits and demands no unqualified response, no unconditional yes; it elicits, rather, a yes qualified by noes. In this case, the critique of the symbol is provided not by the material of the symbol itself (as is done in the symbol of the crucified Jesus as the Christ) but by the negations that qualify the affirmative decision of those who become part of it.

Tillich's two ways of protecting against idolatry in the apprehension of the coming of the kingdom of God were, then, the concept of *kairos* and the qualified mode of affirming the coming reality. That these may not be sufficient to distinguish a theology of politics from utopianism or demonry can, I think, be granted. Indeed, it seems clear to me that, once the symbol of symbols, which relativizes all symbols, has appeared, only an ontology of forgetting—an ontology showing the place of the forgetfulness of the difference between conditioned and unconditioned—can explain how the literal and the symbolic can converge nonidolatrously in the symbol of the kingdom of God. Such an ontology is a task Tillich's theology of politics poses. But this is not the place to take up that task. We can conclude, rather, with the observation that, whatever tasks remain, Tillich's theology of politics, by steering a course between secularity and idolatry, enabled him and the like-minded—those who felt the power of the holy in the *kairos*—to respond to it with a daring and courage that could survive defeat and disillusionment.

PART THREE

The Question of Pluralism

14

THE ARGUMENT FROM
FAITH TO HISTORY

ONE OF the distinctive traits of Paul Tillich's Christology was his position that faith can guarantee that there was an actual historical person on which the New Testament picture of Jesus as Christ is based.[1] Critical studies of this position concur in the conclusion that his argument from the faith-certainty "Jesus is the Christ" to a certainty of the actual historical reality of the Christ is defective. Representative of such studies are Dwight Moody Smith, "The Historical Jesus in Paul Tillich's Christology," David Kelsey, *The Fabric of Paul Tillich's Theology*, and my *Reflection and Doubt in the Thought of Paul Tillich*, all of which present arguments that the certainty of faith cannot lead to a certainty of historical existence.[2] Tillich held the position that faith cannot guarantee the details about the historical person who is the basis of Christian faith, not even the detail of his correct name, but it can guarantee that there was an actual historical person at the basis of the New Testament's picture of Jesus as the Christ. If we examine Tillich's original argument in view of the criticisms offered, it becomes possible to reconstruct an argument for the historicity of Jesus as the Christ which, though similar to Tillich's, more clearly avoids the criticisms that his formulations invited. The present essay will set forth a reconstructed argument from faith to history after first surveying the criticisms that Tillich's version of the argument received.

The Criticisms

Smith's essay of 1966 was one of the first to put the issue clearly without unduly misrepresenting Tillich's position at the outset.

Almost all of the earlier criticism of Tillich's Christology mistakenly asserted (despite explicit statements to the contrary in the *Systematic Theology*) that Tillich regarded the historical existence of the Christ as a matter of complete indifference for faith. Smith correctly noticed that quite the contrary is the case; the historical fact to which the name of Jesus of Nazareth points is indispensable to the Christian faith. It is just that claim, however, which Smith questions. He asks whether it is really possible "for faith per se to assure itself of the reliability or even the historical basis of this biblical picture of Jesus as the Christ," and he suggests that, "as impressive and attractive as Tillich's argument may be, his attempt to insist on the historical dimension of Christian faith while allowing faith itself to put that historical dimension beyond any possible critical questioning is not entirely convincing" (pp. 135, 136–37). Smith bases his subsequent criticism on the principle that, if no single item in the tradition can be guaranteed historically, then the tradition as a whole is equally subject to doubt: "If any single item of the tradition may be false (i.e., unhistorical or misleading), it is logically possible that all may be false" (p. 137). This criticism interprets Tillich's position as making a distinction between the dubitability of a particular item and the certainty of the whole, a distinction which is supported partly by the comparison Tillich draws between the New Testament picture of Jesus and an expressionistic painting but which, as this present essay will show, is not the essential one for understanding Tillich's argument and its tenability. Smith draws the conclusion, as have critics generally, that there is an inconsistency in Tillich's position. "It is clear," he writes, "that [Tillich] wishes to say that faith guarantees the reality of the object of the New Testament witness" and yet "his own argument seems to demand . . . the concluding concession that the personal life attested in the New Testament may be unhistorical, not merely that he may have had another name" (p. 138). In an effort to overcome such an inconsistency, Smith offers another proposal for using the category of "biblical picture of Christ" so as to have it "directly and significantly informed by historical-exegetical study," where such study does not purport to be "a piece of objective historical research, but rather a theological historical investigation" (p. 142) which neither predetermines its results nor disregards its presupposition that Jesus did exist. Such an investigation, however, could not guarantee a historical basis for faith; and Smith concedes that his proposal is not "watertight," for it does not "seal out the bothersome question about the possible non-existence of the personal life attested by the biblical picture of Jesus as the Christ" (p. 143). It presupposes that existence, but presupposing it does not exclude the possibility that the presupposition is not true. Smith does not see how Christian theology can avoid remaining vulnerable with respect to that possibility. Here is the point at which he, then, differs most sharply from Tillich; for Tillich's argument from the Christ-symbol to historical actuality of the man on which it is based is meant to be a safeguard against just that vulnerability which results from making presuppositions without founding them explicitly.

Michael Palmer has added a piece to the criticism by suggesting that, because of the way it uses the *analogia imaginis*, Tillich's Christology has been "supplanted by ecclesiology";[3] for—Palmer argues—the interdependence of the factual and receptive elements in the event "Jesus as the Christ" seems to result in a view not only that the church is constitutive of the event but that apart from the church there can be no testing of the verity of it (p. 293). He admits that "Christology as ecclesiology" is "far from Tillich's intentions," but he thinks that it may result nevertheless as the "logical conclusion of [Tillich's] own arguments." The reason is that Tillich has provided no clear indication of how the experiential evidence of faith, which is the immediate experience of the transforming power of the New Being, can necessarily "incorporate belief in an historical occurrence, much less assure it" (ibid.). Contrary to Tillich, then, he holds that, as long as we insist that there was an actual historical person to whom the Christian kerygma refers, such an insistence can be made only as a historical claim based on historical evidence alone. If the claim is not so based, the continuity of the " 'power' initiated by the concrete manifestation of the New Being in existence cannot be affirmed" (p. 294). Even though faith and historical knowledge are not the same, faith can claim immunity from historical criticism "only at the cost of circumventing the importance of Jesus' earthly ministry" (ibid). In the end the "theoretical risk" remains that the biblical critic may find evidence to show the Messianic interpretation of Jesus' life and teaching as "inconclusive, inadequate, or indeed, non-existent" (p. 295). Thus, in any event, Tillich is "overstating his case when he holds that historical research is irrelevant to the assertion that Jesus is the Christ, since otherwise it is difficult to see why Jesus is a reality and not an ideal category" (p. 288).

Palmer agrees that Christology does imply certain factual statements. Thus, the statement "Jesus as the Christ is the bearer of
the New Being in existence" does imply the statement "A man
(denoted by the name 'Jesus') lived, had disciples, and died." For
otherwise we should have no way of distinguishing between appropriate and inappropriate statements about the subject. Yet
Tillich's assertion that faith can guarantee not only the factual
element (that there was a person who was the Christ) but also the
"essentials of the biblical picture" seems to be an attempt to have
it both ways. First Tillich maintains that the biblical picture was
"forged in the situation of faith," which prevents it from "being
examined historiographically"; then he maintains that the "biblical picture makes historical claims" (p. 290). But—Palmer asks—
how can Tillich be certain that the biblical picture "concerns an
individual who existed apart from the picture"? (p. 291). Like earlier critics, Palmer thinks we cannot be certain; "Tillich's argument demands not only that the 'personal life' of the New Being
may have had another name but that the life itself may be unhistorical" (ibid.). The *analogia imaginis*, which holds that there
is an analogy of image between the historical person and the biblical picture, is open to the same objections since it too is "dependent upon the statement that faith alone can guarantee the historical basis of Christology" (ibid.)—that Jesus as the Christ "is
not a fictional figure but an actual historical person."

Palmer's argument, then, seems to reinforce the conclusions
that have usually been drawn by the critics. The basis of the criticism is a principle that Smith states thus: "The fact that transfor-
mations of a sort take place by faith in Jesus Christ does not in
any way guarantee the historicity of faith's object."[4] It is not at all
inconceivable that a fictional symbol might have such transforming power; nor is it unthinkable that the biblical picture of Christ
might completely lose its transforming power if evidence were
given that the Messianic figure never existed historically. Palmer
strengthens this criticism by assuming, with Tillich, that the
New Being does imply a historical figure as its bearer and by
showing that, even so, the *analogia imaginis* cannot have the importance Tillich attaches to it, for nothing prevents us from regarding the view of its historical sources as a "reflection of this
experience projected back into history" (p. 292). Do we have the
guarantee that the man pictured did in fact overcome the estrangement of existence? Or that the experience of transforma-
tion we have is distinctly Christian? What Tillich has done, ac-

cording to Palmer, is let the believer (the subject) determine what the object of faith is (by considering it to be what it is known as instead of what the actual ministry and person of Jesus were). And, in effect, that relocates the empirical basis with "the recognizable and appropriable life of the community of the New Being" (p. 293), or incorporates Christology into ecclesiology.

The objection to how Tillich relates faith and history and to the function he assigns the *analogia imaginis* in this setting is a strong one, the more so as we can, point for point, make a similar case for the figure of Hamlet, although we do not base our decision about whether Hamlet was an actual historical figure on Shakespeare's play; we base it on other considerations.[5] Nonetheless, I think the argument can be reformulated so as to withstand these criticisms because all of them overlook the fact that one does not argue here on the basis of the general relation between faith and history alone; the decisive basis is provided by the specific material of the religious symbol "Jesus as the Christ."

These criticisms make clear the two problems which must be overcome in reconstructing the argument that Tillich sought to employ. First, we must show how it is possible to take account of subjective difference in the argument itself without invalidating the cogency of the argument. Second, we must distinguish between an argument that follows from the material of a specific religious symbol and an argument that follows from the character of religious symbols as such. On both of these points, Tillich seems to have seen somewhat more clearly than many of his critics; and yet, even so, his formulations do not successfully meet the problems.

Reconstructing the Argument

The first task in setting out the argument from faith to history is to ascertain at what point it begins. Strangely enough, this rather obvious requirement is regularly ignored—not entirely, to be sure, but enough so as to obscure the cogency of an argument from faith to historical actuality. The starting point is determined by whether Jesus as Christ is or is not a religious symbol for the person using the argument. Palmer implies that taking account of this consideration will put Christology on a subjective basis, making it a part of ecclesiology. That that is not necessarily the case (although it may by default happen so) I think the further development will show. In any event, the beginning consideration is this: if Jesus as Christ is not a religious symbol, no argument can be constructed to lead to the certainty that the figure named actually existed. But if it is a religious symbol, the argument can be made. In starting (but not in ending) the argument we do, therefore, abstract from those for whom Jesus as Christ is not a religious symbol. Our habit of mind is to do otherwise, since we ordinarily think that an "argument," to be compelling, must disregard differences between particular subjects who might view it. We usually think that a logically sound argument must be equally convincing to any thinker. The principle that this habit implies is sound enough—an argument, to be convincing, must indeed be convincing to anyone capable of following it. But that principle does not demand that we start a given argument at a place where all subjectivity is neutralized; it demands only that, if we abstract from a certain kind of subject at the beginning, we must somewhere along the way return to pick up what we have at first left out.

If the first step in constructing the argument is to abstract from the subjects for whom the symbol is not a symbol, the second step is to determine what follows, by way of argument, for the remaining subjects. Let us give the designation of B to a subject for whom the symbol is a symbol, and the designation of A to a subject for whom the figure is not a symbol. Then, if the biblical figure of Jesus as Christ is actually a religious symbol, B must ask whether the figure is presented in the biblical narrative as an ideal construction or as an actual man. Clearly he is presented as an actual man. Though there are mythical traits involved, no one would say that the biblical narrative speaks of Jesus as though he were only a mythical image or a constructed ideal. Since that is so, B cannot maintain that he does not know whether Jesus as Christ was a historical reality. He does know it as certainly as he knows the content of the symbolic figure. Thus, the conclusion which can be drawn at this step is that B cannot both maintain a symbolic relation to the figure of Jesus as Christ and also deny that the figure was a historical man, for such a denial would deny the symbol. The two stand and fall together. As long as B's free response is in fact drawn by this particular figure—that is to say, as long as he does indeed stand in a symbolic relation to it—so long does he also know with certainty that Jesus the Christ was a historical actuality and not an ideal construction. This is so, not because of the character of religious symbols as such, but because of the particular content of this symbol. What it expresses is precisely that the eternal and the temporal have come together in an actual historical man; the symbol embodies the eternal in an actual human life. To say that Jesus as Christ was not historical is to deny the connection the symbol expresses; it is, therefore, to deny the symbol. The purpose of an "argument" at this point is to permit B to see that that is so. For when he sees through the fact that his claim not to know with certainty that Jesus the Christ was historical contradicts the symbol, he also sees that the denial is a contradiction of his being B as well.

In this phase of the argument it is shown that B can be as certain of the historical existence of Christ as he is certain of himself as B (that is, as one who stands in a symbolic relation with the figure of Jesus as Christ). This is what Tillich in 1911 called the "dogmatic proof" that Jesus the Christ was a historical actuality.[6] Since the criterion employed is the law of noncontradiction, no historical research can affect the argument. The certainty of B's being B and of the historical actuality of Jesus the Christ stand and fall together. But at this stage in the argument, A, who by definition is the subject for whom the figure is not a symbol, can neither affirm nor deny what the symbol expresses because he does not know its symbolic meaning as symbolic. B can deny the historical reality of the figure presented only at the cost of contradicting the explicit content of the symbol; and if he maintains the denial after seeing through the contradiction, the price is a contradiction of his standing as B. In Kantian terms, the certainty here is a practical one—B can be as certain of the historical actuality of the Christ as he is certain of his own being B. How certain that is we shall discuss presently.

A third step in constructing the argument is to make clear what is and what is not proved by the argument thus far. There are two points on which clarity is needed: first, the matter of the historical actuality of Jesus and, second, the kind of certainty that B's being B has. The argument is that although B can know from the specific material of the symbol that the Christ-figure was an actual human being (for otherwise the symbol contradicts itself), he cannot know from the symbol alone that that man was Jesus of Nazareth. From the content of the symbol one can infer that there was some man at some time and place who was the Christ. Whether that man was Jesus of Nazareth can be known to the degree of probability that historical research allows. Thus, B does know with certainty that the Christ was actual as some man, that there was someone who was Jesus the Christ, the New Being under the condition of existence; but he knows only in terms of historical probability that the man's name was Jesus and that the man lived about the time and place that Jesus of Nazareth did. Faith, or the state of being *B* rather than *A*, guarantees one kind of historical fact but not another kind. It guarantees the historical actuality (*Wirklichkeit*) but not the factuality (*Tatsächlichkeit*) of the Christ figure. Factuality is a task for historical research, and our knowledge of it never exceeds probability. Actuality is implied in the religious symbol itself because the symbol of Jesus as Christ entails the historical actuality of the figure.

The historical actuality is as certain as the religious symbol of Jesus as Christ. But how certain is that? This is the second issue needing clarification. If Jesus as Christ is symbolic for *B*, *B* is as certain of it as he is of his own being. Such a certainty we may call "absolute" but not "unconditional." It is absolute because *B* cannot deny the truth of the symbol without denying his own being as *B*. It is as impossible actually to deny one's own being as it is impossible formally to deny the laws of identity and noncontradiction; for just as a formal denial of the logical laws must employ those very laws, so an actual denial of the symbolic meaning of my being must actually employ that very meaning. But such certainty is not unconditional because *B* coexists with others for whom the symbol is not a symbol at all or is a false symbol; and he can also think of a time when he might no longer be *B*. This is to say that a denial of the historical actuality of Christ is possible, even though *B*, as *B*, cannot consistently make such a denial. *B*, who can be as certain of the actuality of the Christ figure as he is certain of his being *B*, cannot be certain that he should be *B*, rather than *A*, or that there might not come a time when he is no longer *B*. Those others—*A*, or *B*'s imagined non-*B*—for whom the symbol is not a symbol or is false, constitute a denial of the truth of the symbol that *B* affirms.

Thus, although *B* cannot deny the symbol, the symbol can be denied by anyone for whom it is not a symbol or is a false symbol. Because such people do in fact exist—and even if they did not, they could be thought to exist—*B* cannot systematically escape dealing with the negative of his affirmation. That is the import of the existence of others who are not *B*. They present the negation of what *B* affirms, so that even when *B* cannot directly make the negation himself, he can assert that the negation is made, and can be made consistently, by anyone who is not *B*. Hence, he must deal with the possibility that Jesus the Christ was not a historical reality and that accordingly B is currently a living lie because his "absolute" certainty is in truth false.

Yet this demand upon B seems impossible to fulfill. How can B, who cannot make such a denial himself, deal with the denial as a real possibility? How can he, as it were, escape from his own skin? This question takes us to the fourth step of the argument. At the first step, we may recall, the negator (A) was excluded; we abstracted from his situation in order to start the argument with the concrete location of B. Now, however, we return to A, for A comes into the view of B as the one who is what B is not. The question to be decided is whether A or B (or both or neither) is the "living lie" in the sense that what they are "absolutely" certain of is in truth false. And—to keep the line of argument clean—this question must be decided without leaving the location of B. B, without ceasing to be B, must be able to look at himself and A "objectively." How can he do so?

Obviously, he cannot do so by appealing to the symbol's continuing power to impress itself upon him as true and to draw from him a free acknowledgment; for that would be arguing in a vicious circle. What he must do is ask whether the symbol itself contains a reference to the negative possibility embodied in the existence of A. Does the symbol express anything about the meaning of the existence of A (that is, of one upon whom the symbol makes no impression or from whom it draws a negative response)? At this turn in the argument another specific feature of the Christ-symbol comes into play to conclude the argument. Like the reference to historical actuality, this feature too does not belong to religious symbols as such but to this religious symbol. The feature in question is that of "cross"; for it is the crucified Jesus who is the Christ. When this fact is applied to the argument, it incorporates a self-relativization in the symbol. The "cross" within the symbolic material relativizes the material, and simultaneously the symbolic relation to it, by stamping them as the finite entity and relation in which and through which the eternal appears. But in doing so, it also gives the symbol an unconditional certainty beyond its "absolute" certainty for B. How so?

The unconditional certainty of the crucified Jesus as Christ is rooted in the fact that this symbol anticipates and accepts the possibility of its being denied, and it does so in such a way that the negator, qua negator, in his own way states the very truth that the symbol too expresses. This is doubtless the most difficult (not to say the most dismaying) turn in the argument, but its validity can be made clear so long as we bear in mind that not just any symbol, but the specific symbol of the crucified Jesus as Christ, has this characteristic. *B* has posited the possibility that he, not *A*, is the "living lie" and that therefore the one he calls the Christ is not the Christ. That is the extreme form of self-doubt, or self-reflection. *B*, who has posited this, asks, "What follow if I, not *A*, am the 'living lie'?" And he makes the remarkable discovery that *B*'s being that "living lie" is just what is accepted by the symbol itself, so that this extreme self-doubt is a confirmation instead of a refutation of the symbol's content. Thus, if it is true "objectively," beyond the difference between *A* and *B*, that the symbol which *B* calls true is false, it is still true in relation to *B* because it expresses that very possibility. To reduce the matter to its simplest terms, we may say that normally a symbol is either true or false (and accordingly, either *B* or *A* is the "living lie"). If the symbol is true, *A* is the "living lie" and *B*'s position is the "objectively" appropriate one. If the symbol is false, *B* is the "living lie" and *A*'s position is the appropriate one. That would be the normal state of an argument based on a symbol. The peculiarity of the symbol of the crucified as Christ is that if the symbol is true (which entails that *B* is in accord with it), then *B* is nonetheless the living lie just because what the symbol does is affirm *B*'s estrangement from the truth. It is *B*, not *A*, who says, "We are all sinners," and says it not apart from but in view of the symbol. Thus, the certainty of the symbol no longer depends upon *B*'s certainty of his own being; it lies in the way the symbol discloses itself as comprising *B* and his opposite and of tagging *B* as the opposite of what *B*, as only *B*, is. As responding to the symbol, *B* is *B*; but in view of the actual content of the symbol *B* is also non-*B*. He is himself and also beside himself.

This turn marks the transition from absolute certainty to unconditional certainty, in which the truth of the symbol no longer is contingent on self-certainty. *B* does not know, except within the range of probability suggested by the durability of his present character and situation, whether the symbol of Jesus as Christ will continue to be symbolic for him in the future. He does know with certainty that, even if it should cease to be symbolic for him, the cessation will not deny the truth symbolically expressed; it will, instead, confirm that aspect of the symbol expressed by the "cross" in the symbolic material.

We notice now what has happened at this step in the argument. *A*, who was disregarded at the beginning, is now included as *A* within the range of B, and yet the argument from the symbol to the historical actuality of the Christ still stands, true not only subjectively but transsubjectively for B. Thus the transition from absolute to unconditional certainty enables the argument to revert to and include the possibility it rejected at the beginning—the existence of A. The argument which could not begin by taking account of a person for whom the symbol was not a symbol can end by including his position in the argument; for he is the negative possibility whose actuality is embraced by the symbolic figure.

Possible Criticisms

How this reconstructed argument meets the various criticisms that have been made of Tillich's version can be shown by reference to Kelsey's study.[7] Kelsey has correctly drawn together some of the "factual" statements about Jesus that Tillich makes—such as that the person who was the Christ must have been the "only perfectly healed man" and that he must have suffered and died (pp. 98–99) and been without unbelief because "only if his actions satisfied these conditions could Jesus (if that is his name) have so 'impressed' the original disciples" (p. 100). Kelsey concludes that this is "an astonishing argument for Tillich" because "on his own grounds it can have no theological significance because it concerns itself with making claims about a historical figure while theology is supposed to be concerned with explicating the meaning of religious symbols and myths" (ibid.). Yet this conclusion, and the criticism that follows from it, is very probably incorrect, even with respect to Tillich, for the reason that like other criticisms of Tillich's position, it overlooks the fact that Tillich's argument is implicitly related to the peculiar character of this religious symbol. Thus the contrast between "claims about a historical figure" and "the meaning of religious symbols and myths," which is the source of Kelsey's "astonishment" at Tillich's argument, might hold in general; but the distinctive feature of the Christ symbol is that it fuses the symbolic and the historical so that a denial of the historical actuality is ipso facto a denial of the symbol. Some religious symbols permit their disengagement from historical actuality; the Christ symbol does not. But whether or not Kelsey's criticism is valid of Tillich's formulation, it will not weaken the reconstructed argument presented above.

In the end, Kelsey asserts, the comparison of the biblical account of Jesus with a picture "is self-defeating" because "it is used to make contradictory claims"—it is used to deny that historical fact-claims are part of the meaning of the picture and it is used as the basis for an argument about what "must have been" the nature of that personal life, and this latter is an argument making historical fact-claims (p. 101). That criticism too vanishes as soon as we distinguish between two meanings of "historical." The word can refer to empirical factuality (Tillich's *Tatsächlichkeit*); but it can also refer to empirical actuality (*Wirklichkeit*). The reason why, in Tillich's argument, faith cannot "guarantee" that the Jesus portrayed in the New Testament was in fact named "Jesus" is that such matters belong to historical factuality, which is forever problematical and ascertainable only in degrees of probability. That he existed, however, and that he lived under conditions of existence without being in bondage to them (his "sinlessness" and willing death) belong to the historical actuality implied in the Christ-symbol—which is to say that if we deny those things, we simultaneously deny the symbol. Thus, whereas it is possible to deny that the Christ was ever an actual man, it is not possible to do so without at the same time denying the symbolic meaning of the symbol Christ; but, on the other hand, it is possible to affirm or to deny that the historical person who was the Christ had the name "Jesus" without affecting the symbolic efficacy of the Christ-symbol.

In character we should liken Tillich's argument to a Kantian "practical" argument rather than, in Kelsey's terms, to a covert quest for the historical Jesus; for the sense of "what must have been so" about Jesus is that the certainty of the historical actuality (the necessity in the "must have been") is directly proportional to the certainty of the being of the person who stands in living relation with the Christ-symbol. The effort is not to smuggle in historical facts without having to subject them to historical investigation and critique; it is, rather, to define the content and limits of an argument that moves within a given symbolic relation.

The principal distinction which critics have overlooked is that Tillich's argument is not based upon religious symbols as such but upon the specific character of the symbol of Jesus as Christ. This is evident in Kelsey's remarks. In the reconstructed argument presented here, I have tried to forestall that oversight by making the distinction explicit. There has also been a continuing

tendency to collapse the distinction between factuality and actuality. Even so careful a study as that of Kelsey does so. One may
very properly argue that Tillich draws the line between the two
incorrectly. Indeed, on occasion, he himself seems unsure of where
exactly it should be drawn.[8] One might, therefore, attempt to argue that (say) the name "Jesus" is part of the historical actuality
and not a matter of problematic factuality or that "sinlessness" is
not part of the actuality but of the factuality of the person—
though it is difficult to see what basis there might be for such a
claim. Such arguments, however, do not affect the validity of the
argument from the Christ-symbol to historical actuality, which
moves from the givenness of a living symbol to historical actuality and includes the negative argument in a fourth step.

The preceding reconstruction of the argument from faith to history takes account of two themes which the criticisms of Tillich
and perhaps Tillich's own formulation have neglected. The first
theme is the distinction between what can be argued in general
about religious symbols and what can be argued in particular
about the symbol of Jesus as the Christ. The movement from faith
to history, or from the content of religious symbols to the content
of historical actuality, cannot be made on the basis of the character of religious symbols as such. It can be made only by appealing
to the specific material of the one symbol under discussion; it is
that material which is here decisive.

The second theme is that the argument must explicitly take account of the subjective difference between those for whom the
symbol is a symbol and those for whom it is not. Only by making
that subjective differentiation can we see precisely where the argument starts, where it ends, and how it achieves its transsubjective validity. Tillich's argument is clearly post-Kantian in the
sense that it does not assume (as most of his critics have) that critique is either subjectively neutral or arbitrary, but in his formulation it does not entirely evade valid criticism. In the form in
which it is presented above, the argument is a tight one; and I
think it withstands current counterarguments. For there are only
two conceivable ways of differing with what is said in the argument, and neither of those ways is an actual refutation. Thus,
I can differ with it by denying the symbolic character of the symbol; for if the symbol is not true, then the historical reality of
the figure is not certain but subject to historical investigation.
Or I can differ with it by denying that the figure in the symbol
does indeed portray a connection between the eternal and histori-

cal such that the eternal becomes embodied in a historical personal life.

The first denial, however, is only the position of A, which is already taken into account in the argument. If I make the second denial, B can correctly reply: "But then you are not speaking of the same symbol as the one I am speaking of." This double-pronged reply rests on two supports: the relation between the eternal and historical in the specific material of the symbol Jesus as Christ, and the self-relativizing character of the symbolic material which makes a transsubjective certainty possible. In traditional theological language, it rests on the incarnation and the crucifixion as essential components of the meaning of Jesus as Christ.

But what of the objection, stated by Palmer and others, that Tillich's argument (and perhaps the argument here presented) is based upon a reading of the symbol that is not in accord with the Christian theological tradition? Is that objection too anticipated by the argument? I think it is; for if the objection is meant as a theological objection, and not merely a historical comparison, it is answerable in the same way as the criticisms already treated. "In accord with the Christian theological tradition" must be a paraphrase of "true concretely," and as such it fits into the same argument as other versions of counterargument.

The conclusion that an invulnerable argument from a faith-symbol to a historical actuality can be constructed may take us by surprise, but it is apparently unassailable. If one takes argumentation seriously at all, it is possible to show that because the Christ-figure is a living symbol, the Christ was an actual historical man. Only one must bear in mind that we cannot, in Kantian or pre-Kantian fashion, abstract from the factor of subjective difference in the argument itself.

15

PLURALISM IN THEOLOGY

THEOLOGICAL PLURALISM—the notion that there are different but equally legitimate systems expressing the one content of faith—has concerned ecumenical discussion in two ways: first, as a fact that had to be acknowledged, and second, as a problem for reflection. This second task is the more difficult of the two, as one can notice in several studies that seek to provide an overarching unity for the fact of a plurality of systems in theology.[1] These studies marked an advance over the stage of ecumenical discussion in which the fact of plurality was acknowledged but not incorporated into a theory of unity. They can provide a basis here for asking, broadly: Is there a theory by which the plurality of theologies can be ordered in relation to the one affirmation that is their ground? Can we develop a systematic pluralism, or must we choose between plurality and systems?

Attempts to answer such questions are of importance not only for ecumenical discussion but also for understanding the nature of philosophical and theological thinking. Instead of merely acknowledging unity and difference in some way or another, they strive for an explicated theory of unity in diversity, or a pluralistic systematic, in which diversity is justified and yet ordered systematically. The difficulties of such an undertaking are too patent to need elaboration. But the effort needs to be made, for such a systematic ordering of diversity is of decisive importance for the formation of an ecumenical theology. The task becomes even more important when non-Christian theologies are included in the scope of the "ecumenical" and the last traces of a common theological affirmation seem to be lost; then the plurality seems to be unmanageable theoretically. So long as we are speaking of an ecumenical Christian theology, the ideal of a recognizable common center in the Christian gospel serves as a point of orientation for diverse expressions. But if we trespass beyond the Christian boundaries, the question of a theory that incorporates radical diversity in a single systematic becomes both more problematic and more pressing.

Among the studies of this sort of pluralism, those of Piet Fransen and Walter Capps best combine critical sensitivity, historical detail, and comprehensive scope, although neither of them has been developed beyond some initial proposals. Fransen derived his three "dogmatic ways" of psychological description, essential analysis, and existential analysis both from the theological tradition and from a reflection on the nature of human being, and he illustrated them with examples from the history of theology. By delineating the advantages, dangers, and limitations of each method, his "critical reflection on theological methodology" also suggested the interrelation of the three ways. This is obviously more than an acknowledgment of pluralism; it is a critical analysis of its origin and scope, which constructs a context in which each of the three dogmatic ways can operate independently and yet in interconnection with the other ways.

Capps, too, outlined, and illustrated with specific examples, a theory for charting, or "negotiating," the plurality of theologies. He distinguished his work from interconfessional studies by endeavoring to provide a comprehensive theoretical context for identifying and mapping theological varieties, historically and systematically. If interconfessional studies had shown, for example, that apparent differences between Thomas and Luther on freedom or between the Council of Trent and Barth on justification could be interpreted as differences in conceptual articulation but not in basic affirmations, they enabled us to see a unity where formerly we could see only difference. But Capps raised the further question: How does one determine whether two different ways of formulating things are differences in conceptual type instead of differences in basic affirmation? By what principle does one establish whether differences in conceptual formulation are really differences in type or only differences in vocabulary? For "negotiating" theological differences it is not sufficient to be able to define a unity and diversity in some way or another. It is necessary to show that the definitions of unity and diversity, as the context within which differences are adjudicated, are systematically, or methodically, derived also. This is especially true if the ultimate aim of interconfessional studies is to provide a scheme for addressing all of the representatives and all of the issues that might be involved, and if the means for finding unity in difference are as important as the results.

By directing attention to this task, Capps and Fransen have attacked a problem more basic than that of reconciling interconfessional differences. Unlike Fransen, however, Capps recognized that this task is a work of reflexive analysis which need not have the same norms as theology or philosophy itself. Fransen called it a critical work, to be sure; yet he put it apparently under the same criteria that theology or philosophy itself might have.[2] Capps asked that theology "be equipped to undertake a critical exercise in comparative theological reflexivity," which, as we shall see, does not stand under the same rule as theological or philosophical reflection.[3] For this reason, Capps's essays afford a better focus for developing a systematic pluralism.

As a principal source for a comprehensive theory of the one and the many Capps used Robert Brumbaugh's study of the *Parmenides,* a treatise which he regarded not only as an index to the distinct types of philosophy that have appeared in the Western world but also as a key for constructing a single reflexive system of the plurality of systematic theologies.[4] In *Plato on the One* (1961) Brumbaugh interprets the several hypotheses of the *Parmenides* as an index of the different ways of ordering related items in philosophical systems. Capps suggested that they are also an index to possible theological systems, since "theological patterns" are likewise "forms of order which imply distinct relations of a 'one' and a 'many.'"[5] Such a connection between philosophical and theological types is warranted, Capps believed, because there is a structural "compatibility between two formative relations" in Greek philosophy and Christian theology,[6] namely, the relation of being and becoming and of God and the world.[7] In both of them it is a question of ordering the one and the many, and in both of them the relationship involved is asymmetrical. That is to say, in Christian theology God is the one to whom the world is related as the many, just as in Greek philosophy being is the one to which becoming is related as the many. The asymmetry implies that the way in which the many is dependent upon the one differs from the way in which the one is dependent upon the many; the "dependence of world upon God is not identical with the dependence of God upon world."[8]

Capps found that Brumbaugh's interpretation of the *Parmenides* did, therefore, have "theological overtones" because the axioms which serve as guides to possible systems in philosophy apply also to theology. For example, the theological counterpart of a philosophy in which the "unit of existence" is a transcendent entity is a theology like that of Pseudo-Dionysius in which we have to do with a "God who is known primarily by contrast with that with which [God] stands in relation." Again, if the "unit of existence" is a specific form, the theological counterpart is a theology like that of Thomas Aquinas, in which the part-whole relation is fundamental—"God is looked to schematically to support the interrelationship between kinds of things."[9]

The theological and philosophical axioms are not simply identical, of course. Behind the formation of theologies is a process of selecting from philosophically possible axioms those which accord with the demands of the faith which theology expresses, Not all philosophical axioms would qualify. Some might, for example, contradict the asymmetrical relation between God and the world; if they did, they would not be suitable for Christian theological systems. Apart from this, however, the theological axioms, which are the bases for distinct systems, are not different in kind from the philosophical ones. Indeed, by adapting a phrase from Henry Duméry, Capps understood the task of systematic theological reflection to be that of "choosing . . . a philosophy in view of faith's reflection." The philosophical scheme provides a form for the fundamental dispositions of faith. The two together compose systematic theology, as distinct from prereflective faith on one side and philosophical reflection on the other side.[10]

Thus the *Parmenides*, in Brumbaugh's interpretation, provides us with "types of formal order" with which to sketch out theological systems in advance, by prefiguring the types of formal order, even though we must allow for the "constructive, and nonformally creative, influences of kerygma" upon any scheme.[11] The use of Plato's *Parmenides* extends, moreover, to the *interrelation* of the various theologies. Here, too, the structural similarity of the asymmetry in Plato's being and becoming and in Christian theology's God and the world supports a dialectical relation among the types. Asymmetry between the one and the many implies that no single system in the plurality of systems can articulate the asymmetrical relation completely. The emphasis of each needs to be complemented by the others. Thus, systems in which change is dominant need to be complemented by systems in which stability is dominant. Only in their mutual participation is the asymmetry of God and world or being and becoming dialectically expressed.[12]

It is important to notice that Capps's scheme, more sharply than others, recognizes and employs the distinction between second-order (reflexive) analysis and first-order systematic reflection. Systematic reflection articulates the basic disposition or affirmation of faith; reflexive criticism analyzes the possible types of systematic reflection and their interrelation. The latter is a metatheological discipline. The distinction is important because it makes clear that the analysis and adjudication of confessional differences and unities can operate from a position not identical with either of the positions being analyzed; this fact has been largely obscured by the conception of the "circle" within which theological thinking is said to move. When theological issues are argued or analyzed only at the first level of reflection, the theological axioms cannot be further adjudicated. Once the disputes have been reduced to the axioms underlying each party's position, discussion must give way to the formation of "schools," which may or may not tolerate each other.

This is not necessarily due to narrowness, as Fransen suggested;[13] it comes from not having reached a stage where reflexive criticism is possible. No matter how broad-minded or generous it is, systematic reflection cannot transcend its own axioms. Thus, the post-Reformation controversy concerning justification cannot be adjudicated by first-order reflection even when the different axioms involved are disclosed. The axioms simply clash at crucial points. One axiom determines that theology shall say nothing which allows a human being to have confidence in himself when faced with divine judgment. The other axiom determines that theology shall say nothing which seems to exclude human participation in the work of salvation. The axioms color the concepts of justification differently on each side and determine what can be said differently on each side. Because they are axioms of first-order reflection, they cannot be reconciled; at the most those who hold them can tolerate each other or one of them convert the other. There is no way for first-order reflection to make a distinction between God-for-us and God-for-them (you) except by equating the former with the true God and the latter with a false or partly fictitious God. Such a clash of first-order axioms cannot be adjudicated until theology not only reflects the content of a community's faith, ordering its affirmations according to some systematic principle, but also reflectively analyzes this systematic reflection, recognizing it as one of a number of possible choices of axioms and consequent patterns. Then the conflict of first-order axioms is adjudicated by locating both axioms in an overarching system of reflexivity.

Reflexive analysis, it should be noted, does not provide a theological synthesis of opposing theologies. It does not synthesize because it functions at a metatheological level. It can organize but not synthesize.[14] It differs from the kind of typological analysis represented by H. Richard Niebuhr's *Christ and Culture* because it does not take its reflexive categories from theology itself, and it differs from a philosophy of religion or a "history of religions" analysis because it does seek to adjudicate, to "negotiate," the plurality of theologies and to do so in the name of theology. That is to say, since theological systems are transcended—i.e., "viewed" from a position "above" them—not only by the faith which they always inadequately express but also by metatheological analysis, such an analysis offers a path to unity that is different from efforts to synthesize theology into one systematic whole (a task no one would consider possible or desirable today) as well as from efforts to achieve practical or institutional cooperation among representatives of divergent theologies. It offers, in short, a systematic pluralism.

Summary of Results

We might, then, summarize the results of the studies of pluralism in theology in the following points: they recognized that the depth-content of faith can be given a variety of reflecting articulations each of which is as legitimate as the others. Capps and Fransen also endeavored to develop a methical way of defining the number and interrelation of the various types. Whereas Fransen did this by a kind of ontological analysis, Capps did so by connecting the asymmetry that characterizes the relation between God and the world in the Christian faith with the relation between the one and the many in Greek philosophy, which has been the chief storehouse for Christian theologians reflecting on their faith. In addition Capps suggested that such analytical work is carried out by "reflexivity," not by systematic reflection itself. Since this is an important recognition, too often overlooked in interconfessional studies, I have detailed some of the consequences which follow from it—that such analysis is not theological synthesizing but metatheological organizing, and that it differs from typological analyses as well as from *Religionswissenschaft.*

The shortcoming of these studies, however, was the fact that they did not propose a radical pluralism. They justified the pluralism that follows from the variety of ways of *reflecting the object* of faith (that which is being affirmed), but they were silent about the pluralism that follows from the variety of ways of *responding to the presence* that elicits thought. The one is the pluralism related to the faith-object, the other the pluralism related to the faith-presence. Furthermore, these studies allowed a range in possible reflective systems that is not complete because it does not contain the kind of reflective system whose consistency lies elsewhere than in a specifiable pattern.

In order to see the nature and significance of these two limitations, it will be helpful to begin with a diagram and two general considerations.

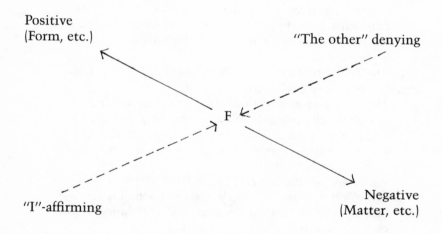

Positive
(Form, etc.)

"The other" denying

F

"I"-affirming

Negative
(Matter, etc.)

Explanation:

1. *F* represents the faith to which reflective or responsive thought is related: it is that in which the depth-content, or the transcendent, concretely appears; it is that *object upon which* I reflect and *the presence to which* I thinkingly respond.

2. The solid line represents the polarity of positive (pure form, the one) and negative (pure matter, the many) which defines *the*

structure of objectivity implied in a pluralistic reflection of one object of faith.

3. The broken line represents the polarity of "my" affirmation (yes) and "the other's" negation (no) which constitutes the *structure of freedom* implied in a pluralistic response to one presence that elicits free responses.

4. The ultimate, or the One, as the depth to which faith is related, appears *in* this structure in all of its parts, but it is not equated with any single part of the structure in contrast to the other parts. This is why opposed systems based on opposite axioms (e.g., "the One is in the many," as opposed to "the One is pure form apart from the many") are equally legitimate.

5. This ultimate depth is "other than" the structure diagrammed, in a double sense:

   a. It is other than the positive alone or the negative alone. (As other than form, it can be identified provisionally with material; as other than material, it can be identified provisionally with form.) The same remark applies to the polarity of freedom: "my" yes and someone else's no.

   b. It is other than the *contrast* between positive and negative and between affirmation and negation. That is to say, it is not only other than the *elements* in the structure diagrammed but also other than the *relation* of "togetherness" contained in the structure.

6. The direction of the arrows in the solid and broken lines is meant to indicate the following:

   a. The opposing patterns of reflection either exclude each other or dialectically supplement each other. A positive pattern, e.g., implies a *negation of a negative* pattern. Hence, each kind of pattern is only a partial expression of the depth-content which it reflects.

   b. With responses the case is different: "my" affirmation implies *my affirmation of the other's negation;* and "his (or her)" negation implies "his" *negation of "my" affirmation.* Hence, each response is *total.*

   c. Viewed from the standpoint of reflexivity, therefore, the fullness of the reflection of the depth-content is expressed by the dialectical interaction between the *partial* reflections, whereas the fullness of the response to the presence eliciting free responses is contained in the *totality* of "my" affirmation without "my" negation (since "his" negation is an aspect of "my" affirmation). Thus, reflection oscillates between the positive and negative poles whereas response rests with the one pole alone ("my" affirmation without "my" negation; "his" negation without "his" affirmation)—each response a center of freedom.

This diagram should help to visualize the several points I wish to make in two general considerations.

The first consideration has to do with the origin of, and the structure implied by, a pluralistic set of patterns. One origin of pluralism, as the diagram above indicates, lies in the fact that faith is one and theologies are many. Faith has a depth-content that can never be exhausted by reflection, and it gives rise to a plurality of reflections upon the object which embodies that depth-content. The ultimate One that appears concretely in the object embodying it (= object-F), is thus not the numerical one in contrast to the numerical plural; it is, as in Plotinus and Duméry, the inexhaustible, unspecifiable depth which is grasped by all articulations though exhausted by none.

The numerical one and the numerical many designate the poles of the *structure* implied in a plurality of reflections; other designations of the same polarity are: form and matter, positive and negative, static and dynamic. The nature of systematic reflections is such that its basic axioms can be drawn from either of the two poles but not both simultaneously. Thus, systems based upon an axiom identifying God with a static absolute and those identifying him with infinite adaptability cannot absorb each other, and no single reflective system can be built upon both axioms at once. Yet both axioms express something of the truth of the depth-content which is affirmed by faith. Hence, only in the mutual participation of the discrete systems based upon these different axioms can the content of that depth be expressed. None of the systems can directly include the others, but they are all equally possible choices. Since no synthesis of all of them—no total systematic theological reflection—is possible, the complete articulation of the content of faith is contained only in the dialectical participation of the several patterns in one another. This is the origin of the pluralism which reflexive analysis describes and justifies— there are many systems and no single one of them is *the* system nor can they all be synthesized into one whole system of reflection. In the explanation to the diagram, I have referred to this as the structure of objectivity.

This model—the dialectical whole constituted by the set of equally valid and mutually participating systems based upon opposite axioms—does not, however, include the whole range of possibilities between the positive and the negative. Specifically, it does not include that kind of reflection which could be represented by a "no-pattern" in any given set of patterns. If the ultimate One to which reflection and faith are directed legitimates both positive patterns (e.g., those based upon a static absolute—the One as apart from the many) and negative patterns (those based upon process—the One as *in* the many) because it is the depth-content which is other than either or both of them, it also legitimates a no-pattern. That is to say, it legitimates a kind of reflection in which the consistency is found not in an axiom and its consequences (whether positive or negative) but in the originating act of the person who is doing the reflecting. The continuity of such a system lies in the fact that it is "I" who think it through, even if the pattern which results from my thinking it through, because it does not accord with specifiable positive or negative axioms, would have to be called nonpatterned—a no-pattern in relation to the rest of what is included in the set of patterns.

Such a no-pattern may usually be overlooked because we tend to assume that it is the opposite of systematic reflection: we consider a reflective system whose consistency lies only in the thinking "I" to be arbitrary and nonsystematic. But this is not necessarily the case. Certainly, there are people who think nonsystematically and make choices arbitrarily without thinking them through. There are others—and among theologians Karl Barth and Martin Luther might be cited as representative cases—whose thought is systematic though it cannot be defined in terms of specifiable patterns.[15] The consistency of such thought is based upon there being continually present in the thought the one who is thinking; it is a consistency of *act*, which cannot be translated into a homomorphic pattern.

What warrants our recognizing this, too, as a systematic reflection is the fact that the ultimate One is not only the opposite of the positive and negative patterns in turn, but also the opposite of the *opposition* between positive and negative. If God is in this sense *totaliter aliter*—not only other than the positive forms and negative forms of reflection but also other than the otherness contained in the positive-negative relation—a complete set of dialectically related patterns must at some point include a no-pattern. The fact that they have not made such an inclusion is the first reason why the existing studies of pluralism are not yet radically or completely pluralist.

The second reason leads to our second preliminary consideration. Studies of pluralism have been based upon a structure defining the objectivity of reflection. This structure is constituted by the basic polarity between positive (form) and negative (matter). But there is also a structure of freedom that is implicit in the plurality of responses made to a presence that elicits response. This structure has not been regarded at all in studies of pluralism.[16] It is constituted by the basic polarity between "my" affirmation (my freely given yes in response to the presence) and "his" negation. The polarity in responsive thinking, which corresponds to the polarity of positive and negative patterns for reflectively grasping object-F, is that of yea-saying and nay-saying to the One as present (= presence-F).

Here we have uncovered the other half of the whole structure underlying pluralism: the structure of freedom, in which the polar opposites are the yes (on "my" part) and the no (on the other's part) to any given proposal (a presence-F, which elicits a response). What holds for patterns of reflection also holds for different responses. There can be a variety of ways of saying yes (just as there can be a variety of positive patterns of reflection) and a variety of ways of saying no (like the variety of negative patterns of reflection). But the pluralistic structure is constituted by the basic opposition between the yes and the no of response, each of them a free response to one presence. The depth-content given in an object (= object-F) is drawn into opposite patterns of reflection. Similarly the depth given in a presence (= presence-F) elicits opposite responses from "me" and from "him (the other one)." The fact that they are both free responses indicates that the ultimate One to whom the response is made transcends affirmation and negation just as the ultimate depth-content transcends the positive and negative patterns and their relation of opposition. Both the affirmation and the negation are legitimated by that One.

To retrace the steps we have taken in these two preliminary observations: among the possible patterns of reflection we must also include a no-pattern; otherwise we have not covered the full range between positive and negative. Moreover, we must define the structure of pluralism not only with respect to reflection upon object-F but also with respect to response to presence-F.

Without taking account of both aspects of plurality we cannot
fully account for or describe a pluralist systematics. Any model of
pluralism must, then, take into account these considerations.

Given the double structure here implied—that of objectivity
and that of freedom—we need add only that a simple gauge of
how much plurality a reflexive model allows is the extent to
which it includes negativity. The minimal form of negativity in
the patterns of reflection is the otherness of the opposite patterns; the maximal form is the no-pattern. The minimal form of
negativity in free response is a variety of ways of saying yes; the
maximal form is a total no to what is proposed. A radically pluralist model must, of course, include the maximal forms of negativity in both cases.

Can there be a reflexive model of such radical pluralism at all?
To give a provisional answer to this question we might at least
note that, if it is not possible to order actual freedom, as well
as the patterns and no-pattern of reflection, in some reflexive
scheme, the objection that systematic thinking is always totalitarian would, I should think, be well founded. We should then
concede that pluralism is not theoretically manageable; it is the
surd, the permanently indigestible fact, for theoretical thought.
The issue, of course, is not whether we can give plurality *some*
intelligible order but whether we can really order the freedom it
involves in reflection as well as responsive thinking.

Is it possible to think in total terms without thinking in totalitarian terms? The dilemma for ecumenical theology here, toward
the solution of which the models of plurality are offered as a
means, is only a focus of the dilemma of a technocratic and world
society. On the one hand, some kind of total thought (planning,
systems-analysis) is the only thing that prevents the consequences
of free action from destroying the freedom and the reflections on
ultimate content from stifling the content. On the other hand,
total thought seems inevitably to become totalitarian. Only if it
is possible to order actual freedom and to pattern the depth of
content can this dilemma be avoided. This is the fundamental
question for pluralist systematics; and it is the reason why the
undertaking is more than a question of technical scholarship. Until we have seen, at least in principle, how to analyze actual freedom, any model of systems, no matter how adequate it is for the
formal and material details of systematic patterns, runs the risk of
excluding the one thing that keeps it from being a heteronomous
new orthodoxy in a more complex guise.

Toward a Radical Pluralism

Where then shall we begin in order to construct a model that is radically pluralist? We can reduce this specifically to the question of how to construct a model that includes the plurality of *actual freedom*. We need to take our clue, not from the God-world relation in which the freedom of the human subject is not thematically present, but from some question that exhibits the plurality of subjective freedom. This means a case in which (a) there are at least two subjects, acting in opposite ways; (b) neither can do what the other does, though both are equally legitimate; and (c) the form and matter of what they are dealing with remains constant. In other words, two subjects are differentiated from each other here only by their *act*, not by the content with which they are involved nor any objective forms they employ.

Such cases are intimated in a number of places in traditional material. Consider, for example, the relation between a penitent and a confessor in giving and receiving absolution. Assume that the formal and material content of absolution is the statement that the penitent is forgiven. If we consider only this content, the statement, if it is true at all, is true no matter who speaks it. If one is forgiven, one is forgiven; and my saying the opposite will not alter the state of affairs. If, however, we consider the situation in which the different acts of the penitent and the confessor are set, then it becomes obvious that this is a content which can be spoken by only one of the two parties. The penitent cannot actually say to himself that he is forgiven; it can be said to him by the confessor. Thus, even though the formal and material content of forgiveness is the same whether the penitent or the confessor speaks of it, the actual situation is such that spoken by the confessor it is true, and spoken by the penitent it is not.[17] Here we have an intimation of the plurality of freedom. The only thing that distinguishes the two statements is the subjective difference—a difference which is guarded by the office of the confessor, for an *officium* is to a subject's act what a genus is to an objective being. Moreover, the polar structure is evident here in the fact that "I"-receiving cannot be turned into "I"-giving and another-giving cannot be turned into another-receiving without altering the freedom this situation contains.

A second example is a set of observations about innocence and Messiahship. Buber has said that a man who called himself the Messiah would by that very act show that he is not the Messiah.

Kierkegaard noted that we know innocence only dialectically, as that which we have lost; an innocent person who says he is innocent is already guilty by virtue of knowing the difference between innocence and guilt. This is more than a matter of the psychology of innocence and Messiahship. What is also involved is the real plurality of subjects; something said by one person may be true when the same formal and material content said by another is false, not because the content changes but because the subjects are free, that is, not reducible to each other or to a common subjectivity. Again, the polar structure is evident in this example because the existence of a Messiah requires two subjects: the one who is, but cannot say he is, the Messiah; and the other who is not, but can say the first is, the Messiah.

These examples are intimations of a pluralism of free subjects that becomes of central importance in analyzing answers to the question whether Jesus is the Christ, the Logos, the Messiah. There is an intrinsic connection between christological affirmations and the plurality of freedom; for the answer to the question whether salvation is present in Jesus, is, more than other questions in theology, a matter of free response. This is the *scandalon* of the cross's wisdom, that it is radical freedom, of God and of man. Affirmations or denials here do not depend upon conceptual clarity concerning what is said nor upon the strength with which the case can be argued. When everything has been fully clarified, and all evidence is in, the answer yes and the answer no are still equally possible. As "dialectical" theology in particular recognized, a yes or no has no further human ground than the free response to the word freely coming to one. Accordingly, the factor determining the truth or nontruth of christological assertions is the factor of freedom—freedom of the object to disclose its presence to faith, and freedom of the human subject to respond affirmatively or negatively.[18] To be a *free subject*, although a finite one, requires that a person respond in one way or another, not both, and that one be able to make this affirmation without its being negated by another's negative response to the same object.

Put more sharply: the response here *determines* the truth of what is said. That Jesus is the Christ can be said truthfully by one who sees him as that; that he is not the Christ can be said truthfully by one who does not so see him. Each of them can support the response with a train of reasons as cogent as the other, for the determining factor is not the reason but the free response. This is not to say that response is purely a matter of subjectivism, or "fideism," but that in christology we are dealing with a reality so completely "open" to free response that it can elicit a free no as well as a free yes. Thus, my response is not one I merely decide to make, according to my fancy, but one that is actually elicited by that reality.

Here we have the radical case of the plurality adumbrated in our earlier examples. The formal and material content of the person of Jesus is the same whether he is or is not acknowledged as the Christ. Were we to disregard the difference between subjects in act we should have to say either Jesus is or is not the one who brings salvation; he cannot "objectively" be both. We might, of course, be modest enough to say that "objectively" refers to a perspective available only to God, that the answer is problematic because of the limitedness of our perspectives, and that we might not know for certain whether he is or is not what we say he is; but in the end we should have to maintain that he can be "really" the one or the other, but not both. If, however, the situation involved in the difference between positive and negative responses is what determines the truth or untruth of what is said, and if the issues fundamental to Christology involve the plurality of free response rather than of reflecting patterns, then it is quite possible for Jesus "really" to be and not to be the Christ. For what he "really" is is a presence which elicits a yes and a no, both as free and appropriate responses to him. In other words, it is a case that exhibits a structure in which (a) there are at least two subjects, acting in opposite ways; (b) neither can do what the other does, though both are equally legitimate; and (c) the form and matter of what they are dealing with remains constant.

Since it would be easy to overlook the importance of this point, I want to put it again. What is manifested in the christological Jesus is the depth of *actual freedom*. It bears the same relation to acts of a subject (yea-saying and nay-saying) as God himself bears to the systems of reflection outlined by Capps. God as the One is the depth of what is reflected on; Jesus as the Christ is the depth of the acts of free response. If the depth of what is reflected on legitimates both sets of opposite patterns and founds their dialectical interaction, the depth of the acts of subjectivity legitimates both yea-saying and nay-saying. Hence, "I" who say yes and the other who says no to what is proposed—namely, this man as the Christ, the one in whom salvation for the world is present— bear the same relation to each other as static conceptions and process conceptions of God bear to each other in the model Capps outlined, except that static and process patterns are each *partial* whereas the yes and no are each *total*—a difference which derives from the difference between a structure of objectivity and a structure of freedom.

Consequently, if it is true that a pluralistic model of forms for reflecting the basic disposition of faith moves from a positive pattern to its opposite and finally to a no-pattern, it is also true that a systematic response which starts from the affirmation that salvation is present in Jesus (= the yea-saying on the part of "me") cannot end until it reaches the opposite contention (= the nay-saying on the part of the other), both of them equally legitimated by the presence-F they express. I suppose most Christian theologians have always hoped to convert the nay-sayers.[19] Is this not due to the fact that a recognition of the plurality of subjects has come very late in the history of Western thought, and then only painfully and in part? If it is true that christological thought involves a plurality of sheer freedom, not only a plurality of reflective axioms and patterns, then the relations between a Christian who affirms and a non-Christian who denies the presence of salvation in Jesus is the prototype of pluralistic freedom, and a systematic christology should reflect that fact.

Is it possible to systematize this freedom? Is it possible to negotiate or chart this kind of plurality? I think it is. That it is logically possible is shown by Gotthard Günther's *Idee und Grundriß einer nicht-aristotelischen Logik.*[20] But is it theologically possible? Would this kind of theological undertaking deprive theology of its distinctive character? No, because the alternative is not a leveling syncretism on one side and a genuine Christian theology in all its concreteness on the other side.[21] On the contrary, there is no reason why we cannot engage in a systematic thought in which we avoid abstractive reductionism by maintaining the christological affirmations as both distinctive and fundamental in Christian theology while we also thematically treat the negations of these affirmations and treat them as equally well founded. Systematic consistency demands that I do not simultaneously affirm and negate my point of departure, but it does not prevent me from *affirming another's negation* of that point of departure nor does it demand that I treat that negation as though it were equivalent to my negation.

A recognition of the plurality of actual freedom, and the structure it rests upon, provides us accordingly with the very thing that allows us to escape from the dilemma of a theology which is tolerant at the cost of eliminating its concrete uniqueness and a theology which maintains its concrete uniqueness but is intolerant. If the import of christology—which is the concrete and unique element in theology, the element that is both essential and separative—is that it contains the depth of actual freedom, then it allows the Christian theologian to regard the yes as central to this theology but in such a way that the yes includes another subject's no. What gives this theology the concreteness essential to any living theology is the yes to Jesus as the Christ; what gives it freedom is the recognition that the yes is, because of the polar structure of actual freedom, implicitly also an affirmation of an opposite subject's no.

There is a difference, as we see here, between the way in which the yes and no to presence-F support each other. Each of the systems of reflection expresses a *part* of the whole content; their opposition is based upon the *finitude* of all concepts used for grasping the ultimate content of faith, and their dialectical relation is based on the fact that the ultimate content is more than what finitude contains. In the case of the yes and no to a given proposal, the centering of freedom depends upon being able to say only one and not the other. It is not the case that one's freedom is incomplete until one says both yes and no. On the contrary, there is a totality involved in either response to the concrete presence which represents the depth of freedom.

What happens to diverse expressions of freedom in a reflexive analysis is, therefore, different from what happens to the variety of systems of reflection. From the standpoint of reflexivity each of the first-order reflective systems can be seen as part of a dialectical whole, and the dialectical whole is a fuller expression of the content of faith than any of the parts alone. Thus, trinitarianism as a theological system of reflection, which is like a dialectical whole because it rests on two opposite axioms, expresses more than unitarianism or christomonism or process theology alone. Similarly, Hartshorne's surrelative conception of God is more adequate than a merely absolute or merely relative conception. But in the case of the plurality of response my endeavor to say both yes and no to the christological proposal (that in this Jesus salvation is present for the world) is not a fuller but a lesser expression of freedom. The structure of pluralistic freedom depends upon there being two subjects, each saying, as his own free act, either yes or no but not both. I can, accordingly, think trinitarianly or surrelatively all by myself, but I can respond pluralistically only in the presence of another subject, the nay-sayer.

Hence, when reflexivity analyzes the plurality of freedom and introduces a theology that recognizes that plurality, the consequence is not that a Christian theologian endeavors to say both yes and no to the proposal that Jesus is the Christ. Rather, it is to say only yes to that proposal but to continue with an affirmation of an *opposite subject's negation* of the same proposal. This is where the element of plurality enters and systematically expresses the fact that the nay-sayer is not just one who has not quite seen the truth yet—not a covert yea-sayer, or an "anonymous" Christian—but one whose actual freedom is the polar opposite which, together with "my" freedom, establishes the structure of pluralistic response. The other's no (when it is as free and authentic as my yes) centers freedom as does my yes; and the depth of freedom (not just my freedom, but of the structure of freedom) is the polarity of my yes and the other's no.

To put it differently: in a pluralistic logic of freedom, my affirmation of a given proposal does not entail a negation of another's negation of it. The notion that it is impossible for me to affirm and another person to negate one and the same proposal and for both of us to be wholly right (so far as that is ever humanly possible) is an unwarranted assumption. It presupposes the unity of a "transcendental subject." If subjectivity is plural, systematic thought may comprehend one person's affirmations and another's denials as two distinct themes even when the objective form and matter remain constant.[22]

Indeed, the responsible theologian is then obliged to do more than think through the affirmations systematically; we must also think through *another's negations* in an equally systematic way. In doing so, one speaks for one's own concrete tradition as well as for (and not only *to*) other traditions, without treating representatives of the latter as though they were potential participants of one's own tradition. A principle often stated in ecumenical discussions is that the more deeply one explores one's own tradition, the more one becomes aware of a oneness in faith with those in other traditions. It is doubtful that this is true for anyone conscious of the plurality rooted in the originating freedom of subjects. On the contrary, there will always be cases in which the only affirmation I can make of another's freely held faith is the one that affirms an inaccessible depth in the other's freedom. These are cases in which the other's no is as free as my yes.

This relation of freedom is focused in my recognition that another's negation of my affirmation is not identical with my own negation of it. For what does this imply? It implies a difference between us as subjects that makes the other's freedom inaccessible to my judgment. My systematic response starts with what I basically affirm, but it ends only where I allow the other to negate my affirmation and, in consequence, to determine my place in relation to the other's affirmation. Between this beginning and end there are three distinct themes. The first theme articulates my affirmation; the second theme articulates my systematic affirmation of another's negation of my basic affirmation (which I have formally articulated as the first theme); the third theme—though it could conceivably be part of the second theme—is my affirmation of another's indifference to my basic affirmation.

The first studies of theological pluralism did not get beyond the first theme; the same is true of hermeneutically oriented approaches to pluralism. By taking footing on the distinction between reflexive criticism and systematic reflection, one can open the path to the diversity of ways for conceptualizing a faith, but this does not yet assume the task of affirming another's negation of the protothematic affirmation and of ordering free response. It is important, however, that we learn to do the latter as well, lest systematic pluralism become only a more complex form of orthodoxy. Indeed, to the extent that it can succeed in theologizing in this manner, ecumenical theology will be the vanguard for attacking theoretically the more general problem of ordering freedom in a world society.

16

ONE OF THE MANY AND
THE MANY OF THE ONE

THE TITLE of this essay has in it a double formulation. The first part of the title, the phrase "one of the many," carries connotations that come mostly from ordinary discourse, although there are allusions as well to meanings that come from the history of philosophy and theology; the second part of the title, "the many of the one," is a phrase that would scarcely occur at all in any discourse except that of philosophy and theology when they address themselves to questions at the ultimate horizon of thinking and being. The intention of the whole title is to focus our consideration upon the question of unity and multitude which in fundamental ways is at the intersection of the ordinary and the extraordinary in human experience and which in a special way comes to the fore in what today is often called pluralism. The manifoldness of things, which dominates the normal way of being in the world, is intersected by the occasional sense—not the less important for its being occasional—of their unity.

That something is one of the many is in the first place a limiting idea. So we can say that an individual is only one of the many. "This city is only one of many cities; this religion is only one of the many; this philosophical view is only one among many; this is only one of many opinions; each of us is but one of the many human beings there are, have been, and will be." Such statements can be multiplied indefinitely. They express the recognition, common to reflective experience, of the relatedness of everything at least to other things of the same kind, if not to all other things, and the awareness of being parts of a whole without being the whole itself. That we do not normally convert such statements by saying that the other cities are the many of this one city, the other religions the many of this one, other philosophies the many of this one, other human beings the many of this one human being, and so on, indicates the way in which the singular stands apart from the others—the multitude predominates over the unity. The many others are other ones that on their own are also each only one of the many. The thought "This is but one of the many" comes to mind, then, as the consciousness of the limitations that individuality brings with it, the consciousness of finitude. "These others are the many of the one" would come to mind, if it came to mind at all, as the consciousness of the plenitude that multitude brings with it, the consciousness of transcending the particular, or the consciousness of the whole. What falls away, in other words, in the common experience that each is but one of the many of its kind is an awareness of the participatory and representative aspect of the one; what predominates is the awareness of the limitedness, the exclusiveness, the particularity, of the particular one over against the many as other ones. Plato could even form an epistemological theory on this basis. In the everyday, the soul has forgotten its preexistent knowledge of the universals, so that it can attain to knowledge only when it remembers those unities by recognizing them in the particular ones. To understand means to recall the forgotten universals in the particulars; without such a remembering there is no knowledge or truth but only opinion and seeming. In that theory are reflected two of the several senses that the idea of the one has had in philosophical thought: the one as the particular one, which is meant in our phrase "only one of the many," and the one as the common or universal, which is suggested in the phrase "*the* one of (or in) the many" and to which the phrase "the many of the one" is a pointer.

But my purpose here is not to use the common ways of speaking as a means for giving a diagnosis of existence, not even of contemporary existence, nor is it to trace the philosophical history that arises from the several senses that oneness, as *henosis* and as *monas*, had in Greek thought. It is, rather, to reflect on three ways in which the many-ness of the one and the oneness of the many interplay. (1) One way lies in the interplay between the many names of one concept and the many concepts of one name. (2) A second way lies in the ineffability of the one as one. (3) And a third lies in the hermeneutical relation between the two basic forms of thinking that have shaped the spirit which is doubly heir to the intelligibility of being and to the credentiality of God, and for which the intelligibility of being appears *as* the trustworthiness or credentiality of God and the credentiality of God appears *as* the intelligibility of being.

Concepts and Names

An interreligious discussion today of the question of God points out an interplay of the one and the many by raising in two different ways the question of the unity of subject to be discussed. First, if the discussion is about God, do nontheistic religions and philosophies have anything to say pertinent to the matter? Antitheistic, or atheistic, philosophies are something else. The unity of the subject to be discussed would not be harmed by negative treatments of it. But are there religions and systems of thought which have nothing to say about the matter because neither the name nor the idea of God appears in them at all, either as a matter of affirmation or as a matter of denial? That is one way in which the question of the one and many is raised. In a second way, it takes the form of asking whether the name "God" designates the subject under discussion or whether this name, "God," is but one of many names for a subject primarily designated by a different name. Is the word *God* one among many names for something that we can more properly designate, for example, as "ultimate reality"? These are, I think, two versions of what is basically the same question, the question of the unity of the subject intended by theology.

It is common to seek a unity between theistic and nontheistic philosophies and religions by having recourse to such notions as that of "ultimate reality." Then the unity and diversity have to do with the different ways in which that matter called ultimate reality is understood and shaped, whether in theological terms by reference to the name "God," or in ontological terms by reference to being, or in existential terms by reference to the meaning of being, or in still other terms by reference to names or concepts that are indifferent to the distinction between theology and ontology or between being and meaning. There is certainly warrant for that approach, not only in the phenomenology and history of religion, but also in theologies in which "God" is understood predicatively, as, for example, in the thought of Paul Tillich when "God" is understood to mean what concerns us unconditionally.

Anything that is a matter of unconditional concern is a god, phe-
nomenologically speaking, and the critique of the gods in religion
involves assessing whether any of the things—be they objects or
persons or words or ideas—about which one is or can be unconditionally concerned is really unconditional. A contemporary discussion of God, carried out along these lines, would be an investigation and critique of those matters which are of unconditional
concern today. The critical question in such a discussion is not,
then, whether there is a god but whether any of the existing gods
is truly unconditional. "God" is one name for the unconditional;
there are other names for it as well. The unity is found in the concept of what concerns us unconditionally. The manifoldness is
found in the names that are given to that unconditional. "Ultimate reality" or "the unconditional" is what we are talking
about; "God," "being," and the like are different names for that
reality.

That is one approach. The opposite approach is to regard the
word *God* as the symbol which itself designates the subject of discussion. We might see the nature of this opposite approach by recalling the distinction that Kant made between, on the one side, a
concept that can never be exhausted by any intuition and, on the
other side, an intuition that can never be exhausted by a concept.
"God" can be understood as the concept of the absolute unity—of
"ultimate reality," if we will—which can never be exhausted by
any intuition. From this arises the dynamic between the many intuitions that make the concept perceptible, or partly so, and the
oneness of infinite concept that always exceeds them. But "God"
can also be taken to mean the one intuition that can never be exhausted by concepts. In Kant's language, this is an aesthetic idea;
in our language today, it is a symbol. Treated in this latter way,
the word *God* is not one of the many names for what is conceived
of as absolute unity or ultimate reality but is, rather, the one
name of the one intuition that can never be grasped in a concept.
With the word *God* something is intuited that is always being defined differently but never being defined finally. Every concept is
broken through by the intuition contained in the word *God* as
symbol. For such an approach, "God" names the one subject matter being discussed; "ultimate reality," "unconditional concern,"
and the like, are some of the many concepts that are used in order
to grasp that intuition but without ever being able to do so.

There is a third possibility which, as it seems to me, has scarcely
come into play at all. It is the possibility, suggested already in an

essay written on the logic of the divine names ("Über den Logos: Ein Beitrag zur Logik der göttlichen Namen") by Karl Daub in the early nineteenth century, that the names "God," "Jahweh," "Allah," and the like, which seem to be different names for either the same or a different referent, are in fact the *same* name although they may have different meanings. This is to say that, just as in the world of physical objects the one concept that is represented by the many examples is the same concept (the flower as flower is the same whether it is exemplified in a rose or in a tulip), so in the sphere of the divine names it is the same name, the name of the one, that is represented in the many linguistic figures. Thus, the English word *God* is not a different name from the Latin *Deus* or the Greek *theos*, but it is the same name in a different language. There is one name, in the many linguistic figures, just as there is one concept in the many physical examples in which the concept appears. The point here is that in every language there emerges that name which, in the given language, is *the* name, the one name of the one, and which therefore is the *same* name despite the different acoustic and visual figures *and despite different meanings*, the same name for the same one. The problem of the divine names is, then, that of finding, in each language, that word (acoustic or visual figure with meaning) which, when its meaning is thought and understood, both names and brings to appearance the one.

This, as I said, is a line of thought that scarcely anyone has pursued. Perhaps that means it cannot be followed very far. Or perhaps it means that we are predisposed to put the matter in one of the first two ways without considering this third one even as a possibility. Or perhaps the reason for not following this path is neither the shortness of the path nor our predispositions but that our discussions are perforce carried on in the medium of one language so that we consider the diversity of religions or philosophies but not the diversity of languages. We who speak English may forget the particularity of our own language and not wonder how the word *God* fits into the English language just as a language. Whatever its significance, there is at least this third possibility for exploring the question of the one and the many in the contemporary discussion of God.

The Ineffability of the One

"God" is, in English, the one name of the one, we said. If that is so, then we cannot say that "God" is a name for ultimate reality or for what concerns us unconditionally or for anything else than itself. "God" as the name of the one is "God" as the name for nothing other than God. What can be said of God basically is only that God is God; that is the oneness of God. Yet to say even that "God is God" is to introduce a many into the one by separating the one as subject from the one as predicate. This immediately raises the question of the nature of that manifold which mediates and refracts the oneness of the one and without which the one could not even *be* one. Strictly speaking, the thought of God as God is not a thought of the one; for "God," as the one name of the one, names an inconceivable; that is, it names one that cannot be split into a subject and a predicate without a rupture in its oneness. Yet we can also understand that this is so. That is to say, we can understand that in thinking the one as one we are disrupting its unity as one. The one *is* one in the manifold that interrupts its oneness. We can understand more than we can conceive; we can understand the inconceivability of the one which we conceive *as* the one.

The fact that we can understand the inconceivability of the one as one is a root of pluralism. The question of pluralism is not the same question as what, traditionally, appears in the form of relativism, that is, as the idea that there is no universally recognizable truth, correctness, beauty, goodness, community, or justice but that what counts as such is always only relative to those who are engaged in the knowing, doing, and making connected with these values. The refutation of relativism does not therefore immediately apply to pluralism. That refutation can be put in the form of a question: If all truth is relative to the one pronouncing or ascertaining it, then is the statement that all truth is relative itself (only) relative? If so, then it is self-defeating because it is only a reflection of the one who makes the statement and not a statement about the possibility of there being, or of our knowing, truth that as such is not relative. If, on the other hand, the statement that all truth is relative is not itself relative, then there is at least one truth that is not relative, and so the statement itself— that all truth is relative—cannot be true. It is never clear exactly how many people are ever persuaded by such formal refutations, correct as they may be. But, in any case, that matter is something other than what is expressed in the concern with "pluralism" when one speaks of pluralism in philosophy and theology and means the essential many-ness of the one when it is one and when it is thought and known as the one.

Pluralism has to do, here, with the question of the one and the

many. In its minimal, though highly important, sense it can mean
what Heidegger referred to when he said that every poet has only
one poem to write, but no poet ever writes that one poem, for
every poet is always writing toward, and out of, that one unwrit-
ten poem without ever being able to write the poem itself. The
one poem can never be written as such; the many poems are in-
dicators of it without being that one itself. This sense of pluralism, here applied to the work of those—the poets—who put
truth into words, is of the same kind as that contained in the
Middle and Neoplatonic negative theologies, for which God is the
undifferentiated one, unnamable, unspeakable, and unknowable
as such. The pure identity of God cannot even be spoken, for to
say that God is God is to introduce a two-ness into the one in the
distinction between subject and predicate connected by a copula.
The name "God" serves only as a name for what cannot without
self-contradiction be named. Even naming the unnamable as the
unnamable, to say nothing of naming it as God, is to deny the un-
namability of the unnamable. Hence, strictly speaking, the God
who is purely one can be spoken only to the extent that silence
can speak it, the silence that surrounds and undergirds all speaking. So, for Neoplatonism, the names of God, even the name
"God" and the word *unnamable* as a name or a predicate, are
forms that give voice to silence so that one is to hear them as the
sounds that call attention to silence by breaking it. We can know
the silence as that which is broken by the voice of the words that
name it. The various names of God, even the name "God," serve
that purpose; they call attention to the one, the pure identity, by
showing it as that silence which is broken by the names themselves. To know what is named by the names of God requires the
discipline of indirect knowledge along with direct knowledge,
just as hearing the silence that is broken by the voice requires
the ability to hear indirectly as well as directly, to hear not only
what is said and sayable but also what is unsaid and unsayable.
Heidegger's remarks about poetry run in the same direction. The
poet's one poem is the one that we can hear or read only by listening beyond the actual poems for the silence that they also express. There is this difference, of course, between the poem of the
Heideggerian poet and the Neoplatonic God: in principle, a poet
could write the one poem that fully expresses the word that is
identical with just that poet and with no other, even though in
fact poets cannot do so. Theoretically, a poet could write the one
poem that is the word of truth given uniquely to that poet to say

and others to hear. Not even theoretically, however, could the God who is purely one, pure identity, ever be given a name adequate to incorporate it.

Pluralism in this context has to do with the relation between the one that cannot be said or thought or written and the many words and thoughts and writings that point to it and call attention to it by interrupting its unity. It does not imply a relativism in the sense that any saying is as good as another, or that we cannot judge our own standpoint by something beyond it as a standpoint. It implies a relativism only in the sense that we can always recognize the discrepancy between the many and the one and we can also discriminate among the many in order to ascertain which of them come closer to expressing the oneness of the one. Some poems of a given poet are closer to that one poem than are others. Some names of God, and some judgments about God, come closer to showing the pure oneness of the one than do others. But none of them can ever name the oneness or enable us to know it as such without denying its oneness, just as no spoken word can name the silence without, by its very being spoken, breaking the silence. The one exceeds all of the many that point to it. Pluralism is called forth by the very unity of the one. The one cannot *be* anything at all, it cannot even be one, without this recourse to the many.

Hermeneutics of Thinking

There is another root of pluralism, at least in Western thought, in the history of theontology itself (this is not the onto-theo-logy of which Heidegger speaks), one that lies in the relation between understanding and believing.[1] This is the third of the three ways mentioned at the beginning. The principle that faith seeks understanding and understanding seeks faith, which has been at the basis of theological science since the Middle Ages in the West, is itself a root of pluralism. For what faith intends by the name "God" and what understanding intends by the name "being" are the same in the different, so that the intelligibility of being can interpret the credentiality of God, and the trustworthiness of God can interpret the intelligibility of being.

The hermeneutical scope of this conception of faith as seeking understanding becomes apparent only when the matter of thinking—the matter about which we are always thinking when we think anything at all—is spelled out as the identity in difference between *understanding being* and *believing in (or trusting) God*.[2] To see the import of the formulation, it is not sufficient just to say that faith seeks understanding. It is necessary, in addition, to call attention to the activities and the intentions that are meant by the words *faith* and *understanding*. Understanding always means understanding *being;* and faith always means trusting *God*. Hence, "faith seeking understanding" is a matter of the way in which a *believing in God* "seeks" an *understanding of being*. What is understood is fundamentally always "being," and what is trusted is always in the end "God." The acts are different and the intentions are different; yet there is an identity in this difference that makes it possible for the one to "seek," or be open to, the other, the one that is jointly named as being and as God. It is not that God is being but that the credentiality of God leads into the intelligibility of being and the intelligibility of being into the trustworthiness of God. The proper "object" of understanding is not a thing as it is concretely perceived nor as it is abstractly thought but precisely the "being" that unites the percept and concept. The being of the dog, for example, that we see and know is not, then, a reference to how we perceive it or class it; it refers, rather, to the factor that makes it possible for us to unite our particular perception and our general thought when we understand "this" *as* "a dog."

If understanding being involves a uniting of singular percepts and universal concepts in the way just described, the principle that faith seeks understanding suggests that believing in God "seeks" to understand being. It suggests, in other words, that the understanding of being is also an interpretation of the trust in God—so that the one which is intended both by faith and by understanding is indicated equally originally by understanding and by believing. What we understand when we understand anything is an interpretation of the one we trust when we trust anyone. But this would seem to imply that trusting is, like understanding, an act of thinking in which two different aspects are synthesized. So we must ask: If understanding brings together percepts and concepts, what is brought together in *fides*? If the "being" of a thing means the unity of its singular and universal aspects, what unity is implied in the name "God"?

I should like to propose the thesis that trusting always unites a singular consciousness, which I encounter as the "thou" in my world, with the divine I, so that the act of believing is always one in which the human and divine are united (just as the act of understanding unites what is concretely perceived with what is abstractly conceived). To put it differently: what occurs when we find it possible to trust anyone or anything at all is that we as isolated individuals are enabled to identify ourselves with a selfhood that is universal, and that identification is what is meant by the word *God*. This uniting of singular and universal is different from that of perception and conception but has the same structure, the structure of an act of *thinking*. To be able to trust or to believe means to be able to identify a singular self-consciousness with an all-inclusive consciousness. Radical trust is then the identity of the single consciousness encountered in a "thou" with the divine I, which can appear not only as an all-inclusive I but also as the not-I that opposes and threatens the human I. That by reference to which the identifying is done is signified by the name "God" (in the same way that the name "being" signifies that by reference to which the unity of singular percept and universal concept is achieved). God is the unity of the divine and human as being is the unity of singular and general. Hence, to trust at all is to trust God, just as to understand at all is to understand being; understanding being is the possibility of bringing together perception and conception, and trusting God is the possibility of bringing together the individuality of self-awareness and the universality of selfhood as such, or the human and the divine. Mistrust is, similarly, the failure to unite, or the wrong uniting of, the human and the divine, just as misunderstanding is the failure to unite, or the wrong uniting of, percept and concept.

What is implied in the fact that there are these two basic modes of *thinking*—that of *fides* and that of *intellectus*—and that thinking as such is enacted only in one or both of these modes but never in a third mode synthesizing them is a certain pluralism in the structure of thinking itself. If there is an identity in the difference between the believing in God (in the sense of trusting God) and the understanding of being, then the propositions in which faith is formulated can be translated into propositions in which understanding is formulated, and conversely; and they can interpret and test each other even though they cannot replace each other. But the one that is dually named as being, when it is the object of understanding, and as God, when it is the object of trust, cannot be thought as such—it is always that which appears, when it appears, jointly, in one way to understanding and in another way to believing. The act of understanding being is not the act of trusting God; that is true. Yet, because understanding and believing are both modes of thinking, there is an identity between them so that the one which they jointly mean is what it is in the reciprocal interpretation which trust in God offers of the understanding of being and conversely.

The question that arises when one speaks in this way of *fides* and *intellectus* as two basic modes of thinking, not reducible to each other but interpretable by each other, is whether the thought which makes that connection is itself an exercise of faith or of understanding or of both. If believing in God and understanding being are said to *be* two modes of thinking, the very language we use to describe the relation between them suggests that it is understanding, rather than believing, that provides the connection between the two. This is, of course, understanding of a second degree—not an understanding of the being of things but an understanding of what thinking is. But understanding, even when thus potentiated, or raised to the second degree, is still understanding, so that the point of view from which we regard believing and understanding is that of understanding. We "understand" that our understanding and our believing are two modes of thinking; we "understand" the "being" of thinking.

Although the very way in which we describe the matter does, accordingly, suggest that the difference which exists between believing in God and understanding being at the first level does not apply at the second level, we are well advised not to accept this suggestion without further scrutiny. True, when we say what faith and understanding "are," we are giving expression to an understanding of their being. But it is also possible that the difference between understanding and believing is also effective for second-order understanding. If it is effective there, then our understanding of what understanding and believing are is but one side of our thinking of them; the other side is an activity that has the nature of *believing* our believing and understanding. Believing in believing may initially suggest the kind of empty action that critics of "faith in faith"—the view that it is important to believe that believing is important but not so important to have this rather than that content of believing—rightly contemn. But that is not what is at issue here. Rather, it is the question of whether believing in God (what we are doing when we believe in, or trust, anything) can be raised to the second degree as can the understanding of being. The suggestion here is that it can be so raised and that, therefore, the hermeneutical reflection, through which we understand the identity and difference in understanding being and trusting God, is itself not only an understanding of being (the being in our thinking) but also a trusting of God (the God in our trusting).

This is a subtle but an important point. If it is true that the understanding of understanding is still directed toward being (even though it is the being of understanding rather than the being of things understood), it is also true that believing in believing is still directed toward God (though it is the God of believing rather than the God of things or persons believed). At the primary level we understand being by understanding things as being what they are (this as a tree, that as a rose, another thing as a dog, and so on); at the secondary level, we understand being by understanding our understanding as being what it is (the unity of percept and concept). Similarly, we trust God, in the primary sense, by trusting the community of the human and divine in things or persons (alien egos as expressions of selfhood); at the secondary level, we trust God by trusting our trusting as an expression of the community of self. And just as it is "being" that remains the object of understanding at both levels, so it is "God" who remains the object of trust at both levels. The understanding of understanding is an understanding of being; the believing in believing is a believing in God. In that sense the unity of faith and understanding is itself both faith and understanding, and human thinking is pluralistic, a many of one, a difference in identity, at its foundation.

To say that human thinking is pluralistic is to say more than that each of us is a different perspectival point for the way we think of the world. That we are such perspectival points is no doubt true. Every act of thinking is an act emerging from a point, an agent, that has perspectival uniqueness. But the pluralism of thinking, strictly taken, means more than that; it means that thinking as such is expressed in at least two fundamental modes which can never be reduced to each other or to a mode more basic. Thinking as thinking appears only in the form of understanding being and of believing God. The two acts are different from each other; their intentions (being; God) are different from each other; the difference between them cannot be collapsed or absorbed into a higher mode of thinking. In all that, they are irreducibly two. Yet the two move toward each other because each provides an interpretation of the other. What it means to understand being is made clear by trusting God, and what it means to believe in God is made clear by understanding being. What connects the two is not some third mode but the metaphorical power of moving between them in the hermeneutical process.

It is possible to find this line of thought less than convincing. For do we not, after all, find ourselves saying what thinking and believing—now thinking and believing of the second degree—"are"? And in saying what they "are," are we not once again moving in the sphere of understanding rather than of believing? Perhaps. But perhaps we could not even raise that question if there were not a believing in the understanding. At least, we could not leave the question open if there were not that.

NOTES
INDEX

NOTES

1. Onto- and Theo-logical Thinking

1. John Macquarrie, *Principles of Christian Theology*, 2d ed. (New York: Charles Scribner's Sons, 1977).
2. Ray Hart, *Unfinished Man and the Imagination* (New York: Herder and Herder, 1968).
3. Martin Heidegger, *Phänomenologie und Theologie* (Frankfurt am Main: Vittorio Klostermann, 1970), p. 18.
4. Jürgen Moltmann, *Christ the Crucified God*, tr. R. A. Wilson and John Bowden (New York: Harper & Row, 1974), p. 215.

2. The Identity of God and the Crucifixus

1. Georg Picht and Enno Rudolph, eds., *Theologie—Was ist das?* (Stuttgart: Kreuz-Verlag, 1977); Eberhard Jüngel, *Gott als Geheimnis der Welt* (Tübingen: J. C. B. Mohr [Paul Siebeck], 1977).
2. Karl Daub comes closer in his formulation that being as thinking is the essence of God and thinking as being is the existence of God (*Philosophische und theologische Vorlesungen*, vol. 6 [Berlin: Verlag von Duncker und Humblot, 1841], p. 63).
3. Picht and Rudolph, *Theologie*, p. 512.
4. Ibid., p. 513.
5. Ibid., p. 514.
6. *Kirchliche Dogmatik* II/1 (Zollikon-Zurich: Evangelischer Verlag, 1958), p. 288.
7. See chap. 4, below.
8. Jüngel, *Gott*, p. 402; emphasis original.
9. Ibid., p. 403.
10. Ibid., p. 402; italics original.
11. Ibid., p. 403.
12. Ibid., p. 404 n. 25.
13. Ibid., p. 403.
14. Ibid., p. 399.
15. Quoted ibid., p. 382.

3. The Being of God When God Is Not Being God

1. Dietrich Bonhoeffer, *Act and Being*, tr. Bernard Noble (New York: Harper & Row, 1961).
2. Karl Barth, *Kirchliche Dogmatik*, IV/1 (Zollikon-Zurich: EVZ-Verlag, 1960), pp. 201–4 (hereafter *KD*).
3. Whether the abuses of deconstruction can shed light on anything I am not certain. But one can be greatly entertained by a report of one such abuse: see Barbara Grizzuti Harrison, "Ah, Nihilism!" *Harper's*, September 1981, pp. 88–93.
4. That "destruction" has not attained conceptual clarity yet is perhaps indicated by there being no entry for "Destruktion" in Braun and Rademacher's lexicon, although there is one for "Konstruktion"; see Edmund Braun and Hans Rademacher, *Wissenschafts-theoretisches Lexikon* (Graz, Vienna, Cologne: Verlag Styria, 1978).
5. Martin Heidegger, *Sein und Zeit* (Tübingen: Max Niemeyer Verlag, 1963), p. 22 (emphasis original). The English translation, *Being and Time*, by John Macquarrie and Edward Robinson (New York: Harper & Row, 1962), gives the pagination of the German original as well.
6. This is a point that Hans Jonas treats in his interpretation of a Pauline passage ("The good that I would . . .") under the question of who the "I" there is ("The Abyss of the Will," *Philosophical Essays* [Englewood Cliffs, N.J.: Prentice-Hall, 1974], pp. 335–48; published also in James M. Robinson, ed., *The Future of Our Religious Past* [New York: Harper & Row, 1971]).
7. The "transcendental schema" is the "third thing," which is both intellectual and sensible, homogeneous, on the one hand, with the category and, on the other, with the appearance (*Critique of Pure Reason*, B177/A138).
8. See L. M. Vail, *Heidegger and Ontological Difference* (University Park: Pennsylvania State Univ. Press, 1972), p. 158.
9. *KD*, I/1, pp. viii, ix (Foreword).
10. Eberhard Jüngel, *Gott als Geheimnis der Welt* (Tübingen: J. C. B. Mohr [Paul Siebeck], 1977), p. 385.
11. Martin Heidegger, *Identity and Difference*, tr. Joan Stambaugh (New York: Harper & Row, 1969, two-language ed.), pp. 113, 114.
12. The term first appears in *Vom Wesen des Grundes*, but the difference is already mentioned in *Sein und Zeit*, p. 4. See Vail, *Heidegger*, pp. 5, 105.

4. Being "As Not"

1. "Mein Interesse ist auf den Doppelsinn der Beziehung von philosophischer und theologischer Hermeneutik gerichtet. Einerseits scheint ja die theologische Hermeneutik ein Sonderfall der philosophischen zu sein, insofern als sich deren wichtigste Kategorien, die der Rede, der Schrift, der Erklärung, der Interpretation, der Verfremdung, der Aneignung usw. dort wiederfinden; ihr gegenseitiges Verhältnis ist also das einer allgemeinen Hermeneutik zu ihrem Teilbereich. Andererseits besitzt die theologische Hermeneutik spezifische Merkmale, die den Universalitätsanspruch der philosophischen Hermeneutik, wie er zum Beispiel von Hans-Georg Gadamer formuliert wird, in Frage stellen. Hier erscheint das Verhältnis der beiden Hermeneutiken umgekehrt: die philosophische wird Organon der theologischen Hermeneutik" (Paul Ricoeur, "Philosophische und theologische Hermeneutik," *Evangelische Theologie*, Sonderheft, "Metapher: Zur Hermeneutik religiöser Sprache" [Munich: Chr. Kaiser Verlag, 1974], p. 24).

2. Paul Ricoeur, *The Rule of Metaphor*, tr. Robert Czerny (Toronto: Univ. of Toronto Press, 1977), p. 7.
3. "Listening to the Parables of Jesus," in *The Philosophy of Paul Ricoeur*, ed. Charles E. Reagan and David Stewart (Boston: Beacon Press, 1978), p. 239.
4. When one says or thinks the word *I*, one becomes the referent of the word. In that sense, the very word *I* instantiates what it means; it is an ontological word with reference to actual thought or speech. In correlation with the word *I*, the word *God* instantiates the negation of the self; God means the not-I that is instantiated in the speaking or thinking of the name, the "other" of the I, in the same fashion as the "I" instantiates the subject. In this sense, again, the word *God* is ontological. One cannot really think the meaning, or understand the word spoken, without at the very same time instantiating the negation it means. This is the same relation as that between the name "the kingdom of *K*" and the name "the kingdom of God," with the exception that the noun "kingdom" does not instantiate what it means in the way the pronoun "I" does. Every intelligible noun, of course, does show the reality it means to the mind—if someone says the word *kingdom*, and I understand what it means, I cannot help thinking of a kingdom. But "I" and "God" present their referent not only to mind but also in reality, at a certain time and place, namely, those of the speaker or thinker.

5. *Does Saying Make It So?*

1. Martin Buber, *Werke*, vol. 1, *Schriften zur Philosophie* (Munich: Kösel-Verlag, 1962), p. 79. Subsequent citations appear in text.
2. This may need correction. Paul Tillich reported, for example, that he had once asked Buber whether "God" was a *Grundwort* and that Buber had replied in the affirmative. (This reference is contained in a transcript, now located in the Tillich archives at the Harvard Divinity School, of a lecture Tillich gave in 1954 before the Cooper Union Forum in New York.)

6. *Hegel and Theology Today*

1. Karl Barth, *Protestant Theology in the Nineteenth Century*, tr. Brian Cozens and John Bowden (London: SCM Press, 1972), p. 390.
2. G. W. F. Hegel, *Werke in zwanzig Bänden* (Frankfurt am Main: Suhrkamp, 1970–79), 17:297, 298.
3. Letter of 3 July 1826; quoted in Eberhard Jüngel, *God as the Mystery of the World*, tr. Darrell L. Guder (Grand Rapids, Mich.: Wm. B. Eerdmans, 1983), p. 90.
4. See ibid., p. 82.
5. Hegel, *Werke*, 10:23 (= *Enzyklopädie*, §381, Zusatz).
6. See Michael Welker, "Barth und Hegel: Zur Erkenntnis eines methodischen Verfahrens bei Barth," *Evangelische Theologie* 43, no. 4 (1983): 312.
7. See Gerald A. McCool, ed., *A Rahner Reader* (London: Darton, Longman & Todd, 1975), p. xxvii.
8. Barth, *Protestant Theology*, p. 420.
9. Robert W. Jenson, *The Triune Identity: God according to the Gospel* (Philadelphia: Fortress Press, 1982), p. 136.
10. Hegel, *Glauben und Wissen*, in *Werke*, 2:289.
11. Ibid., p. 290.
12. Jüngel, *God*, p. 73.
13. Thomas J. J. Altizer, *Total Presence* (New York: Seabury Press, 1980).

7. Schelling's Impact on Protestant Theology

1. In a reference I have not tracked down, Georg Huntemann, *Die dialektische Theologie und der spekulative Idealismus Hegels: Ein Beitrag zur Geschichte des Kampfes um das finitum capax infiniti in der neueren Theologie* (Syke, Federal Republic of Germany: G. Knaurs Buchdruckerei [Anton Petzold], 1957), mentions Ludwig Lambinet as one who regarded Barth as a *Fortbildner* of Schelling's philosophy (p. 5).
2. Eberhard Busch's *Karl Barths Lebenslauf* (Munich: Chr. Kaiser Verlag, 1975), in the two index references it has to Schelling, indicates a link between Barth and Schelling by way of Kutter but otherwise none (p. 111).
3. Huntemann concludes that each of the dialectical theologians (Barth, Brunner, Gogarten, Bultmann) traversed a course which, starting with an attack on speculative idealism (Schelling against Hegel), increasingly approximated Hegel's philosophy as the theology matured (*Die dialektische Theologie*, p. 133).
4. Paul Tillich, *Briefwechsel und Streitschriften*, ed. Renate Albrecht and René Tautmann (Frankfurt am Main: Evangelisches Verlagswerk, 1983), p. 76.
5. Ibid.
6. Paul Tillich, *On the Boundary* (New York: Charles Scribner's Sons, 1966), p. 52.
7. Ibid., p. 83.
8. Ibid., p. 51.
9. Tillich, *Briefwechsel*, pp. 114, 115.
10. Ibid., p. 130.
11. F. W. J. Schelling, *Philosophie der Offenbarung* (Darmstadt: Wissenschaftliche Buchgesellschaft, 1966), pt. 2, lecture 25, pp. 37, 39.
12. See Tillich, *Systematische Theologie* (1913), printed in John P. Clayton, *The Concept of Correlation* (Berlin and New York: Walter de Gruyter, 1980), pp. 253–68.
13. Hirsch rightly (and shrewdly) pointed out that one cannot escape having a system fall victim to the judgment of history just by incorporating into it its self-judgment: "For even the device of looking this judgment in the eye, and the knowledge of how to make it the basic paradox of the system, does not make it immortal" (Tillich, *Briefwechsel*, pp. 130 f.).
14. Paul Tillich, *Systematic Theology* (Chicago: Univ. of Chicago Press, 1951–63), 2:111.
15. This connection has been traced recently by H. Frederick Reisz, Jr., "The Demonic as a Principle in Tillich's Doctrine of God: Tillich and Beyond," in *Theonomy and Autonomy*, ed. John J. Carey (Macon, Ga.: Mercer Univ. Press, 1984), pp. 135–56. On another point of connection one might be inclined to think that Tillich's rejection of the statement "God exists" (in contrast to the statement "God is") comes from Schelling, since Schelling had made the same point. But textual evidence indicates that the more direct connection is with Heidegger; for Tillich does use "Gott existiert" (although with a paradoxical sense) in his early works on the philosophy of religion.
16. Karl Barth, *Kirchliche Dogmatik* II/2 (Zollikon-Zurich: Evangelischer Verlag, 1959 [1942]), chap. 7 (hereafter *KD*).
17. In *KD* II/2 Barth observes that Daub's not being able to do anything more with Judas than repeatedly to damn and decry him as "'the sinner without equal'" shows only how impotent German idealism was in view of the center of the New Testament, namely, that in the figure of Judas "sin is made righteousness, evil is made good." "Das Ja *folgt* nicht dem Nein wie bei Paulus, wie bei den anderen Aposteln, sondern das Nein selbst und als sol-

ches *ist* das Ja" (The yes does not *follow* the no, as it does in Paul and the other apostles; the no itself and as such *is* the yes) (p. 559).

18. Eberhard Jüngel, *God as the Mystery of the World* (Grand Rapids, Mich.: Wm. B. Eerdmans, 1983).

19. I. A. Dorner, *A System of Christian Doctrine*, 4 vols. (Edinburgh: T. & T. Clark, 1888–90).

20. Ibid., 1:251, 253.

21. Ibid., p. 406.

22. Alfred Jäger, *Gott: Nochmals Martin Heidegger* (Tübingen: J. C. B. Mohr [Paul Siebeck], 1978), p. 284.

23. Georg Picht and Enno Rudolph, *Theologie—Was ist das?* (Stuttgart: Kreuz Verlag, 1977), pp. 20 f.

24. Schelling, *Philosophie der Offenbarung*, lecture 5, pp. 75 f.

25. Ibid., pp. 7, 8.

8. The No to Nothing and the Nothing to Know

1. Paul Tillich, Lecture at Free University of Berlin, p. 1. G. Siemsen copy. In Tillich archives, Andover-Harvard Divinity School Library.

2. Barth wrote in English to Adelaide B. McKelway on 21 August 1963: "I like it to hear, that Paul Tillich is satisfied about the manner your husband has treated him. This is exactly what I wished: that that necessary attack on Tillich's abominable theology should be made in the indirect way of an absolutely fair representation of its trend and particularities." On 3 December of the same year, he wrote to Tillich, on the occasion of the latter's visit to Basel: "It is for me a very special phenomenon that we understand one another so well and cordially at the human level, but materially—and don't try to offer me a synthesis; in so doing you would only strengthen me in my opinion!—we can only contradict and oppose each other from the very foundation up" (Karl Barth, *Letters 1961–1968*, ed. Jürgen Fangmeier and Hinrich Stoevesandt, tr. and ed. Geoffrey W. Bromiley [Grand Rapids, Mich.: Wm. B. Eerdmans, 1981], pp. 123, 144.

3. Paul Tillich, *Kirchliche Apologetik*, in *Gesammelte Werke*, ed. Renate Albrecht (Stuttgart: Evangelisches Verlagswerk, 1959–75), 13:46 (hereafter *GW*).

4. Karl Barth, *Kirchliche Dogmatik*, II/1 (Zollikon-Zurich: Evangelischer Verlag, 1958), p. 715 (hereafter *KD*). On the question of whether dialectical theology brought into being a new kind of personality, Tillich wrote, in 1945, that Barth "sought to save Christian personality from secular disintegration and totalitarian mechanization" but did not "produce a new type of personal life" and, instead, "left the field to the fanatical dynamics of the totalitarian 'impersonal personality'" (Paul Tillich, *The World Situation* [Philadelphia: Fortress Press, 1965], p. 40).

5. Karl Barth, "Von der Paradoxie des 'positiven Paradoxes,'" in Paul Tillich, *GW*, 7:231.

6. Tillich, "Kritisches und positives Paradox," *GW*, 7:217. Barth, "Von der Paradoxie des 'positiven Paradoxes,'" p. 226. Tillich's essay, along with the replies of Barth and Friedrich Gogarten and an epilogue of the editor of *Theologische Blätter*, Karl Ludwig Schmidt, are now printed in the new critical edition of Tillich's major works: Paul Tillich, *Main Works/Hauptwerke*, vol. 4, ed. John Clayton (Berlin: Walter de Gruyter, 1987), pp. 91–116.

7. Karl Barth, "Das Wort Gottes als Aufgabe der Theologie," in *Anfänge der dialektischen Theologie*, ed. Jürgen Moltmann (Munich: Chr. Kaiser Verlag, 1962), pt. 1, p. 217. Horton's translation blunts the point here: Barth's "defeat [*Niederlage*] of all theology and all theologians" is turned into the

"frustration of every ministry and every minister." See "The Word of God as the Task of the Ministry," in Karl Barth, *The Word of God and the Word of Man*, tr. Douglas Horton (London: Hodder & Stoughton, 1928), p. 214.
8. Barth, "Wort Gottes," p. xvi. The formula of his "'biblicistic' method," he wrote, was simply: "Think! [*Besinn dich!*]," which he would apply to his reading of Lao Tzu or of Goethe if it were his office to interpret them (p. xv).
9. "Nur lediglich darin, daß die Verneinung der göttlichen Existenz völlig nichts ist, liegt der Unterschied seines Daseins von anderer Dinge ihrem" (The only difference between the existence of God and the existence of other things is that the denial of God's existence is completely nothing) (Immanuel Kant, *Der einzig mögliche Beweisgrund zu einer Demonstration des Daseins Gottes*, in *Werke in sechs Bäden*, ed. Wilhelm Weischedel [Darmstadt: Wissenschaftliche Buchgesellschaft, 1963], p. 737).
10. Barth, *KD*, III/3 (Zollikon-Zurich: EVZ-Verlag, 1961), pp. 400–402, 406.
11. "This [namely, that every dialogue between religions is "accompanied by a silent dialogue within the representatives of each of the participating religions"] produces (as I can witness) both seriousness and anxiety" (Paul Tillich, *Christianity and the Encounter of the World Religions* [New York: Columbia Univ. Press, 1963], p. 58).

9. *Constructing Theological Models*

1. *Christian Scholar* 46 (1963), reprinted in Dallas High, ed., *New Essays on Religious Language* (New York: Oxford Univ. Press, 1969), pp. 54–96. Subsequent relations appear in text. My quotations are from the latter publication.
2. One might then—to take another example—construe the change in Christian theology that occurred with the Reformation as a change in theological theory (from the Latin to the German God-concept) with a retention of the basic theological model (in which case it was a "theological" revolution), or as a change in high-level models (from a personal being "having" justice to one who "imputes" righteousness) with a retention of the theory (in which case it was a "religious" revolution), or even as a change in both (in which case it was a religious as well as a theological revolution).
3. Ian Ramsey, *Religious Language* (New York: Macmillan, 1957), *Models and Mystery* (London: Oxford Univ. Press, 1964), *Christian Discourse* (New York: Oxford Univ. Press, 1965). Also see Ramsey, ed., *Words about God* (London: SCM Press, 1971), pp. 202–23.
4. See *Words about God*, p. 222 n. 2, where Ramsey explains that one of his reasons for using "model" rather than "image" is that the latter seems "to have too strong a psychological ancestry and to beg or to by-pass too many epistemological and ontological questions"; and pp. 211 ff., where he explicitly takes up the question of the objective reference of theological models.
5. For this account of Tillich, see my *Reflection and Doubt in the Thought of Paul Tillich* (New Haven: Yale Univ. Press, 1969), pp. 56 and 125 f. (the second way of theonomous metaphysics is the one I take in the present essay to be the formation of a model), pp. 22 and 119 f. (on the derivation of ontological categories, including freedom and destiny), and the various references to Tillich's works given there.
6. What is important here is not the terminology (since "ontology" and "metaphysics" are often used interchangeably or in other senses than those stated here) but the distinction itself.
7. Paul Tillich, *Systematic Theology* (Chicago: Univ. of Chicago Press, 1951–63),

1 : 163; cf. p. 169 ("this awareness [of self-relatedness] can only be denied in a statement in which self-relatedness is implicitly affirmed"). Tillich's description of the formation of ontological concepts (p. 164) does not make so clear the difference between metaphysical generalization and ontological deduction as does his actual procedure or his derivation of "self" (p. 169).

8. The Latin prefix *con* sometimes has a doubling connotation (*con-scientia*), which is intended in "conjunctive." The structural poles of a domain are "joined" by that domain itself, but they are "conjoined" by the depth. So the "juncture" between man and God in the religious relation of such activities as prayer or worship is different from the "conjuncture" of "being itself" as the depth of that relation. It is this aspect that puts the notion of "conjunctive" into the vicinity of the dialectical notion of "spirit" in speculative idealism as well as in dialectical theology.

9. An example is William Pollard, *Chance and Providence* (New York: Charles Scribner's Sons, 1958). As there presented, the model needs adapting, since Pollard's view seems to suggest something of a world behind this world.

10. Paul Tillich, "System der Wissenschaften nach Gegenständen und Methoden" (1923), in *Gesammelte Werke*, ed. Renate Albrecht (Stuttgart: Evangelisches Verlagswerk, 1959–75), 1 : 109–293; and Hans Wagner, *Philosophie und Reflexion* (Munich-Basel: Ernst Reinhardt, 1959), are two examples of works which do undertake that sort of determination.

11. The Book of Job might serve as a good point of departure for a discussion of criteria used to determine the truth of theological models. Job's model could be formulated as "God rewards uprightness and punishes wickedness." The model takes material from the primary domain of subjective experience, as constituted on the one hand by my activity (what I do) and on the other hand by my passivity (what I suffer) as the two poles of the basic structures of such experience. The theological connective for the poles is "God rewards" or, as the case may be, "God punishes." Its function is to unite personal action and personal suffering by a depth manifest in them. The normal unity of the two in subjective experience is the fact that "I" am the subject of both. The unity in the theological model is that of God's activity, specifically his punishing and rewarding, which relates my deeds to my sufferings indirectly. My deeds do not cause my sufferings except indirectly by God's activity. If that is the theological model, then the Book of Job presents a case in which the model is subjected to experiential testing and breaks down because it does not make Job's experience subjectively intelligible; it does not provide him with a way of dealing with the transcendence present in his subjective experience (God's activity is inscrutable), nor does it give him an intelligible view of his experience from the standpoint of that transcendence. The model breaks down because the particular connection of the two poles of experience (doing and suffering) that it makes is contradicted by actual experience. For the model makes the suffering of misfortune intelligible by connecting it to the doing of evil—not directly, to be sure, but indirectly; it does not suggest that evil-doing causes my suffering as such but that, indirectly, by way of the transcendence present (God's activity), the two are connected. The model "God punishes the wicked" would not be refuted by a case in which a wicked man escapes punishment, for one could always say that he may yet be punished. But it is refuted by a case in which the suffering of misfortune is not preceded by the doing of evil, as Job contends is true of himself. The debate between Job and his counselors is a debate between those who would hold to the model by maintaining that Job must have done some wickedness in secret and Job who maintains his innocence at the cost of the theological model. The pro-

logue to the book might then be regarded as an effort to reinterpret the model (God's punishment is only apparent) without discarding it altogether. And Job's own answer may be seen as his making a dialectical use of the model, which prior to the decisive experience had expressed the depth of subjective experience as intelligible, now is used to express that same depth precisely as unintelligible; the answer Job gets from the Lord is only the answer that Job does not need or have a right to an answer—or, according to a different reading of the book, that Job can behold the answer, without being able to put it into words, in such wondrous phenomena as the instincts of the ostrich which "deals cruelly with her young, as if they were not hers" (Job 39:16). This particular illustration provides a good point of departure—even if it does not tell the whole story of testing theological models—because it presents a model that seems clearly to be empirically testable, although, of course, it is not experimentally (scientifically) testable.

12. Paul Tillich, *The Future of Religions* (New York: Harper & Row, 1966), p. 87.

12. Goethe's and Berlioz's Faust

1. One illustration will serve to indicate the relation of Goethe's text to Nerval's translation (which stays close to the text) and Berlioz's text (which is freer than a translation). From scene 15:

Goethe's text:

> *Meine Ruh' ist hin,*
> *Mein Herz ist schwer,*
> *Ich finde sie nimmer*
> *Und nimmermehr.*

Nerval's translation:

> *Le repos m'a fuie! hélas!*
> *la paix de mon coeur malade,*
> *je ne le trouve plus*
> *et plus jamais.*

Berlioz's text:

> *D'amour l'ardente flamme*
> *consume mes beaux jours.*
> *Ah! la paix de mon âme*
> *a donc fui pour toujours!*

13. Demons, Idols, and the Symbol of Symbols
in Tillich's Theology of Politics

1. In Paul Tillich, "Zur Theologie der bildenden Kunst und der Architektur," *Gesammelte Werke*, vol. 9, ed. Renate Albrecht (Stuttgart: Evangelisches Verlagswerk, 1967) (hereafter *GW*), Tillich explains that the reason why architecture is mentioned separately in the title is its double-sided character:

"Das Kirchengebäude ist Zweckbau und Symbol in einem" (p. 352). The negative consequence thereof is that the purely technical purpose can be separated from the symbolical character or the symbolical character used in such a way as to corrupt the integrity of the structure. The positive consequence is that the necessities bound with the technical purpose place a check on archaistic traditionalism.

2. Ibid., p. 353.
3. Ibid., p. 355.
4. Paul Tillich, *Systematic Theology* (Chicago: Univ. of Chicago Press, 1951–63), 3:311 (hereafter *ST*). In his open letter to Emanuel Hirsch in 1934, he referred to the period in Germany as a time when political affairs were gaining "a significance surpassing all others," and that was a reflection of his view of the importance of Religious Socialism; but the statement in *ST* is more general. See "Open Letter to Emanuel Hirsch," in *The Thought of Paul Tillich*, ed. James Luther Adams, Wilhelm Pauck, and Roger Lincoln Shinn (San Francisco: Harper & Row, 1985), p. 354.
5. Paul Tillich, "On the Idea of a Theology of Culture," in *What Is Religion?* ed. James Luther Adams (New York: Harper & Row, 1969), p. 167; "Über die Idee einer Theologie der Kultur," *GW*, 9:21.
6. Paul Tillich, *The Protestant Era*, tr. James Luther Adams (Chicago: Univ. of Chicago Press, 1948), p. xxi.
7. Tillich wrote to Hirsch that in the present "struggle for what is coming" theonomy will "face more defeat than victory" but a *gläubiger Realismus* prevents a person from seeing a fulfillment in some romanticized event ("Open Letter," p. 363).
8. Ibid., p. 362.
9. Utopianism, demonry, and idolatry (as well as supranaturalism) are, in different places, characterized as making something conditional unconditional. But in their proper sense, the three concepts are different. The *demonic* is the irruption of the power of the depth of being (the "ground" and "abyss") in such a way that its creativity is used in the service of destruction. The *divine*, which is the opposite of the demonic, is the irruption of that creative power in such a way that it serves the creation of new forms. Both of them are simultaneously creative and destructive of forms; the difference is that the demonic creates forms in order to destroy all forms, whereas the divine destroys forms in order to create new forms in which the old are salvaged. The demonic and the divine are two manifestations of the *holy*. An *idol* is something conditional elevated to the status of the unconditional; it is something given in space and time that has been consecrated as such. *Utopianism* is idolatrous when it regards a particular view of the fulfillment of history as though it were not affected by the ambiguity of other views; it idolizes not something that is but something that should be so.
10. "Der Staat als Erwartung und Forderung," Tillich, *GW*, 9:123. An English translation of this essay is in *Political Expectation*, ed. James Luther Adams (New York: Harper & Row, 1971), pp. 97–114.
11. Tillich, *GW*, 9:123.
12. Ibid., p. 124.
13. What Tillich in his theology of culture in 1919 had called the *Gehalt* which breaks into the form (and content) of reality and which is the key to reading the theology of culture is called the "depth" or "depth-dimension" or "substance" in later years. The methodological guideline is given in the formulation of 1919—"the *Gehalt* is grasped in the content [*an dem Inhalt*] by means of the form [*mittelst der Form*] and given expression."
14. "Verantwortliche Schau des Staates ist da, wo der Staat gesehen wird unter dem Blickpunkt eines sinngebenden Prinzips, das dem gegenwärtigen Staat

seine Tiefe und seine Grenze gibt. Nur in einer solchen Schau ist Erwartung und Forderung machtvoll und spannungsreich geeint" (*GW*, p. 124).

15. "Das Verhältnis von Theologie und Politik kann niemals durch ein 'und' gekennzeichnet werden," Tillich wrote in "Um was es geht: Antwort an Emanuel Hirsch," in *Briefwechsel und Streitschriften*, ed. Renate Albrecht and René Tautmann (Frankfurt am Main: Evangelisches Verlagswerk, 1983), p. 216.

16. Tillich told Hirsch that what he as a theologian ought to have done was "to find the theological word that sobers those who are intoxicated [by their enthusiasm] without depriving them of courage and daring" ("Open Letter," p. 366).

17. A. James Reimer, "Theological Method and Political Ethics: The Paul Tillich–Emanuel Hirsch Debate," *JAAR Supplement* 47 (1979): 182.

18. Emanuel Hirsch, "Christliche Freiheit und politische Bindung: Ein Brief an Dr. Stapel und anderes," in Tillich, *Briefwechsel und Streitschriften*, pp. 204, 205.

19. Tillich, "Das Dämonische: Ein Beitrag zur Sinndeutung der Geschichte," *GW*, 6:42–71. The opening paragraphs of this essay have a singular intensity among Tillich's analyses of history: "A talk about the demonic is followed by wildness or emptiness or both," but Tillich will "dare to speak of that of which one cannot speak with impunity, the demon" (p. 42). Tillich probably did not change his position on the demonic, but it is noteworthy that elsewhere he speaks of the "divine" as the mediation between the demonic and the human, just as "theonomy" is the mediation between autonomy and heteronomy and "prophetic" a mediation between sacramental and secular (*On the Boundary* [New York: Charles Scribner's Sons, 1936], p. 81). In the *ST* there seem to be only a few echoes of the early conception that the demonic and the divine are two sides of the holiness of God—here, where the idolatrous and demonic are almost synonyms, the accent falls on the fact that elevating something conditional to the unconditional, which can occur when an institution or person denies its own involvement in the ambiguities of history, is what brings about the demonic or idolatrous. Thus, Tillich speaks of the "idolatrous adherence [on the part of a community of faith] to its own historically conditioned symbols [by excluding competing symbols]" and goes on to remark that "whenever the Spiritual Presence makes itself felt, the self-criticism of the churches in the name of their own symbols starts," something "made possible because in every authentic religious symbol there is an element that judges the symbol and those who use it" (*ST*, 3:206); and he also speaks of the "demonic quality" of papal leadership given to it when it does not acknowledge the ambiguity of itself (3:207). In none of these instances does the demonic appear as the destructive side of the manifestation of the holy.

20. Tillich, *On the Boundary*, pp. 78 f.

21. Tillich, "Open Letter," p. 372.

22. *Kairos* in the unique sense "describes the moment in which the eternal breaks into the temporal, and the temporal is prepared to receive it"; what happened in the unique *kairos* "may happen in a derived form again and again . . . creating centers of less importance on which the periodization of history is based" (*Protestant Era*, p. xix). In the 1920s there is already a shift toward a christological usage of *kairos*; but the debate with Hirsch seems to be the point at which the question comes to a head.

23. Ibid.

24. Tillich, "Kairos and Logos" (1926), *GW*, 4:43–76; see esp. pp. 57 and 73 f. The *kairos* is absolute in placing one before the decision for or against the truth;

it is relative in one's knowing that this decision is possible only as a concrete decision, a temporal destiny.
25. Tillich, "Open Letter," pp. 386 ff.

14. The Argument from Faith to History

1. The first, basic statement is contained in the fragment of an address, "Die
   christliche Gewißheit und der historische Jesus," which Tillich delivered
   in 1911. It is published in Paul Tillich, Briefwechsel und Streitschriften, ed.
   Renate Albrecht and René Tautmann (Frankfurt am Main: Evangelisches
   Verlagswerk, 1983), pp. 50–61. In On the Boundary (New York: Charles
   Scribner's Sons, 1966) Tillich refers to this treatise as "the documentary
   proof" of his change of interest away from the theology of mediation and its
   apologetics to church history and the problem of historical criticism (p. 50).
   In the treatise he suggests a "dogmatic proof" that Jesus the Christ exists. It
   is not a dogmatic proof based on the authority of Scripture, or on the providence of God, or on the actual effectiveness of a reality; instead, it is a proof
   developing the proposition that "it belongs to the essence of the Christ to
   be actual" (p. 8). The fragment available does not present the full proof, for
   it ends after a critique of Herrmann's dogmatic proof based upon the over-
   powering impact of the person of Jesus. Within the systematics this question appears in Systematic Theology (Chicago: Univ. of Chicago Press,
   1957), 2:97–118.
2. D. Moody Smith, "The Historical Jesus in Paul Tillich's Christology," Journal
   of Religion 46, pt. 2 (1966): 131–47. David Kelsey, The Fabric of Paul
   Tillich's Theology (New Haven: Yale Univ. Press, 1967), pp. 98–101. Robert
   P. Scharlemann, Reflection and Doubt in the Thought of Paul Tillich (New
   Haven: Yale Univ. Press, 1969), pp. 110–12.
3. Michael Palmer, "The Certainty of Faith and Tillich's Concept of the analogia
   imaginis," Scottish Journal of Theology 25 (1972): 279–95.
4. Smith, "The Historical Jesus," p. 138.
5. Scharlemann, Reflection and Doubt, pp. 110–12.
6. See note 1.
7. Kelsey, The Fabric of Paul Tillich's Theology, pp. 98–101.
8. In "Die christliche Gewißheit" (1911) Tillich regards doing miracles and being
   resurrected as nonessential: they can be contested without affecting the
   Messianic predicate. He is uncertain whether Messianic self-consciousness
   is essential, although he thinks it is. He considers complete sinlessness
   (willing death) indispensable.

15. Pluralism in Theology

1. Walter H. Capps, "Plurality of Theologies: A Paradigmatic Sketch," Religious
   Studies 3 (1967): 355–67; "Harnack and Ecumenical Discussion," Journal
   of Ecumenical Studies 3 (1966): 486–502. Jean Daniélou, "Unité et plu-
   ralité de la pensée chrétienne," Etudes 312 (1962): 3–16. Piet Fransen,
   "Three Ways of Dogmatic Thought," Heythrop Journal 4 (1963): 3–24, reprinted in Intelligent Theology (London: Darton, Longman & Todd, 1967),
   1:9–39. Michael Novak, "The Philosophical Roots of Religious Unity,"
   Journal of Ecumenical Studies 2 (1966): 113–29. Herbert W. Richardson,
   "A Philosophy of Unity," Harvard Theological Review 60 (1967): 1–38, re-

printed with slight changes in *Toward an American Theology* (New York: Harper & Row, 1967), chap. 4. W. Seibel, "Der eine Glaube und die Vielfalt der Dogmen," *Stimmen der Zeit* 169 (1961–62): 264–77. W. A. Visser 'T Hooft, "Pluralism—Temptation or Opportunity," *Ecumenical Review* 38 (1966): 129–49. For some of the historical background see Claude Welch, "God, Faith, and the Theological Object," *Harvard Theological Review* 59 (1966): 213–66. And for philosophical counterparts, see Richard McKeon, "Philosophy and Method," *Journal of Philosophy* 48 (1951): 653–82; idem, "Principles and Consequences," *Journal of Philosophy* 51 (1959): 385–401. Henry Alonzo Myers, *Systematic Pluralism: A study in Metaphysics* (Ithaca, N.Y.: Cornell Univ. Press, 1961). Kenneth L. Schmitz, "Philosophical Pluralism and Philosophical Truth," *Philosophy Today* 10 (1966): 3–18. Since the time when these references were assembled, the literature on pluralism has grown considerably, most of it taking an approach through hermeneutics rather than through systematics; but Walter Watson's *The Architectonics of Meaning: Foundations of the New Pluralism* (Albany: State Univ. of New York Press, 1985) is a recent systematic study in the style of McKeon.

2. Cf. Fransen, *Intelligent Theology*, 1:37.
3. Capps, "Harnack," p. 497.
4. Capps, "Plurality," pp. 355–67.
5. Ibid., p. 357.
6. Ibid., p. 359.
7. Walter Capps, " 'Being and Becoming' and 'God and the World': Whitehead's Account of Their Early Association," *Revue Philosophique de Louvain* 63 (1965): 572–90.
8. Capps, "Plurality," p. 358.
9. Ibid., pp. 356, 360, 361.
10. Ibid., p. 356, and "Harnack," p. 497.
11. Capps, "Plurality," p. 358.
12. One obvious omission in Capps's sketches is that he treats only one form of systematic reflection. On the one side he has the kerygmatic affirmations, the nonsystematic expression of faith's fundamental disposition; and on the other side he has philosophical articulations, systems based upon fundamental axioms, which, when conjoined with the disposition of faith, constitute theological systems. The tools for systematic reflection are philosophical. But this ignores the question whether there is a systematic character to mythology and whether mythology is a form of reflection; it also ignores the question whether the sort of theology that consists of a narrative of God's acts is a reflection on faith and is systematic in its own way. I think these questions have to be answered affirmatively. Still, this opinion would not constitute a major objection to Capps's analysis.
13. Fransen, *Intelligent Theology*, 1:33.
14. Of course, theological synthesizing goes on too. Some interconfessional studies, such as the works of Hans Küng on justification and on the church, are theological syntheses as well as reflexive analyses. A theological synthesis occurs when a theological axiom is discovered that transcends and embraces formerly opposed axioms. Synthesis takes two opposites into a higher unity at the same level of thought. Hence, only theology can synthesize theological axioms; reflexive analysis cannot. Again—to cite other examples—the confessional statements of the *uniert* churches in Germany are syntheses of Reformed and Lutheran axioms rather than second-order organizations of different theologies. By contrast, the unity of the World Council of Churches is, or has been, an institutional organization of different theologies which is neither a theological synthesis nor a reflexive analysis. In contrast both to institutional connections of disparate theological

axioms and to theological syntheses, reflexive analysis provides a meta-theological connection, a connection in thought, of theological axioms and systems. When reflexive analysis replaces, or is added to, federations of communities representing different theologies, theology is taken into a context which, though it is not theological reflection, is still a context of reflexive thought and is not alien to theological reflection—it is metatheological.

15. Capps does include Luther among his illustrative examples, but not in a way that catches the element of freedom in his theology. Luther is taken as an "'atomist'" ("Plurality," p. 362, cf. p. 359), one whose primary interest is not in the "unitary" or the "all-comprehensive" but in "the particular, the peculiar, the individual," the "irreducible substratum whose authority is beyond challenge" ("Harnack," p. 499). But certainly it is the divine freedom, rather than singularity or individuality, that is the systematic thread in Luther's theology. Cf. his attitude on the christological and trinitarian syllogisms as discussed by Occam and d'Ailly: Bengt Hägglund, *Theologie und Philosophie bei Luther und in der occamistischen Tradition* (Lund: C. W. K. Gleerup, 1955), pp. 47 f.

16. This is true of both levels, reflection and reflexive analysis, but I am limiting my discussion to the first level, partly for reasons of space and partly because transferring to the second order would not involve any problems new in kind.

17. This example should not be confused with a case that appears similar but is not. "I have blue eyes" would be true when spoken by some but not when spoken by others. However, this is due to the fact that the reference changes with the different speakers. If "I have blue eyes" is true when spoken by A, it is also true when B says to A, "You have blue eyes." By contrast, a confessor can say to A, the penitent, "You are forgiven," and it is true, but the penitent cannot say to himself or herself, "I am forgiven."

18. In his discussion of Judas, Karl Barth, *Kirchliche Dogmatik*, II/2, (Zollikon-Zurich: Evangelischer Verlag, 1959 [1942]), p. 559, comes very close to maintaining the equivalent standing of negative and positive responses—this is the closest that "dialectical" theology comes to having worked out the structure of pluralistic freedom.

19. Cf. Markus Barth, "What Can a Jew Believe about Jesus—and Still Remain a Jew?" *JES* 2 (1965): 383.

20. Gotthard Günther, *Idee und Grundriß einer nicht-aristotelischen Logik* (Hamburg: Felix Meiner, 1959). See pp. 15, 85, 135, and passim.

21. Visser 'T Hooft, "Pluralism," sees the alternative in this way. So he can conclude that pluralism must not mean complete relativism, or syncretism, but "a truly open situation in which all have the right to persuade all and in which we respect in each other the seriousness and sincerity with which convictions are held and expressed" (p. 141). Cf. A. A. Gilbert, "Religious Pluralism: A Jewish View," *Theology Today* 19 (1963): 510–22, esp. p. 510. Also K. E. Skydsgaard, "Israel, the Church, and the Unity of the People of God," *Lutheran World* 10 (1963): 345–51.

22. It might be objected that what I am speaking of here is not a pluralism but only a dualism of subjects. This is not the case, for just as recognizing diversity in objects depends not upon being able to recognize more than one or two distinct objects but upon recognizing the differences between being and nonbeing (i.e., objectivity and its opposite; as in the doctrine *creatio ex nihilo*), so the recognition of plurality in freedom depends not on recognizing two distinct subjects but upon recognizing transcendental freedom ("I" in the act of affirming) and its opposite (the "other" negating, equally transcendentally). Plurality of subjects and objects rests upon this polar structure of sheer positive (being; "my" yes) and sheer negative (nonbeing, the "other's" no).

16. One of the Many and the Many of the One

1. In Heidegger, ontotheology is a reference to a kind of metaphysics: one in which the difference between being and entities (*Sein* and *Seiendes*), the difference between God and being, and the difference between the general and the supreme (the one "overall" and the one "over all") is overlooked, or left out of account, or "forgotten."

2. The following paragraphs are an abbreviated and slightly altered version of a line of thought developed in an essay in *The Whirlwind in Culture: Frontiers in Theology*, ed. Joseph L. Price and Donald Musser (New York: Meyer and Stone, 1988), pp. 224–36.

INDEX

Absolutism, 96

Actuality, *see* Factuality

Adler, Mortimer, 145

Aesthetic idea, 219

Afterthinking, 3, 8, 10–13, 18; of death, 16; possibility of, 22; transition to, 21, 22, 29

Alienator, 61, 65; function of, 62

Altizer, Thomas J. J., 90

Analogia entis, see Being, analogy of

Analogia imaginis, 185–87

Analogy, 17, 18, 23, 24, 26–28; and model, 128

Analysis, reflexive, 199, 213, 242 f.

Anselm of Canterbury, 44, 82; on proof of God, 119, 120

Antimetaphysical, 45

Antinomy, 76

Anxiety, 123, 167, 169, 236

Apollo and the Muses, 154

Aquinas, *see* Thomas Aquinas

Architecture, 168, 238

Argument, practical, 194

Aristotle: on being, 41 f., on dialectic, 36, on liberal arts, 141 f., 146, 153

Art, 84, 150, 163; as achievement and as failure, 157; theology and, 111, 154 f., 168

Arts, liberal, *see* Liberal arts

As: hermeneutical and apophantic, 10

Asymmetry of God and world, 199–201

Atheism, 31, 45, 46

Augustine of Hippo, 30, 145, 146

Axioms of systems, 200–206

Bach, Johann Sebastian, 157 f.

Bacon, Francis, 152

Barth, Karl, 3, 26, 45, 67, 198; characteristics of, 110 f.; on analogy of being, 42; on Anselm's definition of God, 24, 44; on evil, 234 f., 243; on God's freedom, 92; on Hegel, 80, 87; on Mozart, 160 f.; on natural theology, 31; on theology and music, 154 f.; on Tillich's theology, 111–14, 235; on Trinity, 88; Schelling's influence on, 92 f., 98 f.; theological model in, 133 f., 206; supranaturalism of, 112, 117 f; *see also* Election

Being: abyss of, 102; analogy of, 24, 42; and becoming, 199; and God, 8, 16, 37, 123, 124, 225; and God in the theistic picture, 31, 45; and thinking, 5 f., 37, 104; appearance of, 19, 25; as donated by language, 11, 154; as object of understanding, 7, 224; as presence, 36; as referent of statement, 58; as synthesis, 7, 19; as the word *is,* 38; as thinking, 33, 231; as unity of percept and concept, 19; as unthought, 36, 39, 43; coalescence of biographic and dramaturgic in, 59; concept of, 41, 99, 103; definition of, 4, 7, 19; finite and infinite, 41; forgetting of, 30; grace and positivity of, 25, 160; ground of, 19, 25, 101, 103 f.; holy, 8; intelligibility